Leadership in Post Compulsory Education

Inspiring leaders of the future

D1322138

JILL JAMESON

 David Fulton Publishers

Also available:

In at the Deep End
A survival guide for teachers in post-compulsory education
Jim Crawley
1-84312-253-7

Mentoring Teachers in Post-Compulsory Education
A guide to effective practice
Bryan Cunningham
1-84312-316-9

Teaching 14–19
Everything you need to know about learning and teaching across the phases
Gina Donovan
1-84312-342-8

Teaching in Post-Compulsory Education
Policy, practice and values
Anthony Coles
1-84312-233-2

Teaching Business Education 14–19
Martin Jephcote and Ian Abbott
1-84312-254-5

This book is dedicated to my mother, Phyllis Jameson,
with love and heartfelt thanks for all you are and have done.

David Fulton Publishers Ltd
The Chiswick Centre, 414 Chiswick High Road, London W4 5TF

www.fultonpublishers.co.uk
www.onestopeducation.co.uk

David Fulton Publishers is a division of Granada Learning, part of ITV plc.

First published in Great Britain in 2006 by David Fulton Publishers.

Note: The right of the individual contributors to be identified as the authors of their work has been asserted by them in accordance with the Copyright, Designs and Patents Act 1988.

Copyright © Jill Jameson 2006

British Library Cataloguing in Publication Data
A catalogue record for this book is available from the British Library.

ISBN 1 84312 339 8

Typeset by Servis Filmsetting Ltd
Printed and bound in Great Britain

Contents

List of figures and tables

Figures

Tables

List of interviewees

Lynne Sedgmore

Lynne Sedgmore, CBE, MSc, BA, PGCE, MCIM, FRSA, has been Chief Executive of the Centre for Excellence in Leadership since 2004. She was previously Principal of Guildford College, during which time the College was the only UK FE College listed in BT's Vision 100 index as one of the UK's most visionary companies, was awarded bronze for the Business Excellence Model, and achieved the Good Corporation kite mark for 'ethical organisation'. Lynne has been a member of the National Bureaucracy Review Group, Sweeney Task Force, and Chair of the FE *Success for All* National Advisory Group. Lynne was awarded the CBE for services to education in 2004.

Dr John Guy

Dr John Guy, OBE, PhD, BSc (Hons) has been Principal of The Sixth Form College, Farnborough, since 1992. After graduating in Chemistry in 1971, John researched Crystallography (PhD) in 1974 at Birmingham University, following which he was a Research Fellow at St. Edmund's College, Cambridge University (1974–76). John has been a Council Member of the Sixth Form Colleges Employers Forum (1994–97), Association of Colleges Board Member (1997–2000) and on numerous committees of the FEFC, LSC and DfES. He served on the Tomlinson Committee on 14–19 Reform, chairing the Assessment Sub-Group. In 2002, Farnborough Sixth Form College was named as one of the first four LSC Beacon Colleges. John was awarded the OBE for services to education in 2001.

Dr David Collins

Dr David Collins, CBE, MA, PhD, DMS, DipEd (Admin), has been the Principal and Chief Executive of South Cheshire College, a Beacon College in Crewe, since 1992 and is a member of the College Finance, Organisational Development, Quality and Standards and Search Committees. He leads the national programme *Induction for New Principals* at the Centre for Excellence in Leadership. A recent Ofsted inspection graded South Cheshire College as 'outstanding' in ten curricula and three cross college areas – leadership and management, social inclusion and support for students. David is a Visiting Professorial Fellow at Lancaster University and was awarded the CBE for his work in FE in 2005.

Ruth Silver

Ruth Silver, CBE, FRSA, MA, Dip Ed, studied Psychology and Literature at Glasgow and Southampton Universities as an NUM scholar, and trained at the Tavistock Institute. Principal of Lewisham College, Ruth has written and broadcasted extensively, and is highly committed to inclusiveness and excellent standards of provision for learners, especially those facing multiple challenges. Ruth was awarded a CBE in 1998 for services to further education, and is an adviser to the Select Committee in the House of Commons. In 2004, she became Visiting Professor of Educational Development at London South Bank University. She is a Commissioner on the Women and Work Commission, and in 2005 became a member of the Parliamentary All Party Skills Commission. Ruth is Chair of the NEAFE/LSC 'Faiths in FE' chaplaincies group and a former member of the Liddle Working Group on the planning and funding of Learners with Learning Difficulties.

Anne Morahan

Anne Morahan is Education Manager from HMP Dover Immigration Removal Centre. In October 2004, Anne was selected from more than 1600 nominations to win the Centre for Excellence in Leadership STAR Award for Outstanding Management of Learning for her innovative and flexible approach to managing learning at the Centre for students who come from more than 70 countries. Anne and her team use learner surveys to identify detainee needs and are always amending learning provision appropriately, recently introducing stress management classes.

Professor Daniel Khan

Professor Daniel Khan, MA, FCCA, FAIA, is the Principal and Chief Executive of the Grimsby Institute of Further and Higher Education. In October, 2004, Daniel was selected from more than 1600 nominations to win the Centre for

Excellence STAR Award for Outstanding Leadership for his visionary and charismatic leadership of Grimsby college. By working with local, regional and national committees, Daniel has ensured the college combines commercialism with learning provision, and continues to meet community needs.

Bob Challis

Bob Challis completed the interview for this book a few days before his retirement as Principal at Abingdon and Whitney College, a role he fulfilled with great success and inspiring commitment to student achievement throughout 15 years from 1989 to 2004. During Bob's time as leader of the College, many changes and improvements were achieved. Bob worked closely with the governors and staff of the College to achieve a Grade 1 (outstanding) for Governance in the FEFC Inspection of 1997–98. The College was the only institution in the South East to achieve Accredited status prior to the setting up of the LSC in 2001. Following success in inspection, Bob led the College effectively through the challenges of a merger of Abingdon College with Whitney College. Carried out during 2000–02, this amalgamation set up new, dynamic further education provision for the people of Oxfordshire. Bob led the new institution – Abingdon and Whitney College – to achieve many successful changes.

Dr Andrew Morris

Dr Andrew Morris, PhD, BSc (Hons), is Director of the National Educational Research Forum. Earlier in his career, Andrew worked for 19 years in sixth form and FE, initially as a lecturer, then as Deputy Director of Islington Sixth Form Centre and Director of Marketing and Development at City and Islington College. As LSDA Research Manager (1996–2003), he led the LSDA Research Strategy, was Chair of the National Planning Group of the LSRN, and Editor of the *Learning and Skills Research Journal*, first known as *College Research* (1998–2004).

Wendy Moss

Wendy Moss is Manager for the Centre for Teacher and Management Training at City Lit in London, and previously Project Manager for Talent Central, funded by London Central LSC (2001–2003), a capacity building project training literacy, numeracy and ESOL teachers. Wendy works with the National Research and Development Centre, the Research and Practice in Adult Literacy Group, and is a consultant for national research evaluating teacher training. Wendy won a STAR award for outstanding cross-sector provision in 2004.

Talmud Bah

Talmud Bah is Associate Director for Second Wave Centre for Youth Arts, based in Deptford. He is also a freelance urban arts/education specialist. Talmud first became involved in Second Wave in 1997. Prior to becoming Associate Director he has been a learning mentor and New Opportunities fund coordinator for The John Roan Secondary School, an adviser, trainer and tutor to the Laban Centre, The Albany/Art of Regeneration/Royal National Theatre, a mentor trainer for the Greenwich Directorate of Education, and has worked for numerous youth arts organisations across London. Talmud is also a recognised Sifu/Master of martial arts and founder of his own system.

Foreword

❝I am delighted to introduce this new book about leadership, which aims to inspire leaders of the future in post-compulsory education. The post-compulsory sector faces many challenges. It now caters for more than 6 million learners over the age of 16 in further and higher education colleges, adult and community education centres, work-based training providers and prison education departments, and it has a budget of over £8 billion. Yet by 2007, about 60% of the leaders in the sector will retire. There is therefore a 'succession crisis', which is being addressed by the new Centre for Excellence in Leadership (CEL), set up by the Learning and Skills Council. In this book, a number of models of leadership are explored. It reports on ten interviews carried out in 2004–05 with experienced educational leaders from across the UK, whose work was recommended in different ways: by Ofsted, the LSC STAR award process or, more quietly, by individual members of staff, governors and students, as providing examples of outstanding leadership. I welcome this work to inspire new leaders of the future for the benefit of those adults and young people who are learners.❞

Baroness Tessa Blackstone
Vice Chancellor of the University of Greenwich

Acknowledgements

With grateful thanks to all the leaders who were interviewees and advisers for this book: Talmud Bah, Bob Challis, David Collins, John Guy, Daniel Khan, Anne Morahan, Andrew Morris, Wendy Moss, Lynne Sedgmore and Ruth Silver. Thanks to Baroness Tessa Blackstone for the Foreword, to the Centre for Excellence in Leadership for permission to reproduce the *Leadership Qualities Framework*, to Pencil-Sharp Editors and to Tracey Alcock of David Fulton Publishers. Also to Shirley Leathers for her efficient, humorous administrative assistance and to Dr Tricia Meers and Bill Goddard for their support. Special thanks to my mum Phyllis, to Kevin and Imogen, Celia, Peter, Sarah and Arthur for making available so willingly and patiently their time, support, resources and help for this book.

Finally, I want to thank many friends and colleagues who have debated concepts of educational leadership with me tirelessly, including Professors Yvonne Hillier, Ian McNay and Patrick Ainley, Francia Kinchington, Barbara Chandler, Suzanna Stein, Bernadette Katchoff, Linda Karlsen, Susan Baylis, Christine Rose, Simon Walker and Malcolm Ryan. I thank also, for formative educational influence, colleagues in the Greenwich Lifelong Learning Partnership, Adult Learners' Working Group, 14–19 Greenwich partnership, the LSDA/LSRN LSE Regional offices, staff and members, colleagues in Abingdon and Whitney College, City and Islington College, the former Islington Adult Education Service, the LOCN Board of Trustees, Kent Thameside Learning Steering Group, North Kent Area Investment Framework Education and Skills Working Group, Shooters' Hill Post-16 Centre Governing Body, Bexley College Governing Body, the Arts Learning Partnership, JISC eLISA and BFI Movie Memories projects, and colleagues in the University of Greenwich School of Education and Training, and its partner and network colleges, who have supported and helped me in the post-compulsory education sector, to which, after 30 years' experience, I hope to contribute a work that will, in some measure, help future leaders.

Introduction

❝We must become the change we want to see in the world.❞
Mahatma Gandhi

Leadership is still an enigma, more talked about than understood, more investigated than proven. We still struggle in puzzled fascination with leadership. What is it? Who 'owns' it? How do seemingly excellent leaders achieve what they do, time and again? Why are apparently poor leaders the way they are? Are these qualities 'fixed', or can we change them? What is 'good leadership'? Is there a menu for it? Where is this?

We still don't really know what leadership is. It eludes comprehensive definition. Yet there is so much interest in leadership in the post-compulsory education (PCE) sector and, within this, Learning and Skills (LSS), that the time seemed ripe to examine leadership from a fresh perspective. It seemed time for authentic leaders in PCE to speak out in invigorating, diverse, distinctive ways. In this book, you can 'hear' the voices of leaders whose influence many welcome as exceptional. Here you can consider perspectives on leadership, collected together for leaders of the future.

Reviewers we consulted about leadership in PCE said it wasn't a good time for a comprehensive textbook or 'guru' guide to leadership in post-compulsory education. Reviewers felt that there is no *one* way to sum up effective leadership in the sector, and may never be. We may always want to celebrate an invigorating diversity of achievements in leadership. Reviewers felt a

> The key to successful leadership today is influence, not authority.
> *Kenneth Blanchard*

large number of staff, perhaps particularly in further education (FE), had lost heart in the concept and practices of management and leadership, and would not, *at all*, appreciate being 'preached at'. Some felt there had been so many problems with 'top-down' prescriptive 'managerialism', since the incorporation of FE colleges in 1993, that changes were needed. It would be good, they felt,

1

to have a fresh look at leadership from an individual, reflective point of view, considering new perspectives and situated examples from leaders with a good record in PCE, in the context of new initiatives such as the work of the Centre for Excellence in Leadership (CEL), set up for providers funded by the Learning and Skills Council (LSC).

Leadership is, in fact, regarded in prior literature as a notoriously tricky and elusive concept to define comprehensively. Gregory, writing in 1996 on the development of effective leadership for change management in FE colleges, cited Marshall (1995), noting 'reservations and scepticism about whether there is – or indeed if it is even possible to make – a value-free definition of leadership' (Gregory, 1996, p.47).

Northouse (2004) echoes this disinclination to pin down a generalised definition of leadership, noting it 'has many different meanings' (Northouse, 2004, p.2). Yet he discerns four main elements in 'leadership'. It:

1. is a process
2. involves influence
3. occurs in a group context
4. involves goal attainment.

By focusing on such generalised descriptors, Northouse arrives at the following definition: 'Leadership is a process whereby an individual influences a group of individuals to achieve a common goal' (2004, p.3). Whether or not we agree with Northouse, most would agree that leadership generally is considered to require 'followership' of some kind.

However, we might also want to take the heat off individuals and consider placing emphasis more on groups, envisaging leadership as a series of sets of relationships of influence. Leadership could then be defined as: 'Shared understandings of relationships of influence within a leadership context, operating dynamically in a series of processes to achieve mutual goals.'

Strictly hierarchical leader-follower theories, especially heroic models, begin to seem increasingly 'last century' as Bob Challis said when I went to interview him (see Chapter 14). Lacking relevance in a postmodern world influenced by quantum mechanics, strict hierarchical transactional models seem now to be outdated. We may query whether leadership is, also, always located in 'individuals'. A group of individuals may lead others, whether formally or informally. Leadership may also be considered *a field of interactive relationships of influence*, in which many individuals, leaders and followers, play different parts leading different, specialist areas, in a series of ongoing dynamic processes.

Leadership is about relationships in a heterarchy

Field (2002), also attempting to define leadership, in comparison with management, analysed images on the Internet representing 'leadership' (187 images) and 'management' (186 images), deciding that:

> Leadership is about taking action and communicating values in the context of a relationship. It is not about reinforcing the status quo and . . . reliance on hierarchy . . . leadership is different from management . . . leadership applies to all kinds of people at all levels in organisations . . . leadership is about relationships.   (Field, 2002)

Keith Grint observes that, in successful leadership situations, relationships are effectively situated in a *heterarchy* in which communication occurs via an egalitarian 'exchange model', rather than in a hierarchy with linear 'top-down' expectations of command and control in a 'transmission model':

> Power is not so much a possession but a relationship . . . A heterarchy is a movable hierarchy where people would replace leaders on a temporary basis . . . leadership occurs throughout the organisation and is not constrained to the formal positions in the hierarchy . . .
>   (Keith Grint, speaking in a televised interview with Bryant, 2004)

This key area of relationships is linked also to new quantum thinking about science, as Wheatley notes in her study of leadership:

> Nothing exists independent of its relationships, whether . . . subatomic particles or human affairs . . . relationships are a growing theme in today's leadership thinking.
>   (Wheatley, 1999, pp.163–4)

To engage with relationships, leadership development needs to occur not only at the level of behaviour, but also in the consciousness of leaders, as Blank (1995, p.22) reminds us. The development of awareness of self, others and of situations is a key component of leadership. To what extent has this been addressed in PCE leadership research and theory?

Relative sparseness of research on leadership

Well, not much, so far. Jackie Lumby and Tim Simkins recognised in 2002 a 'relative sparseness of research and publication in the field of leadership and management within further/technical education' (Lumby and Simkins, 2002, p.5). The field has, during past years, begun to grow rapidly, influenced by new initiatives from the Learning and Skills Research Centre (LSRC), the Learning and Skills Development Agency (LSDA), and the Centre for Excellence in Leadership (CEL). There seems little doubt that it will grow again in size and complexity during the next several years. There is much work to do in LSS leadership development, as Lumby *et al.* report in their recent study (2005). This applies particularly in the areas of transformational and distributed leadership as well as to diversity initiatives, in terms of understanding organisational processes, knowledge of systemic principles and theories, skill in relationship building and developments in leaders' awareness of self and others.

Reviewers for this book reported a general disillusionment with top-down coercive styles of management, in particular, post-incorporation 1993, combined with a history of generally low levels of awareness of followers' needs by those in senior management. We therefore felt it was time to open the window to new ways of thinking about leadership, and let in a bit of fresh air into the somewhat overheated debate about targets for performance.

The kind of reductive 'performativity' Avis and Bathmaker (2004) describe, which Hargreaves (2003) characterises as 'government-by-target', has, many hope, largely run its course. Although targets for performance are and will remain 'an essential part of the toolkit', we can observe with Hargreaves (2003), Ball (2003) and Avis and Bathmaker (2004) that current examples of the over-regulation of PCE institutions are ultimately counter-productive. 'You cannot fatten a turkey by weighing it,' as some educators have observed, citing this old saying in wry criticism of over-zealous target-setting bureaucracy. And if what gets done in some institutions is only what is measured, perhaps we need to widen out our measuring tools, handling all with greater wisdom and insight. In such a 'fabulous place to be' as this sector (see Chapter 11, interview with Ruth Silver), it seems well worth it to make every effort to inspire new faith and hope in the potential for excellent new leadership to be developed over the next few years.

A new politics of hope for post-compulsory education leadership

In contrast to the culture of performativity, Avis and Bathmaker (2004) have in fact proposed a new 'politics of hope' for post-compulsory education, 'characterised by an aspiration towards critical and democratic practice'. In recognising that such hope must not just be a vaguely 'romantic possibilitarian' empty discourse individually enshrined in solipsistic wooliness as 'reflective practice' (Avis and Bathmaker, 2004, p.301), these researchers assert that new hope must be grounded in real, situated, whole-sector structural proactive critique of professional practice. Can we discover a new politics of hope of this kind for leadership in the sector?

There and back again: reporting from journeys to ten institutions

In this book I report from my journeys to ten institutions across the UK between August, 2004, and April, 2005, to gain views from leaders in the field about their own, situated, specific experiences of leadership. Reviewers said they wanted to hear the opinions of excellent leaders: they would like to read about views from across a number of different parts of post-compulsory education. We listened to reviewers, and so provide here some reflections from ten leaders who kindly met me to discuss, for this book, the question of leadership in post-compulsory education and its future.

What is post-compulsory education? The 'Yes, but . . . and' sector

Post-compulsory education is that field of post-16 education, sometimes loosely termed 'lifelong learning', which is concerned mainly with FE entry to Level 3 sub-degree work undertaken by post-compulsory age learners. In prior work on post-compulsory education research with Professor Yvonne Hillier of City University (Jameson and Hillier, 2003), we summed up the diversity of the PCE sector by saying that it mainly comprised 'educational provision for post-compulsory age learners at sub-degree level in a range of post-16, adult and extra-mural education and training institutions', noting also the 'large amount of provision we could call "post-compulsory" in higher education, especially in full and part-time extramural, adult and evening classes.'

We noted also at that time that the 'PCE sector educates the largest number of learners in the UK' (Jameson and Hillier, 2003, p.2). The diversity of PCE is nowhere more present than in the general FE colleges sector. Stanton and Morris (2000), celebrating the 'inclusive' strengths of colleges, and noting the need for FE-based research to inform colleges, observe that FE '. . . has been described as the "Yes, but . . . sector"', citing Stanton's earlier work on FE colleges:

> Does it provide for most 16–19 year olds? Yes, but the vast majority of participants are over 19. Is it the most important provider of vocational education? Yes, but it also provides the majority of 'A' Levels. Are most students part-time? Yes, but FE is also the biggest provider of full-time post-compulsory education and training, with more students than schools and universities put together.   (Stanton, 1997, p.15)

If Stanton and Morris describe FE as the 'Yes, but . . .' sector, we could perhaps describe post-compulsory education as the 'Yes, but . . . and' sector, since PCE is larger than and includes FE.

In the 'Yes, but . . . and' sector, not much has changed overall since 2003 with regards to the quantity of learners, diversity of provision, size of the sector and its importance nationally (NAO, 2005). What has been changing very much, though, is a new emphasis now being placed on learners aged 14–16, and the link with school provision in the 14–19 qualifications amendments which, with some regrettable limitations, followed the Tomlinson Committee Report and its recommendations (2004). What has also developed in significance is a significantly greater emphasis on both quality and leadership in the implementation of *Success for All* (DfES, 2002). The overriding importance of leadership initiatives within this is reported by the National Audit Office in their recent report on strategic leadership within the sector, which is highlighted as a key area within the four main strands of *Success for All* (NAO, 2005, p.8).

Definitions and terminology for the 'Yes, but . . . and' sector

In the definition of 'post-compulsory' education, I refer to post-16 institutions such as FE colleges, sixth form centres, adult and community education, prison education, training and voluntary institutions funded within the LSS. However, there is a certain valuable fuzziness about the defining boundaries of 'post-compulsory education', including higher education (HE) as well as 14+ provision. In terms of the distinction between 'PCE' and 'PCET', I use the arguably broader term 'PCE' to refer to all post-compulsory education and training provision.

The 'other' sector, adaptively layered: a 'not-school, not-university' sector

A relative vagueness in terminological usage creates a constantly redefinable space for the 'being-ness' of PCE or PCET to be debated, tested and contested. The conceptualisation of 'PCE' or 'post-compulsory education' (whether and/or not 'training') and/or 'further education' and/or 'learning and skills' in woolly terms as 'the other' sector (more easily named as '*not* schools' and '*not* higher education') reinforces both its relative marginalisation and its growing importance. So, the term 'post-compulsory education' is used as a short form here for educational provision in *both* 'post-compulsory education' (PCE) *and* 'post-compulsory education and training (PCET)'. The term 'post-compulsory education' is used interchangeably with 'PCE'. The term 'further education' is used to designate FE college provision within the PCE sector, while 'learning and skills' designates provision funded by the LSC. The 'Yes, but . . . and' concept of PCE covers them all, the short form for which, in this book, is just 'PCE', or 'the sector'.

What does this book provide?

This work was written to be an accessible practitioner handbook for reflection, linked with stories from ten leaders I've met during the past year. The book focuses primarily on *distributed* and *transformational* models of leadership, and on variants of these. I am interested in leadership as a process throughout organisations, rather than one residing only at the top of given hierarchies or in positional roles. The book does *not* seek to report proven research about this conclusively. You do *not* need to learn it off by heart for any exam! I provide a manual for reflection, with some quotations from prior leaders and references, positioned like breadcrumbs, to mark the paths in our journeys of understanding about leadership.

> Exceptional leaders cultivate the Merlin-like habit of acting in the present moment as ambassadors of a radically different future, in order to imbue their organisations with a breakthrough vision of what it is possible to achieve.
>
> *Charles E. Smith*

As a 'visioning' practitioners' handbook on leadership with 'live' stories and quotes from leaders for future leader-practitioners, this work may hopefully provide an aid to reflection. Interviews were carried out on a basis of trust, to provide useful notes and reflections for the future from well-known leaders. All individuals were free to say whatever they wanted. There was no 'party line' when we completed the interviews. There still isn't. The work is therefore a complementary reference volume with selected excerpts from case study interviews, to be read alongside research and development reports, handbooks and textbooks on leadership. The interview extracts provided give a unique account of leadership from the autobiographical points of view – the 'stories', in effect – of some leaders themselves. These leaders were selected from recent successful examples of PCE leadership because in specific ways they have been regarded by colleagues and/or assessed by external agencies as providing outstanding examples of educational leadership. Interviewees' reflections arise from around 250+ collective years of experience in the PCE sector. Together these provide, as Ruth Silver says about the artwork in Lewisham College, 'incitements to thought', catalytic stimuli for reflection on future leadership (see Chapter 11).

The challenge

During my years working in colleges and adult and community education from 1974 to 2000, I noticed increasingly a tendency towards what researchers have called a growing 'managerialism' within the sector. As a senior then executive manager myself in Adult and Community Learning (ACL) and FE between 1987 and 2000, I observed many different aspects of this phenomenon. I, like others, have been professionally and personally concerned about it – as a practitioner,

> The leaders who work most effectively ... never say 'I' ... that's not because they have trained themselves not to say 'I'. They don't think 'I'. They think 'we'; they think 'team'. They accept responsibility ... don't sidestep it, but 'we' gets the credit ... This is what creates trust, what enables you to get the task done.
>
> *Peter Drucker*

former PCE senior manager for 18 years, governor and trustee board member, teacher trainer, academic and writer. A number of instances have occurred in relation to poor or unethical leadership in post-compulsory education during the past decade which have greatly disturbed many colleagues. The literature strongly indicates that I am by no means alone in such reflections. There have been widespread anxieties about excessively controlling, inadequately supportive and ineffectively directed managerial practices in PCE, particularly since 1993. It is time to address the urgent needs for improvements in leadership across the sector.

A step change for excellence in leadership

I also believe that, for this to be effective, such initiatives need to be carried out in ways that genuinely engage, support and develop staff in widespread ownership of leadership. There is a lot more to say

> History is Philosophy teaching by examples.
>
> *Thucydides*

and more to listen to on leadership, to improve PCE delivery. We might listen here to the translation of Lao Tse's words that 'as for the best leaders, the people do not notice their existence'. Who – or what factors – have not yet been listened to sufficiently on leadership in PCE? Who or what have we taken for granted?

The invisibility paradox

There are different kinds of 'not noticing' in terms of behaviour and systems as well as people. Perhaps we do not notice enough the successful examples of PCE leadership right in front of our eyes, performing well every day, assuming success is automatic. We may think successful institutions and people are 'just lucky', privileged by circumstance. Although examples of good leadership may be well known, we don't always *really* notice what characterises them, what causes conditions for success to develop, what the views and actions are of people formative in creating success. It's almost as though these leadership situations are partly invisible, even though we know they're there. Perhaps it all just seems like too much hard work sometimes to acknowledge, understand and emulate ways in which successful leadership situations have been created. It's a lot easier to assume that effective leadership arises through fortuituous circumstance, luck in inspections, clever marketing and a good client group. We are sometimes good at *explaining away* the success of others.

What is more challenging is to recognise that everyone is potentially capable of achieving successful leadership. To say this requires us to work hard to *create* the right conditions and circumstances, staff and resources for leadership success, and to carry out improvements proactively. It's about having the *passion for excellence* and *focus to achieve* that the new CEL has listed as two key criteria in its *Leadership Qualities Framework*, as discussed by Lynne Sedgmore. A passionate desire to achieve high quality, and an appreciation of learning for its own sake, are cited as key factors in leadership by all the leaders here represented. We must *really want*, and plan, to cultivate the development of excellence in provision, and in leadership, in order to begin, in any way, to achieve this.

How to cultivate a pearl, not just an irritated oyster

Given a passion for excellence and focus on student achievement, the kind of 'irritation' to achieve higher standards noted by John Guy (see Chapter 9) can act as the spur to further development and transformation of provision, a desire to *mobilise to impact* and *sustain momentum*, the other two key qualities in the CEL *Framework*. A particular kind of way of creatively engaging with that 'irritation' emerges in effective leadership situations. As David Collins says (see Chapter 10), it's a way of leading and managing the desire to achieve in institutions so that you develop a pearl, 'not just an irritated oyster'.

Eating the menu, not the dinner

What is this 'way' of doing things? It's hard to say. We have a habit of categorising leadership as a 'thing' that can be pinned down and classified rather than as a dynamic, enigmatic series of processes taking place in socially situated communities of organisations. As Prince (2005) observes in her article on Taoism in leadership, we have a tendency in the West towards an active, hierarchical, controlling, classificatory approach to leadership which she compares with 'eating the menu rather than the dinner'. She notes in her article that since 'leadership remains a tantalizing enigma for Western thinkers and practitioners' despite thousands of studies on the subject, we may benefit from considering a Taoist approach towards leadership, 'moving away from codes, prescriptions and specifications much more towards a located and responsive social skill . . .' (Prince, 2005, p.106).

Prince observes that sometimes our Western ideas about leadership tend to be task-focused, whereas Taoist principles are mainly process-focused. The kind of leadership which is 'dispersed and systemic, flowing through the organisation across levels and hierarchies' (see Briggs, 2005b, p.229; Lumby, 2002; Ogawa and Bossert, 1997, p.10), conceptualises the involvement by all staff in decision making as a routine expectation of professionalism. Professional organisations, full of creative energy, high standards of quality, and egalitarian respect for staff, may be the products of truly excellent shared leadership situations. Such organisations foster community ownership of a collaborative mission prioritising student-centred provision, in a friendly place in which people enjoy their work. Does this kind of high quality expertise in leadership already exist in PCE? Well, I argue that through authentic accounts and stories from effective leaders, in situated examples, metaphors and models, we can catch glimpses of some 'ways' (as opposed to one way) in which the process of 'doing leadership' is already highly effective in some PCE institutions.

Quantum leadership; connected energies

Some successful public leaders do their work with a vibrant flow-through of words and actions, simultaneously connected and authentic. The innovative creativity of values-driven expert leadership positively influences organisations. Such experts seem to melt into what they do. Person and task unite in what Ruth Silver might call 'the love of the task' (see Chapter 11), or in a 'creative process' that Talmud Bah (see Chapter 17) describes as being 'like an undefined conscious energy'. Expertise doesn't 'try' to work well: it has an 'always-already' relaxed brilliance which makes the complex task of heading up institutions/groups seem to flow, with easy grace. These leaders perform like Billy Elliot, the talented dancer from a mining community who overcame prejudices towards male dancers in achieving success. Billy felt he 'disappeared', becoming at one with the dance: '. . . Once I get going, I sorta disappear. I feel a change in my body – like fire, like a bird flying, like electricity' (Hall, 2000). The spontaneous energy of effective connections through relationships between people in shared leadership can be interpreted, in quantum leadership theory, as the kind of brilliant performance that happens when 'great groups' operate well together (Wheatley, 1999). However, we may also reflect that, behind such apparently easy expertise, there may be many years of gruelling hard work and sustained, unremitting determination to succeed.

In a fractured postmodern world, in which we observe, with Binney *et al.* (2005) that 'there are no more heroes', only ordinary people struggling against difficult odds to behave with vision, integrity, high standards, respect for others and compassion, we might want to celebrate PCE leaders whose work is characterised by deep expertise and the passionate stewardship of learning. We might especially want to respect the professional love of the task, integrity and rich knowledge informing the work of the educational leaders interviewed here.

> If you want together honey, don't kick over the beehive.
> *Dale Carnegie*

A phoenix-like deep energy in community leadership

There is another category of 'not noticing'. This refers to the category of people not at top or senior management levels, but acting as good leaders at other levels. Some of the most dedicated and talented people in the sector do not put themselves forward, and, perhaps out of self-consciousness, do not want to. Among these are numerous people working with dedication, energy and humour every day in colleges, adult education centres, work-based training providers, voluntary groups, sixth form colleges, ICT centres, libraries,

> First they ignore you, then they laugh at you, then they fight you, then you win.
> *Mahatma Gandhi*

prison education services, advisory services, administrative centres and post-16 agencies all over the UK and beyond. Some of these people are perhaps truly 'the best leaders', at many different levels, whose work seems to go relatively unnoticed, except by learners and staff. Everyone seems to rely on such people, but perhaps takes them for granted. And if such unacknowledged leaders were to be told that we were discussing them in a book, they would probably laugh, and say, 'Me, a leader? You must be joking!' And yet, such staff sometimes have a phoenix-like energy in service of the sector and its communities, despite setbacks, challenges, problems and criticisms – it is these kinds of day-to-day ordinary informal leaders operating at a variety of levels in our institutions that we most need to take notice of and nurture.

In the past few years, a number of initiatives have been launched to acknowledge the work of leaders who hitherto may have been insufficiently recognised. These initiatives include the 'STAR' award process of the LSC, and Beacon Awards schemes organised by the LSC and Association of Colleges (AoC).

The interviews

I am pleased to include in this book interviews with three 'STAR' awardees: Professor Daniel Khan of the Grimsby Institute of Further and Higher Education, Wendy Moss of the City Lit Training Unit and Anne Morahan, Education Manager at HMP Dover Immigration and Removals Centre. In addition to interviews with STAR award winners, I have during the last year been fortunate to have had the opportunity to interview a range of other leaders from PCE in the learning and skills sector whom I and others regard as outstanding in their leadership qualities. I interviewed these people to find out what they think about leadership in the sector. The full list of interviewees is the following:

- Ruth Silver, CBE, Principal of Lewisham College
- Lynne Sedgmore, CBE, Chief Executive, the Centre for Excellence in Leadership
- Wendy Moss, Manager of the Centre for Teacher and Management Training, City Lit
- Dr Andrew Morris, Programme Leader, National Educational Research Forum
- Anne Morahan, Area Education Manager, HMP Dover Immigration Removal Centre
- Professor Daniel Khan, Principal, The Grimsby Institute of Further and Higher Education
- Dr John Guy, OBE, Principal, The Sixth Form College, Farnborough
- Dr David Collins, CBE, Principal, South Cheshire College
- Bob Challis, former Principal of Abingdon and Whitney College
- Talmud Bah, Assistant Director, Second Wave Centre for Youth Arts.

These people are all, in different ways, exceptional for prior demonstration of leadership qualities, in terms of numerous contributions to UK and international education at post-compulsory level. The interviewees are ten examples of leaders from different kinds of institutions in or closely related to the PCE sector. Some interviewees here represented were given national awards or honours for their work in education. Some interviewees have not yet received formal awards for their work, but were recommended to me more quietly by others as examples of outstanding leadership.

With interviewees' permission, key verbatim extracts from the interviews are published here in the case study 'reflections' section of this book. The interviewees whose words are presented in Part Two are leaders whose work, institutions, departments, teachers and support staff have collectively inspired, taught and supported many thousands of people in PCE throughout many years. I thank all the interviewees for their goodwill, patience with my long-winded questionnaires, and the wonderful examples they have given the sector.

The audience for this book

This book is for the leaders of the post-compulsory education institutions of tomorrow, forming a practitioner's handbook about leadership. The book draws on documentary evidence from leadership and management literature, on verbal evidence from the interviews, and from my own reflections and notes about the work of leaders that personally inspired me during more than 30 years' experience of education. Although some of the leaders interviewed here are heads of institutions, not all are. One of their defining features is that they have all, in their own ways, fought against the odds to uphold high standards of excellent quality and ethics, good service to learners and generosity to staff.

I include verbatim extracts from interviewees to guide and inspire practitioners in post-compulsory education and training. In part, the interviews contain intellectual models of leadership, but they are, beyond intellect, also informed by passion, humanity, courage, vulnerability and, especially, by the diligent experience of many years' hard work in the PCE sector. All these leaders impressed me deeply as individuals recognising and acting on the kind of vision enshrined in what Emerson (1803–1882) said – 'Character is higher than intellect. A great soul will be strong to live as well as think.' I therefore provide a 'rounded' view of connected, 'ordinary', humane leadership. This is informed by intellect, professional expertise, action, emotion, cultural and social diversity, and spiritual and moral values, in order that the leaders of the future may prove to be 'all that they can be'.

The use of keywords

At the end of each case study interview chapter, I have used a series of keywords to identify a number of salient facts about the interviewee, institution, sub-sector within post-compulsory education, the institution's geographical situation and some distinguishing features about the kind of provision and the leadership model I have selected to correspond with the case study interview.

The reason for this is that, to an extent, the interviewees were representative of the sector, in terms of phases of education, size of institution, urban or rural character, nature of client group and type of provision. This was done in response to a request from the reviewers for the book. As there were only ten interviewees, however, the level of 'representativeness' was necessarily incomplete (for example, there is no institution from the South West, no specialist or agricultural college, heads of subject departments (who have key leadership roles) were not interviewed, and there was only one kind of specialist institution to represent prison education).

Therefore, this gives only a selective glimpse of some aspects of very effective leadership operating in the sector during the period 2004–2005. In order to make this more useful to those embarking on leadership careers or carrying out improvements to institutions, however, a series of distinguishing features are provided in these keywords to guide the reader.

Summary of book

Following this Introduction, Part One opens with Chapter 1, 'State of play', defining and examining some current perspectives in leadership theory and practice in post-compulsory education. Chapter 2, 'Leadership in education', explores models of educational leadership to provide a background to the interviews with leaders reported later in the book. Chapter 3, 'Leaders or managers?', examines the difference between leadership and management and considers the role of academic leadership and professionalism in relation to this. Chapter 4, 'Equality and diversity perspectives', provides a brief examination of the need for and progress in initiatives to encourage greater equality and diversity of representation in leadership in the PCE sector, while Chapter 5, 'It's all change! Transformations in post-compulsory education' examines some of the massive changes that have affected leadership in the sector. Chapter 6, 'Leaders in trouble – the dark side', considers leadership in the context of failures and problems, while Chapter 7, 'New leaders on the move', provides a round-up of new ideas for future leaders, including the CEL *Leadership Qualities Framework*, verbatim comments from the interviewees and a proposed new model and framework for the leadership. In Part Two, Chapters 8–17 provide ten reports of the interviews with sectoral leaders, including detailed extracts from the interviews themselves. Finally, Chapter 18, 'Endnote', rounds up the book and reflects on experiences gained from the interviews, literature and observations on leadership. The book concludes with some suggestions for future research on leadership in the sector.

About the author

Jill Jameson, PhD, MA (distinction, King's College), MA (Goldsmith's), MA (Cantab.), PGCE (Nottingham, distinction), PGSAD, BA (UCT). Currently Director of Research in the School of Education and Training, the University of Greenwich, Jill was previously the University's senior management Director of Lifelong Learning (2000–2004). Prior to that, she worked in executive and senior management in PCE (1989–2000) in Abingdon College, City and Islington College and Islington Adult Education Service.

PART 1

Leadership in Post-compulsory Education

1

State of play: leadership now in post-compulsory education

> **"Absolute identity with one's cause is the first and great condition of successful leadership."**
> Woodrow Wilson

Leadership now in post-compulsory education

The case for leadership in post-compulsory education (PCE) is examined in this book in relation to a number of factors. These include:

1. the role of the Centre for Excellence in Leadership (CEL) in the UK learning and skills sector, and the CEL *Leadership Qualities Framework*

> The leader's first job is to be a missionary, to remind people what is special about them and their institutions. Second it is to set up the infrastructure for that to happen.
>
> *Charles Handy*

2. selected aspects of the background history of post-compulsory education

3. institutional leadership within the Learning and Skills Council (LSC) funded sector

4. Learning Skills Development Agency (LSDA) and Learning and Skills Research Centre (LSRC) leadership studies

5. selected studies from prior research on leadership in post-compulsory education and more generally in academic leadership studies

6. the different roles played by specific sub-sectors within post-compulsory education

7. the large numbers of current PCE leaders who are about to retire.

As we began to explore in the Introduction, we consider all these factors, together with case study interviews, to answer the following questions:

- What is leadership in post-compulsory education (PCE) and why is it important?
- What are some current issues and models affecting PCE leadership?
- How did ten successful PCE leaders perceive leadership in an interview for this book?
- What lessons might we draw for future leaders from these interviews and reflections?

To achieve this, the book considers leadership in a wide-ranging way in the PCE sector, reporting the views of the leaders in selected case study interviews.

We may have been concerned lately by a tendency to assume appointees to leadership positions are necessarily beneficent, assuming 'greatness' when they step into the empty shoes of a senior post. To counter potential mis-nomers such as the descriptor 'heroic leadership' to those who can't walk on water or fly plane-less yet, we can perhaps recognise that most of us ordinary human beings need to develop leadership strengths within ourselves. Rather than leave things to less beneficent, even mediocre elements, we need to take up the mantle of leadership more widely. If Lawrence J. Peter's concept *The Peter Principle* (Peters and Hull, 1969) – that employees will rise to, and remain at, their level of maximum occupational incompetence – still applies, and if Scott Adams' *Dilbert Principle* (1996) – that incompetent staff may be moved to where they can do the least harm: man-agement – has ever applied, then institutions remain dangerously vulnerable to incompetence in leadership. Are we doomed to live in a Dilbertian and Peter-principled world of promoted incompetents? Or is there something that can be done to redress this?

> Failure to acknowledge and examine the 'dark side' of leader-ship . . . can distort efforts to learn about the leadership process . . . Authentic understanding of leader-ship requires a balanced discussion.
>
> *Clements and Washbush*

Well, for one thing, we could consider more widely increasing the 'talent pool' of leadership, as it is the mission of CEL to do. If we don't take up the chal-lenge of leadership, someone else, who perhaps can't handle this as effectively, might, and we may be forced to endure, relatively speaking, their incompe-tence. Such a view helps us to take responsibility in different ways for our com-munal destiny. It's a lot safer to develop our own leadership strengths than to rely on leaders who might be narcissistic and self-serving. Dourado and Blackburn (2005) cite Robert Hare, psychology professor at the University of

British Columbia, on the tendency of what he terms 'corporate psychopaths' in the upper echelons of management to be:

> Impulsive, arrogant, manipulative, callous, impatient, unreliable, and prone to fly into rages. They break promises, take credit for the work of others and blame everyone else when things go wrong. Wherever you get power, prestige and money, you will find them. They are smooth, polished, engaging and often charismatic.   (Dourado and Blackburn, 2005, p.5)

> ...leadership is ... a process whereby an individual influences a group of individuals to reach a common goal ... a process that can be learned and is available to everyone.
>
> *Peter Northouse*

Hopefully, this kind of 'corporate psychopath' is a relatively rare phenomenon in PCE, but to guard against poor management of all kinds we do need to consider whether the task of leadership is one that should be widely taken up across institutions by everyone capable of authority, rather than just by the sometimes ineptly selected few. Rather than give in to poor leadership as 'victims', it may help us to reflect on Viktor Frankl's first principle for bringing meaning and fulfillment to life, even in the worst circumstances: 'exercise the freedom to choose your attitude'. Frankl's story as a surviving holocaust victim, imprisoned in Nazi concentration camps in World War II, is an outstanding testament to personal courage in the face of terrible suffering. Discussing Frankl's seven principles in relation to work situations, Alex Pattakos outlines these as:

> (1) we are free to choose our attitude to everything that happens to us; (2) we can realize our will to meaning by making a conscious commitment to meaningful values and goals; (3) we can find meaning in all of life's moments; (4) we can learn to see how we work against ourselves; (5) we can look at ourselves from a distance and gain insight and perspective as well as laugh at ourselves; (6) we can shift our focus of attention when coping with difficult situations; and (7) we can reach out beyond ourselves and make a difference in the world.   (Pattakos, 2004, p.5)

To reach out beyond ourselves and make a difference, ordinary heroes need to take up the challenge of leadership, for the sake of quality learner-focused education, in the struggle against disillusionment, cynicism, complacency, apathy and poor quality provision, and to ensure that bullying and autocratic management are not allowed to thrive routinely, as they have sometimes been allowed to do, in our public sector institutions.

What is leadership in post-compulsory education?

The distinction between leadership and management described articulately in professional and academic literature is to some extent replicated in research literature in this field of post-compulsory education. Leadership in this sector comprises processes and actions influencing other people which affect learners in relation to education and training provision within the sector or institution. Our suggestion here is not dissimilar to the general definitions of leadership discussed earlier in the Introduction. We could also share with Northouse the view that leadership 'is a process that can be learned and is available to every-one' (2004, p.11).

A growing number of studies have been and are being carried out in the field of PCE leadership (for example, Briggs, 2005b; CEL, 2004b; Frearson, 2003a, 2003b; Gleeson, 2001; Hill, 2000; Lumby, 1997a, 1997b, 2001, 2003a, 2003b; Lumby *et al.* 2002, 2004, 2005; NAO, 2005; Randle and Brady, 1997a, 1997b; Simkins and Lumby, 2002) including, in particular, *The Leading Learning Project*, a major four-part LSRC-funded study on leadership in post-compulsory education carried out between 2003 and 2005. Evidence, compiled by Frearson (2003a, 2003b) for the first work package of the LSRC project from Adult Learning Inspectorate/Ofsted inspection reports according to the *Common Inspection Framework* (CIF) for post-16 education and training providers, noted the fact that inspection results in 2001–2002 indicated leadership and manage-ment in 50% of work-based learning (WBL) and nearly 25% of colleges were regarded as 'less than satisfactory' (Frearson, 2003a, p.1), according to the crite-ria of the CIF. Other research reports such as that by Hughes (2002) had already revealed that inspection grades for leadership in work-based learning declined dramatically since 1998–99. Hence, Frearson notes that:

It is hardly surprising, therefore, to find leader-ship and management development at the heart of *Success for All*, the government's reform strat-egy for further education and training (DfES, 2002), which announced the launch of a new Leadership College . . .   (Frearson, 2003a, p.1)

> Learning is not attained by chance, it must be sought for with ardour and attended to with diligence.
>
> *Abigail Adams*

We may have been concerned, like Lumby (2003a), that research on leadership in colleges has mainly so far had a limited focus on individuals, government policy and the volitional power of leaders to shape events in a way that gives a 'two dimensional oil painting when what is needed', in Lumby's view, is 'analy-sis of a three-dimensional moving hologram' (Lumby, 2003a, p.291).

Focus of this book

This book contributes to a number of current attempts (for others, see, for example, Bolden, 2005; Burgoyne, 2004; Frearson, 2002, 2003a; Lumby *et al.*, 2004, 2005) to find a 'better understanding of leadership' in relation to post-compulsory education. Specifically, this is suggested through local, historically situated notes from interviews held with ten post-compulsory education leaders during the past year, using verbatim data collected from one-to-one semi-structured interviews with the leaders themselves. Lumby has noted (Lumby and Simkins, 2002; Lumby et al., 2004), in relation to research on leadership and management in 'post-compulsory/further/technical education', that the 'field is currently underdeveloped' (Lumby and Simkins, 2002, p.8), but that there is still a strong 'pressure' from global factors, policy makers and inspectors 'to make step change improvements to leadership in the sector' (Lumby et al., 2004, p.11). I would agree with this.

> ...You never have so much authority as when you begin to give it away. And so leadership becomes a devolved and distributed feature of high-performing organisations.
>
> *Chris Hughes*

There is a need to define PCE leadership with richer individual variety and detail, more subtlety, complexity, flexibility, inclusiveness and creativity. And also with less of the kind of task-centred conformist reductivism, mechanistic checklisting of attainment targets and 'painting by numbers' to a pre-given palate perhaps more characteristic of the kind of 'banking education' culture Paulo Freire found to be destitute of humanity (Freire, 1972).

There is still, of course, always an absolutely vital need to set targets and monitor checklists to measure performance. There is undoubtedly a continuing imperative to manage, monitor and measure all our work in seeking to attain excellence. The institutions whose leaders are represented here all work to systems of target-setting, monitoring and measurement. They have all been successful, often highly innovative, in completing the tasks of setting and maintaining goals, targets, systems and procedures for institutional performance. All would agree such administrative systems provide an essential backbone for effective leadership. Mechanisms for monitoring performance, for example, provide the substructure of management needed for continuing high quality leadership in education. The Ofsted checklists for leadership and management (Ofsted, 2003, 2005) are useful regarding the characteristics distinguishing 'the highest possible standards and achievements', 'clear strategic thinking and planning for improvement', and objectives, demanding targets, values and effective QA systems that mark out high performing institutions.

We could regard such systems as an essential framework, a skeletal underpinning to maintain good quality. However, these are *not* the only thing, not finally the full, living answer, in terms of the 'connected leadership' needed for rich, complex, variable, high achieving, excellently orientated, inclusive

> No question is so difficult to answer as that to which the answer is obvious.
>
> *George Bernard Shaw*

institutions. A focus on learners' needs, on learning and people is required. In addition, *not only but also*, we need to focus on effective quality assurance and monitoring systems, finance and targets, to drive forward good institutional provision.

Unfortunately, owing to the kind of mechanistic mindset that can sometimes develop when people and organisations are pressured to achieve without having time or resources to reflect, it seems we have sometimes begun to take the mechanistic superstructures and substructures of leadership and management for the thing itself. We have perhaps sometimes begun to mistake the paper and ink for the message written on it, or, as Prince observes, 'the menu for the dinner' (Prince, 2005). Referring to Keith Grint's model of leadership as a 'wheelwright', as cited by David Collins (see Chapter 10), we have perhaps focused too much on the spokes of the wheel (the things, skills and resources organisations need) rather than on the essential connecting spaces in the wheel, the autonomous freedoms of spaces for staff, 'that hold everything in place' (Grint, 2000). As Andrew Morris might observe, we have perhaps been focusing for too long on delivery mechanisms, targets, structures and processes, rather than on holistic long-term values for education centred on learning and people (see Chapter 15).

This book therefore urges us to go back and reflect again to find 'the thing itself' in leadership, the connective spaces that hold together Keith Grint's metaphorical wheel. We need to make more space for the vibrant, good quality, intellectually challenging, emotionally rewarding communities of practice (Wenger, 1998), full of excitement, energy, learning and hope, distinctive with diverse people and purposes, that should be – and in some cases already are – our institutions of learning in PCE. Such institutions place an absolute top priority on the success of learners and clients, fostering achievement, enjoyment and happiness in staff and students. But in order to identify and recognise such strengths in and new potentials for leadership, we also need to look at problem areas.

The dark side of leadership

Like Clements and Washbush (1999), we may have observed that the generally positive face of leadership may be marred by darker sides existing in both leaders and followers. We may be concerned that 'dark' sides to the equation between leaders and followers are too little acknowledged. We may be worried about the Adult Learning Inspectorate (ALI) findings in 2002 that:

> . . . of 298 providers of work-based learning inspected in 2001–02, only one received a grade 1 for leadership and management. The leadership and management of 11 per cent of providers were good, but less than satisfactory in 53 per cent of providers. (ALI, 2002)

We may be worried by Ofsted's (2004a) reports that FE colleges have been judged as failing in the area of leadership and management. Let's consider this in more detail.

Ofsted (2004a) reports on colleges

Reports from Ofsted (2004a), analysing three years of college inspections, found that the national failure rate in the inspection of FE colleges was 12%. We may also have been concerned by the reported north-south divide in college leadership and management performance, noting that Ofsted found more than three times as many colleges in the south of England to be 'failing' in leadership and management, in comparison with the north, observing also that 80% of 'failing' colleges are situated south of Edinburgh (Curtis, 2004). Considering that only 8% of FE colleges were rated by Ofsted as 'outstanding', and that 37 out of more than 300 colleges inspected in England since April 2001 were judged to be 'inadequate' by Ofsted, we may be wondering what on earth has been going on with leadership in the sector, and why David Bell, Her Majesty's Chief Inspector (HMCI), reported recently that he labelled colleges a 'national disgrace' as a result of the recent annual inspectorate report (Ofsted, 2004a). Many in the sector have been concerned about this comment. Some, like John Brennan of the AoC (Association of Colleges), have formally and courageously countered this view (Brennan, 2004); still others have vigorously denied both the tone and substance of these criticisms. Curtis (2004) noted the immediate reaction to David Bell's comments, saying that FE colleges:

> Two thirds of UK organisations are suffering from a shortage of highly effective leaders, according to a survey of 664 training managers . . . by the Chartered Institute of Personnel and Development (CIPD).
>
> *Quentin Reade*

> . . . reacted with fury to comments made today by the head of the education watchdog, Ofsted, that they were a 'national disgrace' . . . The general secretary of the Association of Teachers and Lecturers, Mary Bousted, said: 'The impertinent language used by David Bell is totally inappropriate. FE colleges offer a wide range of vocational and academic subjects and provide education for those young people who very often have not been successful at school . . . To criticise FE colleges and lecturers who are doing outstanding work, faced with poor levels of funding, high staff turnover and quite often poor job security, misses the point entirely.'
>
> (Curtis, 2004)

Dispassionate observers of the PCE sector, observing national statistics from the Chartered Institute of Personnel and Development (Millar, 2005, p.1) reporting on staff shortages and weaknesses in leadership across at least two-thirds of UK organisations, may be interested both to put FE college statistics in a wider perspective, and to encourage and assist all PCE, including FE, institutions to achieve vigorous improvements and new growth for widespread excellence in leadership and management to prepare for the future challenges of the succession crisis. FE colleges, and the

> I hope our wisdom will grow with our power, and teach us, that the less we use our power the greater it will be.
>
> *Thomas Jefferson*

PCE sector in general, then, are by no means alone in needing to work on areas for improvement in leadership – a large number of UK organisations in every sector share not dissimilar difficulties.

Underwhelmed by poor leadership, scandals and bullying

In fact, we may have been underwhelmed by some poorer examples of leadership and management observable in every sector of education and training during the past decade. We may have been shocked by notorious stories of unworthy public sector educational leadership. For example, when the story of Colleen McCabe hit the headlines (Vasager, 2003), we learnt that this headmistress stole £500,000 from the school budget to finance her extravagant lifestyle between 1994 and 1999, while pupils shivered in their classrooms from a lack of heating. The fact that this misuse of public funding carried on for five years without being noticed may particularly alarm us.

We may also have been shocked by earlier stories of other education scandals, notably in PCE, especially in FE colleges, in the 1990s. At this stage, market-led funding principles under the Further Education Funding Council (FEFC) began to create a climate increasingly business-focused (Ainley and Bailey, 1997), in which apparent rewards for entrepreneurship encouraged institutional leaders to overstep the boundaries of acceptability. One infamous example was at Halton College, where senior managers spent more than £6m of public funding during a five-year period on overseas trips producing little benefit to the College, as reported by the NAO (National Audit Office) (1999). In yet another example, Bilston College, near Wolverhampton, lost £3.5m after being forced to end franchised provision following mismanagement (Merrick, 2004).

In her study of women managers in FE, Farzana Shain (1999) cited the FEFC statistic indicating that there was a 32% turnover in principals between 1993 and 1996 following a wave of post-incorporation retirements (FEFC, 1998), signalling a general malaise in human relations in the sector. Shain (1999) observed that:

> Six years on from incorporation, funding constraints coupled with increased workloads and decreased pay have placed considerable strain on the FE sector in terms of its industrial relations (Burchill, 1998). Low staff morale amid widespread allegations of bullying, sleaze and serious financial mismanagement have led to calls for greater accountability . . . (Hodge, 1998). (Shain, 1999, p.1)

Analysing abuses of power in relation to what they observed was a generally 'hegemonic masculinity' of the rapid 'shift to an entrepreneurial work culture' in FE, Kerfoot and Whitehead (1998) reported on 'boy's own stuff': the relationship between masculinist work cultures and management in FE post-incorporation 1993. These researchers observed that 'the invisibility of FE' was marked by 'a lack of academic interrogation of the sector' and abuses of power from the ways in which 'the liberal paternalism' of an earlier era in colleges was replaced by:

the 'macho' culture of contemporary FE . . . apparent in more prominent and public accusations of mis-management, impropriety and fraud directed at individual colleges . . . Indeed, the degree and extent of suspected wrong-doing has led to the Nolan committee on standards in public life extending its remit to include FE, and consider new measures to 'root out sleaze and corruption in universities and colleges' (THES, July, 1997).   (Kerfoot and Whitehead, 1998, p.442)

In their report of case studies carried out with 24 male managers in FE colleges, Kerfoot and Whitehead report a shocking story in which a 'really good' female Head of Special Needs, reapplying for her job in yet another restructuring in one college, did not get the post, was 'traumatised' by this, and, being 'a spinster', went home alone that night to suffer a heart attack caused by the stress of this incident, dying a few days later. It appeared that 'nobody had [had] the decency to talk to her' about the loss of her job (Kerfoot and Whitehead, 1998, p.448).

We may wonder how such appalling human relations and abuses of power could ever occur. What to do – what safeguards to put in place – to ensure such scandals do not happen, either in FE in particular or in PCE in general in the future, is therefore a key issue for those concerned with future PCE educational leadership. We cannot answer this fully in this book. It is beyond the scope of any single publication or any single person to address the legacy of these compelling problems, of the situation in FE college management that Kerfoot and Whitehead summed up in 1998 by saying 'all is not well in FE' (p.449). An issue of historical problems with the management in FE colleges and with wider issues of underfunding, invisibility and relative lack of support for or interrogation of leadership and management practices more generally throughout the PCE sector is one that will take years of work by teams of people, with significant expertise and investment in time and resources, to address in full. But now, having briefly considered some aspects of 'the dark side' of PCE leadership, we need to consider another side to this story.

Celebrating real successes

Putting some of the above in perspective, we may want to celebrate some of the significant successes of the post-compulsory sector, particularly in FE colleges, which have been perhaps unfairly represented as 'failing' in dismissive comments about Ofsted inspections. In a swift successful rebuttal of David Bell's comments about FE college inspection results, John Brennan of the AoC published a letter which put some of the stark findings of Ofsted in perspective. Brennan wrote:

> There is an acknowledged, urgent and serious succession planning problem across the sector with significant numbers of leaders ... due to retire over the next five years. There is growing evidence that there are fewer applicants for senior posts ... CEL will support the sector in addressing the problem.
>
> *Centre for Excellence in Leadership*

> The reality is that of the 37 colleges judged to have serious quality failings ... since 2001, all but one that have completed the process of addressing their weaknesses and being re-inspected have now achieved at least satisfactory gradings. There can be no justification for the claim that 12% of colleges are inadequate ... only about 1% of colleges show serious and persistent weaknesses. (Brennan, 2004, p.4)

Brennan went on to point out the many successes of the FE college sector, noting also 'the stunning satisfaction rates revealed in LSC surveys – which far exceed almost every other public service' (2004, p.5), commenting also on ALI's favourable report on improvements gained in work-based learning. An AoC briefing in 2004, reporting John Brennan's views, asserted that:

> Currently, almost 90% of colleges are regarded at least satisfactory, with a healthy 55% having a good or outstanding judgement made about their leadership and management and over 90% of lessons graded satisfactory or better ... the latest LSC survey of college learners shows that 90% of college students ... are satisfied. ... a small rise on last year's stunning result. The fact that ... 11 out of a total 350 plus colleges in England – were deemed 'failing' – is not to be welcomed, but neither is it at all appropriate to dramatise this small upward trend in the way that it has been. It is inappropriate for immoderate language of this kind to be used about a sector which achieves remarkable success in the face of continuing Government underfunding, which is severe enough to affect the experience offered to many learners despite the superb work of staff and managers. (AoC, 2004)

A tribute to the work done in the post-compulsory education sector, including that in FE colleges, was also given earlier in 2004 by Charles Clarke, then Secretary of State for Education and Skills, who said in his keynote address to the LSDA summer conference:

> ... it is important to start by recognising the achievements of the sector, which I think are very substantial and need to be recognised ... college success rates for all

qualifications have increased from 59% in the year 2000–01 to 65% in 2001–02. Now, that is a very significant improvement and it indicates the actual commitment, hard work, energy that has been put in . . . (Clarke, 2004)

Clarke, however, also drew attention to key issues that needed improvement in all areas of post-compulsory education, and set some challenges for the sector including the need for:

1. a really good offer at 14 plus

2. a good means for all adults to be able to address their own lifelong learning needs at whatever level they exist

3. a reform programme for our institutions, colleges working in partnership with adult learning providers, with schools, to ensure that there really is an offer together

In this context of discussing the performance of the sector, and its relationship with questions of leadership and management, we turn now to take a brief look at the framework by which institutions are inspected.

Common Inspection Framework – leadership and management

Ofsted and ALI grade leadership as part of the CIF by which PCE institutions are inspected. Question seven of the CIF asks, 'How effective are leadership and management in raising achievement and supporting all learners?' This CIF question seeks to judge impact, not intention, locating leadership and management firmly in terms of the need for senior staff to facilitate student success, and it does not differentiate between leadership and management. So Chris Hughes, writing in the editorial for the briefing paper from LSDA, a partner in the 2003 launch of the CEL, observed that the Ofsted/ALI inspection regime was in fact really focused more on assessing transactional management than leadership. Chris called for the development of transformational leadership across the sector, saying this could become a 'devolved and distributed feature of high-performing organisations':

> . . . our inspection regime evaluates management not leadership . . . government ambitions for our sector require more than transactional management: they require transformation of performance . . . leadership. . . . for this to happen senior management teams must give away more of the leadership function to curriculum and other frontline managers. You never have so much authority as when you begin to give it away. And so leadership becomes a devolved and distributed feature of high-performing organisations. (Hughes, 2003)

To achieve this, it is clear that many institutions need significant support in order to facilitate further leadership development and innovation, including parity of funding with other sectors. Many PCE organisations still operate a transactional model in which the concept of leadership resides only at the top tier of organisational hierarchy. We need to consider how to move people gradually towards more distributed and transformational models of shared leadership, and, within this, to specify the key criteria for creating successful institutions.

Put learners, clients and staff at the heart of what you do

This book echoes recent calls to put in place developments for more transformational leadership in the sector, and to create, in a spirit of continuous improvement, the kinds of institutions that achieve *more than* all the ticks for inspection. Such institutions are not primed directly and only to perform well in inspections. High achieving leaders and institutions put learners at the heart of what they do. It is because these institutions and leaders are brilliant at what they do, and put learners, clients and staff at the heart of their enterprise, that

> Everything can be taken from a man but ... the last of the human freedoms – to choose one's attitude in any given set of circumstances, to choose one's own way.
> *Victor Frankl*

such institutions also perform well in inspections. They perform well because learners and teachers love to be in them, and love to work in them.

This book suggests we should rediscover the passion for learning and for empowering others with the gift of education that all the leaders interviewed for this book have shown. What is this passion and purpose? This book begins to trace out some elements distinguishing a kind of excellence in leadership and passion for education. Such *leadership situations* are characterised by a strong, values-driven mission and clarity of purpose that focuses on the learners, client groups and staff served by the institutions. They arise from teams working together to provide high quality provision for learners, in support of each other, led by people who have embraced certain ways of operating that mark out good leadership. In later chapters of this book, we explore some of these characteristics.

We need to go beyond glossy imagery in marketing to discover deeper values in leadership beyond glamour and knee-jerk reactions to latest policy initiatives. We need to go deeper into reflective problem-solving regarding the real task of leading PCE to clarify, continuously, through shared dialogues in new communities of PCE leadership practice, what really helps students achieve good results from their learning. The 'performativity' (Ball, 2003) which has shaped the PCE sector for some years may, ironically enough, provide some of the backbone structure of a solution, though professionals may, naturally enough, instinctively distrust this thought. But we need to – and can – *take ownership*, building on current situations in PCE and FE to make more sensible, humane and more locally tailored the wide-ranging 'targets culture'. We need to transform, from existing mechanistic strategic action-planning systems, the body, heart and soul of locally variegated, flexible, original solutions for specific institutions. We need to take greater ownership and care of opportunities for *distributed leadership* in our institutions, to grow new models for a *transformational leadership* culture throughout the sector, or risk further damage to staff morale from an unremittingly reductive focus on the blunt ends of externally imposed goals.

The Centre for Excellence in Leadership (CEL)

The DfES strategy, *Success for All*, launched in November, 2002, is being implemented to improve quality and capacity across the LSS sector. A new Centre for Excellence in Leadership (CEL) for the learning and skills sector was set up in October, 2003, fulfilling a key priority of this strategy, to enable current and new leaders to work towards improved standards in leadership. CEL was launched to serve the 1.6 million staff employed in the LSS sector, aiming to initiate and develop improvements in leadership through training managers at all levels, and to achieve 'world class' leadership by 2010. Government investment of £14.5m over the next three years will allow CEL to set competitive prices for high quality, innovative leadership programmes, operating in collaboration with its main partners Lancaster University Management School (LUMS), Ashridge business school and the Learning and Skills Development Agency (LSDA). In preparation for the launch of CEL, leadership research reports and good practice guides were commissioned and published for the LSC on leadership and management, notably the guide for 'Leadership and management in work based learning' (LSC, 2002) and the survey report 'Tomorrow's learning leaders: Developing leadership and management for post-compulsory learning' (Frearson, 2002).

With Lynne Sedgmore appointed as Chief Executive from April, 2004, CEL was tasked to carry out research and development in leadership in post-compulsory education. As a result, CEL recently published its *Strategic Document* 2004–2006, acting in an advisory capacity to translate into action the LSRC-funded programme reports emerging from the *Leading Learning* series of research projects (Lumby *et al.*, 2004, p.5; 2005). The draft and final reports from work packages two and three of the *Leading Learning* project have recently been published (Lumby *et al.*, 2004, 2005), stressing the need for further research on leadership to inform the work of the learning and skills sector.

The succession and diversity crises

By 2007, about 60% of the current generation of leaders and managers in the college and work-based learning providers of the PCE sector will retire (CEML, 2002; *Guardian*, 2003; PWC, 2002). The LSC caters for all post-16 learners in the UK except those in higher education, with 47 regional offices, more than 6 million learners, and an overall budget of more than £8 billion. More than 3.91 million learners were in council-funded FE in 2002–2003, an increase of 1% on the 2001–2002 figures of 3.87 million. FE colleges are key to post-compulsory education because of the huge numbers of learners in colleges, and the breadth of provision in FE. The fact that so many leading staff are shortly due to retire is therefore a major issue for the future leadership of the sector.

CEL aims to address both the 'succession crisis' and the problems with a lack of diversity and inclusion. An LSDA survey carried out in 2002 (LSDA, 2003) reported that 40% of leaders and managers in FE colleges and adult and community learning institutions were aged 50+, in comparison with only 24% reported in 1997. Senior management in PCE is also predominantly white and male. Numbers of women managers in PCE remained at a stable level between 1997 and 2002, and only 3% of all managers were from ethnic minority backgrounds. There is therefore a significant need to address diversity issues in PCE leadership – I return to this theme in Chapter 4 (see also Commission for Black Staff in Further Education, 2002a, 2000b).

Recently, there has been an increasing emphasis on the importance to effective leadership of staff and student contributions at all levels in education. The question of widespread ownership of leadership in organisations and their mission is the key issue. We need, in effect, a 'step change' in leadership. This can only be achieved, long term, through substantial collective efforts. To contribute positively to this debate, we can highlight key features of effective leadership, examining local, situated examples of good leadership in action. Models of leadership are not necessarily transferable from one situation to another. However, the principles embodied in successful leadership work are, nevertheless, useful to inform the reflections of those working on leadership.

> The quality of a person's life is in direct proportion to their commitment to excellence, regardless of thier chosen field of endeavour.
>
> *Vincent T. Lombardi*

'I want them to be all that they can be'

My personal motivations for writing this book stem from a concern that poor leadership seems so seldom *really* to be differentiated effectively from excellent leadership. I am concerned to sharpen up our powers of judgement, so that we are more attuned, less biased, more sensitive and more knowledgeable in the way we select for leadership posts. I also want to encourage good leadership in general. Some perspectives on leadership have therefore been brought together here to suggest that PCE leadership has the potential to be truly excellent, and that we need to begin work to implement this across the sector.

As Ruth Silver observes, 'Actually, it needn't be like this: it has to be better'. With the optimism of Dr Andrew Morris, we can perhaps find a way to see that solutions are possible: 'Things really can be good, you can overcome obstacles, you really can have excitement, quality and enrichment.' With the curiosity and desire of Dr John Guy to serve learners, we can aim for 'the highest quality academic and vocational education', for our institutions. We can, like Ruth, Professor Daniel Khan and others in this book, focus on providing brilliantly effective, differentiated, responsive provision for learners, because we share the passion for excellence that comes through in Ruth's statement about Lewisham students: 'I want them to be all that they can be'. We can

> Leaders aren't born, they are made. And they are made just like anything else, through hard work. And that's the price we'll have to pay to achieve that goal, or any goal.
>
> *Vince Lombardi*

be as passionate about good management of learning as Wendy Moss or Anne Morahan. We can facilitate solutions for effective long-term transformation with the warmth and creativity of Talmud Bah. We can uphold quality and ethical standards with the sense of fairness and good faith towards students of Bob Challis. And we can care for the sector overall with the professional love of learning and skills demonstrated by Lynne Sedgmore, echoing again with Ruth, 'Actually, it needn't be like this: it has to be better'.

This book aims to inspire people who want to be leaders in PCE institutions of the future, to help practitioners take up and achieve their personal dreams for leadership. I would like this work to inspire those who want to be leaders, but are perhaps as yet unsure of their leadership potential. It is time for a wholesale transformation of leadership and management initiatives across all regions of the sector. This book was written to propose a more open, collegiate, values-based implementation of transformational leadership in the sector. Education provides a precious opportunity for the life enhancement of our students. We should focus on providing the highest possible quality in lifelong learning services for the success of learners, clients and staff, in stewardship of the worthwhile mission of PCE. In short, we should *want leadership in PCE to be all that it can be.*

> A great many people think they are thinking when they are merely rearranging their prejudices.
>
> *William James*

In the following chapters, the interviewees offer a series of thoughts and examples to suggest that anyone, with time, help, support, hard work and diligence, can achieve excellence in leadership. The leaders interviewed for this book are people with diverse backgrounds, men and women from different cultures and races, ages, religions and interests. They differ in many ways, except one – they are all excellent leaders in the post-compulsory education sector, demonstrating passionate commitment to the achievement of that role. Let's listen to what they have to say in Part Two. But, first, we consider a range of models of leadership and related issues in the following chapters.

Summary

This chapter examines the current 'state of play' of leadership in post-compulsory education. We trace briefly the role of prior leadership studies on PCE, observing that there is a need for 'ordinary heroes' to take up the challenge of leadership in the context of a problematic and under-theorised legacy. We define the basic terms and focus of the book, and note that mechanistic target-setting of a post-incorporation 'performative', masculinist and reductive culture particularly prevalent in some parts of the sector, notably FE, needs urgently to be replaced by more variegated, subtle, flexible and creative local leadership responses. We discuss 2004 Ofsted reports on FE college performance, and furious reactions to these comments. We observe that poor standards in leadership, bullying and scandals have occurred, but move on to celebrate some successes of post-compulsory education, considering the appropriacy of measurements for leadership used in the *Common Inspection Framework*. We observe that there is a need to create a culture of continuous improvement, to strive for excellence and purposeful creativity in leadership in the future. Having briefly described the succession crisis, we consider the setting up of the new Centre for Excellence in Leadership (CEL) following *Success for All* (DfES, 2002) and note that CEL has a formative role to play in developing leadership. We discuss the need for a 'step change' in leadership, and round up this chapter by describing the motivation to write this book. Finally, we outline the role of the case study interviews in Part Two, and the fact that these examples of outstanding leadership have been drawn up to provide inspiration for leaders of the future.

Leadership in education

"❝Life is no brief candle to me. It is a sort of splendid torch which I have got hold of for the moment, and I want to make it burn as brightly as possible before handing it on to future generations.❞
Bernard Shaw

Multiple situated leaderships

Leaders are made as well as born. Though it may be difficult to 'teach' leadership, it can be learned. Those like Ackoff (1998) who say leadership, like creativity, can't be taught because it is 'essentially an aesthetic activity' (Ackoff, 1998, pp.23–4), are partly missing the point. Learning leadership, like creativity, can be facilitated, and can grow, assisted by good teaching, coaching and support. Why otherwise are there so many leadership courses being delivered? Are we all wasting our time? I hope not. However, Ackoff may be right in saying leadership cannot be taught *easily* through simple formulae. Perhaps what is needed is the kind of 'slow growing towards understanding' that Andrew Morris observes occurs in deep learning (see Chapter 15).

> Education is not the filling of a pail, but the lighting of a fire.
> *William Butler Yeats*

We should perhaps consider a new framework for 'multiple situated leaderships', conjoining and applying to leadership Howard Gardner's (1983, 1993) theories of multiple intelligences, with Blanchard *et al.*'s (1986) concepts of situated leadership. For, if we can have 'multiple intelligences' recognising different strengths in people's intelligences, why can we not have – indeed, do we not already have – 'multiple leaderships' operating in practice? If there are numerous kinds of effective intelligences, so, also, are there different kinds of effective leadership situations.

Exploring leadership roles

In their recent report on leadership in the learning and skills sector, Lumby *et al.* (2005) also found there was no one approach to leadership in ten case study sites of successful providers. This key report states that a 'mix of transactional, transformational and distributed styles is in operation', and that 'though a transformational style is considered to be the most effective way to improve organisational performance, line managers are more often seen as employing transactional approaches.' The researchers found that distributed leadership operated at case study sites, but was not allocating real power out to lower levels: 'distributed leadership is often distribution of operational responsibilities rather than a distribution of power' (Lumby *et al.*, 2005, Summary). I now explore 'distributed leadership' more fully.

> The main characteristics of effective leadership are intelligence, integrity or loyalty, mystique, humour, discipline, courage, self sufficiency and confidence.
>
> *James L. Fisher*

The paradox of ordinariness

We tend to dismiss leadership qualities observable daily in a range of people all around us. Binney *et al.*, (2005) comment on transformational leadership:

> . . . we found in our research that transformational leadership is a myth . . . we saw many people attempting, none succeeding, in being a transforming hero. The Emperor has no clothes . . . (Binney *et al.*, 2005, p.26)

Yet even if we find, collectively, that 'the Emperor has no clothes', if the model of transformational leadership exists more as an inspirational ideal than a reality, we still have work to be done in our organisations. Therefore, if existing ideal models of transformational leadership do not perhaps quite fit in PCE, perhaps we need to make some new models. Reflecting on the paradox of ordinariness and uncertainties of quantum principles in relation to leadership can perhaps be useful. As Lynne Sedgmore commented:

> Water is fluid, soft, and yielding. But water will wear away rock, which is rigid and cannot yield. As a rule, whatever is fluid, soft, and yielding will overcome what ever is rigid and hard. This is another paradox: what is soft is strong.
>
> *Lao-Tzu*

> Really advanced, outstanding people don't need to tell everybody. They can do it in such a way that they're also very ordinary, very approachable, very accessible. It's that lovely paradox. They are quite outstanding, but also very ordinary, very real. (Lynne Sedgmore, 2005, interview)

New paradigm: a connected transformational leadership field

A new paradigm for connected transformational educational leadership could be based on the idea of the *leadership field* (Blank, 1995, p.30) existing between 'ordinary leaders', at multiple levels in educational institutions, in proactive interaction with leaders at strategic managerial levels. Heroic models and 'guru' techniques for leadership, set up to be superordinate, based on special techniques or people, sometimes fail. However, we can be comforted by the certainty that outstanding leadership does exist in many of our institutions (NAO, 2005, p.45, para 3.8).

We can outline new models for leadership, based on real, connected people working quietly and consistently to high standards. Such staff, sometimes relatively unrecognised and unnoticed, continue to do their work excellently anyway, subtly influencing and tacitly leading everyone around them, performing as in Keith's (1968) paradoxes about leadership:

- People are illogical, unreasonable, and self-centred. Love them anyway;
- If you do good, people will accuse you of selfish, ulterior motives. Do good anyway;
- If you are successful, you win false friends and true enemies. Succeed anyway.

(Keith, 2003 [1968])

Ordinary 'connected leadership' is sometimes overt, sometimes subtle, sometimes publicly recognised, sometimes instinctively operating in the background. Sometimes it operates at top executive level, and sometimes at middle management, team leader, canteen worker or receptionist levels. Real leadership is, paradoxically, simultaneously both about and not about overt power, and can operate anywhere. To quote Binney *et al*:

Real leadership is connected, involved and engaged. It's often more quiet than heroic. Real leadership is about building an organisation slowly, carefully and collectively. (Binney *et al.*, 2005, p.34)

We have sometimes, perhaps, a biased and limited view of leadership, too tied to the idea that, to be recognised as leaders, people must hold an officially recognised position. Perhaps we are on occasion too restricted by outdated perceptions of what 'being a leader' means. We do not always consciously recognise fine leadership qualities being demonstrated all around us daily everywhere. Good leaders can, and do, operate at any and all levels within institutional hierarchies, though they are not always recognised

> I often say that life is like an apple – It falls into your hands. But it won't fall into your hands unless you stand under the tree. You have to find the orchard, find the tree, and then something may happen.
>
> *Charles Handy*

as such. To develop leadership qualities effectively is to develop self-mastery and greater understanding about the true purposes of education, and the mission of the institutions in which we work.

Before retiring from many years as an FE principal, Bob Challis said he had begun to recognise that the role of a principal was a lot simpler and clearer than he had previously recognised. A kind of 'coherence' (David Collins), 'integer' (Lynne Sedgmore, cf. Jung) or 'crystallisation' (John Guy, cf. Bruner) perhaps occurs when people's level of experience, knowledge, maturity, 'values in action' (David Collins) and 'fit' (Ruth Silver, 'the joy of the fit') within the organisation has reached a point in which good leadership seems to 'flow' naturally with the spontaneity of expertise. Hence, when such leaders speak out with conviction, their voice embodies the values of the whole organisation. When Daniel Khan speaks out to 'commit' the college to diversity and inclusion, the 'I' becomes more than himself: he speaks for a community of practice, for a long history stretching back to his early years in the Caribbean, celebrating the power and benefit of education radically opened out to help students achieve the best for themselves.

Values-bypassed leaders, post-heroic questioning, adaptive challenges

In strong contrast to values-driven perspectives, there are many examples of leaders who seem to have had a 'values-bypass', having an ethical deficit or ethical neutrality in their make-up. Trevino et al. (2003) observe that ethical neutrality is problematic in executive leadership, which needs to provide the 'tone at the top' for ethical values in organisations (p.1). Ethically

> Leadership is the creation and fulfilment of worthwhile opportunities by honourable means.
> *Herb Rubenstein*

bankrupt or neutral people operating as so-called 'leaders' often flounder about in messy situations, sanction corruption, turn a blind eye to failure and sometimes engage constantly in more or less self-serving autocratic practices to serve their own ends. As Killian notes:

> Failure by top leaders to identify key organisational values . . . convey those values by personal example, and . . . reinforce them by establishing appropriate organisational policies demonstrates a lack of ethical leadership . . . that fosters an unethical organisational culture. (Killian, 2004, p.10)

Such 'leaders' seem to revel in positional power for its own sake, making use of such power more or less for their own ends, controlling others for the sake of 'proving' how 'important' they are. Morally bankrupt and insensitive, such leaders are operating in numerous situations at international and national levels in political as well as in educational leadership. Perhaps as a result of such noxious autocrats, widespread disillusionment and cynicism with leadership has been a feature of the political and education landscape for decades.

We are in an age of post-heroic questioning, no longer fooled by empty promises and glossy soundbites. Many people no longer have much faith in the concept of leadership, having perhaps had bitter experience of weak, incompetent, mad, bad and even dangerous leaders. Multiple challenges face leaders at every level of public life. As Heifetz and Laurie note:

> ... a strong belief that working hard makes things happen ... a straightforward, plain honesty ... is very good in a leader ... a strong sense of humility.
>
> *Manfred F. R. Kets de Vries*

> More and more companies today are facing adaptive challenges: changes ... around the globe are forcing them to clarify their values, develop new strategies, and learn new ways of operating. (Heifetz and Laurie, 1997)

'Great groups'

The task of leadership has become more urgently difficult and demanding, while the UK and international public has become less and less trusting of leaders, managers and politicians. In this era of doubt and mistrust, a solution to the lack of trust in leaders is perhaps to be found in high performing groups, in which there are also key individual leaders. However, group leadership must be guided overtly by ethical, values-based principles. Recent research indicates that poor ethics in corporations often involves more than one individual (Turner, 2005, p.1) as flawed results can emerge from a 'groupthink' mindset in which teams place group consensus above ethical principles (Thompson *et al.*, 2000, cited by Turner, 2005, p.2).

There was unanimous agreement among the interviewees for this book that leadership is best seen as distributed throughout organisations. This endorsement of the 'team' concept seems generally to be shared in the literature on leadership. Warren Bennis, founding Chairman of the Leadership Institute in California, observed the following about the shift away from charismatic individuals towards 'great groups':

> There does seem to be a kind of paradox between ... individual-centred, personal accountability and the team concept – but I don't think they're actually in conflict at all ... what is going to happen, ... [is] ... groups of individuals coming together to work on particular tasks from diverse areas ... will intensively work together on a project ... being in a group in no way precludes a high degree of individual autonomy ... It's a paradox, but I don't see it as a contradiction. (Powell, 2000, p.34)

Researching creative team processes in project team development, Rickards and Moger (2000) reworked the standard model (Tuckman, 1965) of team development ('perform', 'norm', 'storm', 'form') and its later Tuckman-Jensen variant (Tuckman and Jensen, 1977) to examine conditions for outstanding team performance. Rickards and Moger proposed a new framework for team development in which creative leadership facilitates team factors to break through barriers in team formation and achieve exceptional performance (Rickards and Moger, 2000, p.281). The concept of *teamwork* has assumed greater importance recently than in some of the more individualised models of leadership now outlined.

Models of leadership – a brief overview

Many theoretical models of leadership have been identified previously in the vast literature on this subject, including, though not being limited to, the following 44 models:

• Authentic leadership	• Instructional leadership	• Servant leadership
• Autocratic leadership	• Intellectual leadership	• Shared leadership
• Charismatic leadership	• Invisible leadership	• Situated leadership
• Classical leadership	• Learning leadership	• Situational leadership
• Coercive leadership	• Living leadership	• Spiritual leadership
• Collective leadership	• Managerial leadership	• Strategic leadership
• Community leadership	• Moral leadership	• Super-leadership
• Contingent leadership	• Participative leadership	• Synergistic leadership
• Creative leadership	• Pedagogic leadership	• Systemic leadership
• Democratic leadership	• Person-centred leadership	• Team leadership
• Distributed leadership	• Post-heroic leadership	• Transactional leadership
• Educational leadership	• Professional leadership	• Transformational leadership
• Ethical leadership	• Pseudo-leadership	• Visionary leadership
• Group leadership	• Quantum leadership	• Warrior leadership
• Heroic leadership	• Self-management leadership	

Figure 2.1 Some models of leadership

Leadership studies from the 1900s to the current day reveal that a huge number of leadership models and styles have been classified and researched. We are no closer to a general definitive model or final theory of leadership, however, and we noted in the Introduction that this may not be possible or desirable in any case.

Nevertheless, it is useful to outline a number of key theoretical models of leadership. This is necessarily a selective round-up of a few major theories from the hundreds, even thousands, of existing theoretical models. As Waters *et al.* note, there were, from the early 1970s to the early 2000s, at least 5,000 different studies on educational leadership that 'purported to examine the effects of leadership on student achievement' (2003, p.4). Given the worldwide growth in leadership studies between 2002 and 2005, this is a selective round-up, focusing only on those educational leadership models which seem to be of particular relevance to PCE currently.

Doyle and Smith (2001) provide a useful background summary of the history of 'classical leadership', observing that during the last 80 years or so there have been four major 'generations' of leadership theory:

1. trait
2. behavioural
3. contingency
4. transformational theories

We modify this list to look at the following 'generations' of leadership theory:

- Trait leadership theories
- Behavioural or style leadership theories
- Situational and contingency leadership theories
- Transformational, transactional and charismatic leadership theories
- Distributed and shared leadership

We now briefly trace each of these 'generations' of theory, in addition to 'non-leadership' and laissez-faire leadership, recognising also that to classify leadership neatly is useful but also partly arbitrary, as there are cross-cutting and overlapping trends, inter-generational theories and sub-theories that persist between time periods. We then focus particularly on a number of variants of the *transformational* and *distributed* leadership models, in view of the potential usefulness of these to researchers and practitioners in the learning and skills sector. To round this study out and add further to the debate on leadership, we focus, also, in the ten case study interview chapters, on the following leadership models, which have relevance to the sector:

- servant leadership (Chapter 8: Lynne Sedgmore)
- guardianship and change agency (Chapter 9: Dr John Guy)

- quantum leadership (Chapter 10: Dr David Collins)
- systemic leadership (Chapter 11: Ruth Silver)
- inclusive leadership (Chapter 12: Anne Morahan)
- the skills approach to leadership (Chapter 13: Professor Daniel Khan)
- ethical leadership and coaching (Chapter 14: Bob Challis)
- network and evidence-informed leadership (Chapter 15: Dr Andrew Morris)
- distributed and team leadership (Chapter 16: Wendy Moss)
- creative leadership (Chapter 17: Talmud Bah)

Trait theories of leadership

The concept that successful leaders are marked out by specific definable characteristics or 'traits' is a superficially appealing one in the attempt to find a 'recipe' for 'traits' marking out successful leaders. Early leadership research around 1900–50 tended to emphasise 'trait' theories. Specific elements of leaders' characteristics were identified and described for research and possible replication (Méndez-Morse, 1992).

However, researchers fairly quickly began to recognise that there were no definitively predictable features accurately marking out what kind of characteristics leaders invariably possess. Northouse (2004, p.33) sums up earlier decades of research work on trait theories by listing a number of the traits which research marked out as generally characteristic of great leaders: 'intelligence, self-confidence, determination, integrity and sociability'. However, this is not a definitive list, being exclusively leader-centred (not including teams, situations and followers relating to 'traits'). Furthermore, this kind of approach can result in subjective, limited judgements regarding the characteristics of 'great' leaders, and an over-reliance on models linked to assumed 'fixed' characteristics of a single individual.

Researchers therefore began to realise that even if a definitive 'traits' list could be drawn up, this would not necessarily result in better leadership. 'Trait' theories have been, therefore, to some extent overtaken in the literature on leadership, with the exception of some specific studies in which 'traits' have been examined in new ways, such as in Kellerman's recent book on 'bad' leaders (Kellerman, 2004).

> History has demonstrated that the most notable winners usually encountered heartbreaking obstacles before they triumphed. They won because they refused to become discouraged by their defeats.
>
> *Bertie Charles Forbes*

Behavioural or 'style' theories of leadership

In the 1950s and 1960s, theorists began to recognise 'trait' models were fallible, and to concentrate on the behaviours or 'styles' of leaders. Four main types of behaviours were identified:

1. concern for task

2. concern for people

3. directive leadership

4. participative leadership

(Doyle and Smith, 2001, p.4).

Many managerial courses were designed based on behavioural models of leadership, and the alleged competencies required for effective leadership. The managerial grid of Blake and Mouton (1964; 1978) was devised to diagnose and develop leadership behaviours, with a key focus on the differentiation between (1) task-centred and (2) people-centred leadership. McGregor's (1960) 'Theory X' (hard, controlling, shop floor production management) and 'Theory Y' (soft, participative, linked to the management of professionals) were contrasted in terms of (3) directive and (4) participative styles of leadership. McGregor deduced that Theory Y (soft management) was preferable, but sometimes difficult to implement.

Situational and contingency leadership theories

'Trait' and 'behavioural' leadership studies were followed by 'situational' studies, focusing on situations in which leaders found themselves, in order to determine the characteristics of effective performance and the selection of leaders as opposed to followers. Situational studies were limited both by their local specificity and by limitations in the generalisability of predictions about effective leadership behaviours for transferral from one situation to another. Again, two basic models of leadership within most situations were identified: (1) situational leader behaviour more directed at organisational systems, or 'task-focused', and (2) situational behaviour more 'people-focused'. Effective leaders in most situations tend to perform well on both these dimensions (SEDL, 2005, p.2). The concept that people change their leadership style to suit particular situations is related to Fiedler's idea of 'contingency theory' (Fiedler, 1964, 1967, 1997; Fiedler and Garcia, 1987). This model attempts to match the styles of leaders to particular situations, providing a framework according to 'leader-member relations', 'task-structure' and 'position power' (Northouse, 2004, p.110) to determine whether leadership is effective. However, although there has been much research to support this theory, it has also been criticised as not necessarily accurate in predicting situational effectiveness, requiring much effort to measure leadership.

Transactional leadership

Transactional theories of leadership are based on hierarchical or positional power and involve task-focused directive leadership with similarities to 'management'. Transactional leaders typically clarify tasks for employees, engaging in a 'transaction' or 'exchange' with followers to explain what is required of employees and the 'reward' available for the successful completion of tasks. Northouse (2004) examines models of transformational and transactional leadership and observes that there are two basic components of transactional leadership: 'contingent reward' and 'management-by-exception' (Northouse, 2004, pp.178–9, also citing Bass and Avolio, 1990a).

'Contingent reward' is the 'pay-off' (for example, promotion) that followers gain as a result of successful completion of tasks in a 'transaction' with their leader, while 'management-by-exception', in both 'active' and 'passive' forms, involves critical feedback if tasks are not done according to the transaction specified. Tasks are therefore completed through compliance, based on a somewhat reductive, though often effective, system of 'bartering' obedience and task-completion for rewards: the self-interest of followers achieving 'pay-off' and incentives for effort.

Transactional leaders tend to focus, at an overt level, on management *duties* rather than on human relations issues in leadership: the achievement of institutional tasks is prioritised over visionary goals for both followers and organisations. One of the problems with transactional leadership, therefore, is that it does not tend to inspire followers to achieve more than the task outlined as part of the basic transaction. It is a limited model of leadership, based principally on exchanges, rewards and negative reinforcement (Northouse, 2004, p.179).

Transactional managers may think they are doing a 'good job' getting a series of specified tasks done, but a problem arises when transactional management does nothing else but focus on basic managerial transactions, neglecting other aspects of effective leadership. There is, in such transactional models of leadership, little space for learning and development, or for taking leadership beyond the

> When I despair, I remember that all through history the way of truth and love has always won. There have been tyrants and murders, and for a time they seem invincible, but in the end they always fall, always.
>
> *Mahatma Ghandi*

leaders' own limited conceptions of what is needed, into, for example, a shared community of practice characterised by mutual growth for both leaders and followers.

Transformational leadership

Transformational leadership has been studied since the 1970s. A wide-ranging model encompassing a number of different variants, transformational leadership highlights the potential for individuals to change and improve educational provision. It is linked, partially, with charismatic leadership models and organisational change theories. Transformational leadership tends to be strongly differentiated from transactional, task-focused styles (Downton, 1973; Northouse, 2004). Frearson (2003) notes that:

> in the public sector, where all services are seeking ways to improve provision within constrained resources, there is a growing interest in the transformational role of leaders in improving organisations and the services they provide.

(Frearson 2003, p.7)

> In the space age the most important space is between the ears.
>
> *Anne Armstrong*

Transformational leadership is part of the 'New Leadership' concept put forward by Brymann (1996) which focuses more on emotional and charismatic aspects of leadership than, for example, transactional styles do (Northouse, 2004, p.169). The process of 'transformation' is intended to raise followers' hopes, and to achieve transforming changes in people and organisations. The process is addressed at the 'whole' person within organisations, including emotions, thoughts, values and longer term ideals and plans. Transformational leadership influences followers to achieve more than they ordinarily would. Strong moral values and ideals are encompassed by the model. Many people adhere to the concept of transformational leadership, but the model has also been criticised for relative ambiguity and vagueness (Northouse, 2004, p.185) and, as we have noted already, the proof of its success is still marginal.

In transformational leadership, the leader, having in the first place a strong moral framework from which to operate, establishes, usually collaboratively, an idealistic 'transforming' vision, with a related set of goals and values for the institution. The leader, confident and clear of their own identity in relation to this vision, seeks to change the consciousness of followers to establish their identities and purposes in relation to that vision, and to move the whole organisation forward to achieve the vision. Transformational leadership can enable successes beyond achievements possible under transactional leadership, focusing not only on routine task-focused exchanges between leaders and followers, but also on transforming the culture of the organisation and on followers' needs, developmental potential and values. The transformational approach is, in ideal form, morally beneficial for both leaders and followers, creating a strongly productive organisational culture.

Bush (2003, pp.76–7), describing models of educational leadership, reports, in relation to schools' leadership, the argument by Caldwell and Spinks (1992, pp.49–50) that 'Transformational leaders succeed in gaining the commitment of followers to such a degree that . . . higher levels of accomplishment become virtually a moral imperative.' The potential for transformational leadership to become despotic is, however, noted by Bush in respect of the charismatic or heroic elements of transformational leadership (2003, pp.77–8).

Authenticity in transformational leadership

However, as Northouse observes, transformational leadership tends to utilise and develop a values and moral framework transcending self-interest, placing emphasis on beneficial values for the good of all. Coercive elements of heroic or charismatic models therefore would not fit into the model (Northouse, 2004, p.184). In relation to 'the good of all', however, Price (2003), responding to prior concerns raised about the morality of transformational leadership, and to Bass and Steidlmeier's (1998) distinction between *authentic* transformational leadership and *inauthentic* or *pseudo-transformational* leadership, cautions us about the moral risks of transformational leadership, whether or not

> The great difference between the real leader and the pretender is that the one sees into the future, while the other regards only the present; the one lives by the day, and acts upon expediency; the other acts on enduring principles and for immortality.
>
> *Edmund Burke*

this is labeled as 'authentic'. Price notes that claims for 'authenticity' may, in fact, blind leaders to justify making exceptions from generally observed moral principles. It is therefore important that transformational leaders observe commonly respected moral standards of behaviour and uphold these both for themselves and others: 'Leaders must be willing to sacrifice . . . other-regarding values when generally applicable moral requirements make legitimate demands that they do so' (Price, 2003, p.80).

Lumby *et al.* (2004), rounding up models of leadership development in post-compulsory education, comment on prior research on transformational leadership. This team sums up findings by Crowther and Olsen (1997) and Leonard and Leonard (1999), noting that the transformational model has been regarded as capable of achieving success, being particularly appropriate to education. Lumby *et al.* (2004) note, however, as Bush and Glover (2003) found, that 'transformational approaches are not easily implemented' (Lumby *et al.*, 2004, p.37), and that we need to query 'If transformational approaches are indicated as highly effective and an ideal for many, why then is transactional leadership so common?' (Lumby, *et al.*, 2004, p.149). We could speculate that leaders may default to transactional models in the absence of sufficient training, confidence and external support from coaches and mentors. This is another reason why professional updating and coaching for leaders is so essential.

Charismatic leadership

What is a 'charismatic' leader? The idea of 'charismatic leadership' is similar in some respects to 'transformational leadership'. I distinguish these two, the latter being more elaborated in recent literature (Northouse, 2004, p.171). Essentially, in charismatic leadership, a person's 'charisma' or strong personality, is regarded as dominant. In Weber's original theory (Weber, 1947) of charismatic leadership, a crisis stimulates the emergence of this leadership, but later theorists viewed this as an unnecessary, although perhaps facilitative, condition for its growth (Yukl, 1999, pp.279).

Charismatic leader-inspired 'followers' not only tend to trust charismatic leaders, but also may begin to believe ideals similar to those of the leader. Charismatic leaders put themselves forward as strong role models, having a desire to influence others, combined with confidence and a robust personal belief system, with explicit values. As role models, charismatic leaders tend to exemplify and 'live out' beliefs they espouse, in ways influencing 'followers' and sometimes causing mass identification with the leader. Charismatic leaders may be unconventional, taking risks in the service of their cause (Yukl, 1999, p.293). Charismatic leaders set forward goals for 'followers' to take up and achieve, tending to expect much from them. Obedience to the leaders' wishes characterises 'follower' behaviour: 'followers' may achieve greater knowledge, confidence and success from emulating charismatics with strong value systems and beneficent goals.

Ethical dimensions of charismatic leadership

Ethical dimensions of charismatic leadership are often potent in appeal. Charismatic leaders tend to have a 'mission' to serve, and to scrutinise the contexts and operational situations in which they work. High standards of ethics are therefore demanded and expected of everyone, including the leader themselves. The extent to which these are appropriately and effectively selected varies according to the nature of the leader and the situation. A belief that leaders are accountable for their moral actions tends to underpin effective charismatic behaviour.

Weaknesses and dangers in charismatic leadership

I have qualified my description of charismatic leadership by linking it with ethics, the standards for which are more enduring and clearly articulated than for charismatic leadership. As Yukl (1999, p.294) notes, this is a somewhat ambiguous term. Charisma is subject to potential vagueries of fashion among followers. There is a clear tendency for charismatic leadership to be regarded

> Great spirits have always encountered violent opposition from mediocre minds.
>
> *Albert Einstein*

as 'heroic leadership', an even vaguer term. Charismatic and heroic leadership are both potentially problematic, even potentially dangerous for educational institutions, in terms of reliance on one dominant leader. There is a potential for 'charisma' to be linked to more or less unhealthy personal ambitions and unpleasant personality states. This has been the case in some of the worst examples of unethical leadership in politics and religion. We can think here of examples such as Hitler, Jim Jones of Wako, Papa Doc Duvalier and Robert Mugabe. However, we must note of such destructive characters that the word 'leadership' barely applies. Extreme abuses of power render the term 'leader' problematic and inapplicable. Doyle and Smith cite Heifetz (1994, p.24) in terms of this: 'Hitler wielded power, but he did not lead . . .' (Doyle and Smith, 2001, pp.1–4). I did not focus on charismatic theories in the interview descriptions, in view of the problematic aspects described here. Furthermore, none of the case study interviewees cited the model of charismatic leadership as being of interest or relevance in our discussions.

Non-leadership and laissez-faire models of leadership

The absence of leadership, or 'non-leadership', is similar to negligent varieties of laissez-faire 'hands-off' models of leadership. This can be in a situation in which leaders are simply not there, whether physically and/or mentally, or do not do anything at all to intervene in or be concerned with the processes of running organisations (Northouse, 2004, p.179). They simply default on the job. Sometimes this may be because such leaders are mediocre in their performance, and are escaping the scene, being incapable of the personal struggle, hard work and dedication needed to fulfil their roles. Leaders in these cases may go away for lengthy periods of time, delay making decisions, fail to make any plans for the organisation, neglect to talk to staff, leave jobs undone, fail to set goals for staff reporting to them, and – which is worse – act with punitive retribution if anyone criticises them. There is perhaps one positive aspect to this kind of model – notably, that the leader tends not to be around to interfere with anything 'followers' are doing. Therefore, in the chaos of absent leadership, creative 'followers' may have freedom to be effective. In all other respects, however, this is a negligent, unsatisfactory model of leadership, and results gained under such a style are dependent on how well different parts of the organisation can operate, in despite of and/or without the leader.

Distributed leadership

The underlying concept of 'distributed leadership' is that leadership, power and responsibility are shared among many parts of an organisation, rather than residing solely at the top in the principalship and/or senior executive managers. This model of leadership is therefore literally 'distributed' or spread throughout the organisation in many or most of the formal hierarchical layers of the power structure, and perhaps beyond this into areas without formal roles. Power is also to some extent shared throughout the organisation in a 'collegial' style of operation. The 'distributed' model can operate alongside other models of leadership, notably transformational and systemic models. For some types of leaders who like to control staff and institutions closely, this distribution of power is particularly challenging.

Bush (2003) notes that 'collegial' models of leadership are similar to the concept of 'distributed' leadership, and that '[c]ollegial models assume that professionals also have a right to share in the wider decision-making process' (pp.64–7). Since teachers, as professional educators, operate to standards of professional practice and a commonly held educational value system extending beyond one institution, the distributed leadership model is particularly appropriate in education. Bush (2003) outlines five core features of 'collegial' models of leadership and management applicable also to 'distributed' leadership:

1. the strongly normative nature of collegial models of leadership

2. the authority of professional expertise shared amongst many staff

3. the common set of values shared by people in the institution

4. a representative structure for consultation, appropriate to the size of the institution

5. decision-making based on consensus, and the ethical aspect of collegiality linked to this.

(Bush, 2003, pp.65–7)

Shared leadership

Similar to 'distributed leadership' is the concept of 'shared leadership' put forward by Doyle and Smith (2001, p.1) as a 'social process . . . between people', not necessarily reliant on positional power in organisations. They describe this form of 'everyday leadership' as a natural occurrence between friends, families and other social groups, in which people flexibly influence and lead each other in a community of shared actions all the time. In determining whether or not this kind of shared action in groups constitutes a model of leadership, Doyle and Smith note that such informal leadership must be:

(1) 'inclusive' and (2) 'elevating, leading to enhancements in people's lives', and should also develop (3) 'ownership of problems and issues' (4) 'learning between people' and (5) 'sharing for "the common good" in "open, respectful and informed conversation", including the virtues of "concern, trust, appreciation, affection and hope".'

(Doyle and Smith, 2001, pp.1–7)

This kind of shared social informal leadership can be contrasted with the more formal models of organisational leadership. There are benefits in conceptualising leadership in ways forming an intrinsic part of everyday shared community life. However, this model is also vulnerable to pitfalls, partly from its informality (Doyle and Smith, 2001).

In the following chapter, I explore leadership concepts more fully, with particular reference to the distinction between leadership and management, and the role of academic and professional leadership.

Summary

Chapter 2 describes a range of educational leadership theories and models. The chapter begins with the concept of 'multiple situated leaderships', since learning leadership can be facilitated and can grow. Discussion then focuses on the results of recent research on leadership in the sector which propose that the transformational and distributed styles tend to be more useful for education. Exploring these models, we consider the paradox of ordinariness, and the need for a new kind of conception of a 'connected transformational leadership field' existing between ordinary leaders currently operating to high standards in PCE as unrecognised leaders, and those in positional management power. The importance of values-based and integral perspectives in the work of the interviewees is discussed, in contrast with values-bypassed, ethically problematic leadership, as is the role of 'great groups' in an era of post-heroic questioning. A number of models of leadership are then outlined, including 'trait', 'behavioural', 'situational', 'transformational', 'transactional' and 'charismatic' leadership. The 'transformational' model is discussed as the model of most likely benefit to the sector. The question of 'authenticity' in transformational leadership is considered, and the ethical dimensions and weaknesses of charismatic leadership are explored. A discussion of 'non-leadership' and 'laissez-faire leadership' is followed by a consideration of 'distributed' and 'shared' leadership models. The next chapter is then introduced.

Leaders or managers

> **❝To lead people, walk beside them . . . A leader is best when people barely know they exist . . . When the best leader's work is done the people say, 'We did it ourselves!'❞**
> Lao Tse

Many styles and many paths of leadership

'Why is the subject of leadership so contested and difficult?', we may ask. There are many more than 5,000 volumes of literature already existing on leadership. We may read Richmon and Allison's (2003) inventory of 35 separate theories on leadership, summarised from eight theorists' prior attempts to organise leadership theories, and note their comments that, despite studying leadership for 'over 100 years', the same question remains to perplex us: 'What exactly is leadership, and how can we come to understand it better?' Drawing up a conceptual framework for leadership inquiry, these researchers note that what is needed is a 'better understanding of leadership' (Richmon and Allison, 2003, p.32). This book aims to contribute to this better understanding of leadership. We examine in this chapter the role of 'leadership' versus 'management', followed by 'academic', 'learning' and 'pedagogic' leadership.

What is the difference between leadership and management?

Why do we need leaders as well as managers in post-compulsory education? What is this separation between leadership and management? Is it valid? Are our managers in educational institutions not automatically leaders, and vice versa? People who have worked in this sector for any length of time

> Management means helping people to get the best out of themselves, not organising things.
> *Lauren Appley*

will probably recognise that there are both managers and leaders all around us. There are people occupying positions of managerial power who are only marginally and temporarily respected, sometimes just grudgingly acknowledged, on account of the hierarchical positions they occupy. It seems sometimes that, as soon as their position changes or is lost, overt evidence of respect from other staff vanishes, or even turns into disdain. It would seem that such staff are either (1) tacitly declaring that the manager has not inspired the confidence we normally associate with leadership, or (2) themselves unthinking followers of fashion, automatically falling into the line of 'followership' for the next positional leader.

Why, on the other hand, are some of our leaders not necessarily managers? We can probably all think of people who inspire notable levels of respect and goodwill throughout a whole organisation for many years, but are not in a position of substantial power in any formal hierarchy. We can also think of examples of leaders occupying higher positions of hierarchical power who we do not feel would be comfortable handling the day-to-day organisational tasks a good organisational manager supervises routinely.

A number of influential business theorists writing on leadership and management during the past two decades have stressed the difference between 'leadership' and 'management'. In *What Leaders Really Do*, John Kotter, Professor of Leadership at the Harvard Business School, wrote in 1990:

> Leadership is different from management, but not for the reasons most people think . . . [it] . . . isn't mystical and mysterious . . . has nothing to do with having 'charisma' . . . is not the province of a chosen few . . . Leadership and management are two distinctive and complementary systems of action . . . Management is about coping with complexity . . . Leadership, by contrast, is about coping with change.
>
> (Kotter, 1990, pp.37–8)

For the question, 'What is leadership in relation to management?', there are therefore a widely diverse variety of answers. Distinctions are made between 'leadership' and 'management' as well as between 'leadership' and 'administration'. Richmon and Allison (2003) observe that:

> A leader is not an administrator who loves to run others, but someone who carries water for his people so that they can get on with their jobs.
>
> *Robert Townsend*

> . . . leadership is often imbued with a sense of honour, charisma, loyalty, respect and greatness. (Richmon and Allison, 2003, p.1)

whereas administration is often regarded more prosaically:

> Administration, alternatively, is often seen in a less favourable light, imbued with the perfunctory happenings and utilitarian banalities of organizations and institutions. (Richmon and Allison, 2003, p.1)

Leadership, then, tends to be concerned with longer term vision, mission and strategy of educational institutions, superseding more the day-to-day organisational tasks of managers, sometimes otherwise termed 'administrators'. While managers may be appointed to hierarchical positions of power, they do not automatically take on or correctly fulfil leadership roles, which are generally seen in a more positive, dynamic way.

Some distinctions between leadership and management have been drawn out from other key theorists. Northouse (2004) reflects on the distinctions between leadership and management previously pointed out by Kotter (1990). Northouse notes that management 'emerged around the turn of the 20th century with the advent of our industrialized society' (Northouse, 2004, p.8) and that it 'was created as a way to reduce chaos in organizations and to make them run more effectively and efficiently' (p.8). Hence, Northouse observes that the main task of management is to 'provide order and consistency to organizations', by contrast with the main task of leadership, which is 'to produce change and movement' (p.8).

We can see here that effective leaders inspire, communicate and energise strategic direction in organisations, whereas good managers ensure that operational activities function well. All the interviewees for this book, speaking from practical experience, recognised that leaders function more at the *strategic* level of organisations (whether or not overtly recognised in positional hierarchies) while managers function more at *operational* levels (usually in ways directly recognised in positional hierarchies at different levels). However, all interviewees also noted that it was beneficial for organisations to nurture 'leader-managers' operating effectively at different levels across both domains of activity.

Building on these definitions, we would expect, then, that managers should be engaged in such activities as planning, budgeting, organising, systems, rules and processes design, control and operations, staffing and monitoring. We would expect that leaders, by contrast, should be engaged in visioning, clarification of the 'bigger picture' in which the organisation operates, setting strategic direction, the communication of aims and values, team building, inspirational, motivational and energising activities. We can also note that the job of management is more closely tied to organisational structures, whereas the function of leadership may operate anywhere, and is not necessarily always linked to the formal responsibilities of particular roles.

From the existing leadership literature, two succinct definitions of the difference between leadership and management are the following. The first definition was cited by many interviewees, as they knew it well:

1. '*Managers are people who do things right and leaders are people who do the right thing.* The difference may be summarised as activities of vision and

judgement – *effectiveness* [leadership] versus activities of mastering routines – efficiency [management].'   (Bennis and Nanus, 1985, p.21)

2. 'Management is concerned with creating order and stability, while leadership is about adaptation and constructive change.'   (Northouse, 2004, pp.11–12)

During the interviews with the case study leaders, the question of the distinction between leadership and management in PCE came up. All interviewees clearly differentiated the two concepts, but also recognised that both leadership and management were necessary for the effective running of organisations.

> There are victories of the soul and spirit. Sometimes, even if you lose, you win.
>
> *Elie Wiesel (holocaust survivor)*

The question of 'managerialism' emerged in relation to an excessive focus on targets, but mainly there was a positive recognition of the important role played by management functions. The concept of the 'leader-manager' is therefore useful, as it recognises and beneficially conjoins these two essential dimensions of strategy and operational implementation of organisational functions.

Dissatisfaction with 'New Managerialism'

There has also been during this era an interest in, and growing dissatisfaction with, emerging concepts of 'new managerialism' in leadership studies relating to all fields in education. The word 'management' has been somewhat under pressure from negative connotations during the past decade in post-compulsory education, and particularly post-incorporation 1993, in relation to concepts of 'new managerialism', which was equated with autocratic and dictatorial managerial positions adopted by many senior management teams in colleges following 1993. The rise of 'managerialism' in education has been linked with the production of mission statements, strategic plans, quality systems, marketing plans and targets for accountability (Simkins, 2003, p.228). Dissatisfaction with managerialism encouraged researchers and practitioners to seek alternative solutions to the ongoing need of educational institutions for effective educational leadership. Comparisons have been made (Simkins, 2003, p.228) between 'bureau-professionalism' and managerialism. 'Bureau-professionalism' is a client-centred professional model of educational service in which the teacher-as-professional pays attention to the needs of students, and decisions are made on the basis of the discretion of professionals. By contrast, 'managerialism' prioritises the values and mission of the organisation and its efficient performance through management techniques which seek to achieve outcomes for students as 'customers' in a more business-related model.

Tensions between performativity, trust, and the passion to educate

Tensions therefore grew up in post-compulsory education institutions in the post-incorporation era between the 'performance culture' of an accountability response to external funding and inspection demands, and the 'passion to educate' combined with collegiate trust which hitherto had been a more natural feature of the professional teaching workforce. Blackmore (2004, p.439), in her study of educational restructuring in public sector schools in Australia, describes this kind of 'dissonance' in education. It is the clash between, on the one hand, educational 'performativity requirements based on efficiency and narrowly defined and predetermined criteria of effectiveness and success' and, on the other, 'teachers' professional and personal commitment to making a difference for all students based on principles of equity'.

Discussing the relations between trust and a performative culture in the re-formation of teacher professionalism in post-compulsory education, Avis (2003) observes that target-setting, action-planning performance management operates within a 'blame culture' and:

> . . . is reminiscent of fordist work relations in as much as the worker is tightly surveiled [sic], with attempts to render transparent the details of their practice. Performance management sits well with low trust if not distrustful work relations (Codd, 1999) and, therefore, is at odds with current strictures surrounding the knowledge economy, which emphasise fluidity, non-hierarchical team work, and high trust relations . . . (Avis, 2003, p.324)

The historical outfall from a climate of blame, fear of surveillance and distrust, regulated within increasingly masculinist and bullying forms of management, a background of multiple restructurings, redundancies, failing colleges, and overstressed and overworked staff therefore needed to be addressed across the PCE sector. It was in this context that the new Centre for Excellence in Leadership (CEL) was created (see Chapter 1). It seemed that it was high time for a more supportive framework for leadership within PCE to be developed, if the widespread sectoral improvement aims in the government-led initiative, *Success for All*, were ever to be achieved (NAO, 2005).

> It's amazing how many cares disappear when you decide not to be something, but to be someone.
>
> *Coco Chanel*

Academic and learning leadership in post-compulsory education

Effective, high quality academic leadership is significant in PCE, in view of its role as what Ruth Silver calls 'the adaptive layer' of the education system (see Chapter 11), responding to many parts of the community other areas don't serve. Something of a tension has emerged between 'managerialist' preoccupations of senior echelons of leadership in PCE and the concept of 'academic' leadership, although this is by no means a necessarily conflictual relationship. Educational leadership is, in fact, best focused on the concept of academic leadership *conjoined* to the practices of management, as has been achieved in some institutions.

PCE institutions are essentially focused on the provision of educational services to learners in particular *disciplines* or subject areas, grouped into around 14 or more clusters of subjects. 'Academic' leadership, described sometimes as 'instructional' or 'pedagogic' leadership, is focused on learners acquiring knowledge or skill in a particular subject area. Effective leadership of the *disciplines* learners come to study in is therefore of vital significance. 'Academic' leadership in teaching requires a high level of professionalism, being up to date in the subject area, having expertise and authority within it, and a broad grasp of the current state of play in the field of inquiry and knowledge (Briggs, 2005b, p.232; Busher and Harris, 2000, p.109). Good academic leadership means having highly effective, responsive, continuously improving and adaptable professional competence in pedagogic methods in your subject area, for the benefit of students and other teachers.

Learning Leaders

Moving from the conceptualisation of education as 'academic' in subject-focused terms into a more general description of 'learning', the concept of the 'learning organisation' (Senge, 1990) is of key importance for the learning and skills sector while, more generally, 'learning' is important in the mindset of leaders' ability to be 'learning-able' – that is, being willing to learn throughout their careers. Talmud Bah of Second Wave (Chapter 17) describes this kind of mindset in leadership with the metaphor of 'the white belt' of the beginner; Lynne Sedgmore (Chapter 8) talks about the need for educational leaders to be aware of and willing to learn constantly. Andrew Morris (Chapter 15) compares learning with breathing for its naturalness and vital importance to humans.

Teacher-leaders: pedagogy as leadership

Within the debate on leadership, it is important that both practice and theory have an ongoing role in shaping our concepts and practices. Staff development activities that encompass 'reflective practice' may be used to develop a rich interconnection between the theoretical or propositional knowledge ('know what') and practical knowledge ('know how') of professional educators. The concepts of 'reflective practice' and 'reflection-in-action' derive from Donald Schön (1983). Schön proposed that we should challenge theoretical models of 'technical rationality' with concepts of the deep practical knowledge deriving from the 'tacit' understandings of experienced professionals (Schön, 1983). These concepts have been both much in vogue and much criticised recently. Hayes (2003, p.4), for example, is dismissive of the term 'reflective practice' because of its under-theorised wholesale adoption, while others are concerned that 'reflective practice' may act as a cover for subtle surveillance of staff (see Gilbert, 2001, on the problematic 'rituals of the confessional'). Nevertheless, if appropriately contextualised, theorised and responsibly used, the concept of 'reflective practice' still has value. Lingard *et al.* (2003) describe the role of 'teacher-leaders' in schools: staff whose deep understanding of pedagogic leadership encourages them to be lifelong learners themselves, and to engage with education in the same way students do. Lingard *et al.* (2003) cite Bascia and Hargreaves (2000) on this kind of teacher-leadership:

> An intellectually enriched teaching profession requires . . . leaders who themselves model effective professional learning by examining their own practice and working alongside staff . . .　　　　　　　　　　　　　　　　　　(Lingard *et al.*, 2003, p.43)

Professional practice and leader-manager networks

A model of leadership in which teachers are seen as pedagogic leaders working in collaboration with other professionals is a fruitful one in education. Avis and Bathmaker (2004, p.301) propose a useful model of teacher professionalism that can inform learning leadership. The professional practitioner 'leader-manager' can foster the growth of practitioner 'teacher-leader' staff in institutions in which a culture genuinely informed by pedagogic models of leadership, and by critical collaborative dialogue, has been developed. This kind of organisation tends to be characterised by *a high degree of leader-member exchange* or 'high LMX' (Briggs, 2005b, p.224, citing Howell and Hall-Meranda, 1999, p.683) with a good sense of trust and creative interaction between leaders and team members, resulting in co-operation and good performance outcomes. Briggs notes that in 'sixth form colleges . . . LMX is likely to be high' (Briggs, 2005b, p.224). In our case study interviews, pedagogic leadership is particularly highlighted in Andrew Morris' discussion of experiences in colleges and sixth forms. These echo Briggs' comments on the positive ethos found in many of the UK's 105 sixth form colleges (Briggs, 2005b, p.224). High LMX is also a feature of high performing institutions in other areas of PCE in which there is a strong adherence to the principle of continuous learning, as documentary evidence from a number of the case study interview institutions demonstrates.

Professional leadership – dialogue and coalitions

An organisation managed by leaders possessing sufficient humility to perceive of themselves as learners may be one in which people at all levels can grow and develop. By contrast, in organisations in which fixed hierarchies have been created and in which managers perceive themselves (and are perceived) as much more 'important' or 'powerful' than practitioners, there may be barriers of misunderstanding and resentment between 'managers' and 'academic' or 'professional' staff. Paulo Freire wrote on the need for the kind of interactional dialogue that constitutes a learning culture, or a 'point of encounter' in authentic dialogue and learning, informed by emotional intelligence and a respect for knowledge:

> Men who lack humility (or have lost it) cannot come to the people, cannot be their partners in naming the world. Someone who cannot acknowledge himself to be as mortal as everyone else still has a long way to go before he can reach the point of encounter. At the point of encounter there are neither utter ignoramuses nor perfect sages; there are only men [*sic*] who are attempting, together, to learn more than they now know. (Freire, 1972, p.63)

A distributed model of professional leadership informed by authentic, democratic dialogue with practitioners is one that I return to later in this book. The role of *coalitions* within professional networking and collaborative leadership (Mullen and Kochan, 2000) in the creation of 'communities of practice' (Lave and Wenger, 1990) in PCE provides a useful model for future development. This concept takes 'distributed leadership' to more advanced, creative levels, enabling us to recognise the *coalition* as 'a dynamic and organic creative entity' fostering 'synergy, empowered and shared leadership, and personal and organizational transformation' (Mullen and Kochan, 2000, p.183). Mullen and Kochan note that their concept of the 'coalition' '. . . was conceived using Bolman and Deal's (1993, p.60) advice to 'Empower everyone: increase participation, provide support, share information, and move decision making as far down the organization as possible' (Mullen and Kochan, 2000, p.187) to improve organisational operations. This means empowering leader-managers throughout the organisation in a heterachy or network of interconnected relations, rather than just viewing leadership as residing at the top of a more singular hierarchy of downwards-diminishing power.

Summary

Reflecting on the many styles and paths of leadership, we consider the ongoing problem of leadership definition, recognising the need to have a 'better understanding of leadership'. In moving towards that, we differentiate between 'leadership' and 'management' on the one hand, and 'administration' on the other. The most succinct definition is that 'managers are people who do things right and leaders are people who do the right thing' (Bennis and Nanus, 1985). We discuss this distinction in relation to the case study interviewees, and then move on to consider dissatisfactions with 'new managerialism', tensions between performativity, trust and the passion to educate, and the role of academic, learning and pedagogic leadership in relation to models of professional practice and leader-member networks.

4

Equality and diversity perspectives

❝Only one man in a thousand is a leader of men – the other 999 follow women.❞
Groucho Marx

Equality and diversity in PCE leadership

In the recent Learning and Skills Research Centre (LSRC) report from Lumby *et al.* (2004, 2005), equality and diversity issues feature strongly in terms of planning PCE leadership development in the future. This is a key issue which hitherto has been insufficiently addressed. Lumby *et al.* note that 'effective leadership for diversity requires commitment at all levels', and that training is required for the creation of 'a national framework that will facilitate effective leadership at an institutional level' (2004, p.99). However, this team advises that in general 'the tentative nature of research findings on issues related to effective leadership and development for diversity' is very clear (2004, p.99). Basically, the promotion of equality and diversity in the sector calls for specific, sustained measures to address the unequal representation of women, black and ethnic minorities and people with disabilities for leadership positions at top levels of senior management in particular. This issue has for too long gone unaddressed.

Women leaders in PCE: advantaged or not?

Why are women not yet playing a significant enough role in PCE leadership? Recent evidence suggests that women now have a more important role globally in leadership. Women leaders may now possess some advantages in leadership, it is argued by some researchers. Some disadvantages women leaders have formerly faced may during the past decade or so have been disappearing, in an era in which more androgynous forms of transformational leadership are on the ascendancy.

But do such advantages relate to PCE institutions? Perhaps not enough, and not yet. Evidence from PCE suggests that the chances of career progression may still be blocked for women, particularly in terms of advancing to higher levels of senior management. There is, perhaps, still something of a 'glass ceiling' in predominantly male managerial environments. Let's examine this issue a little more.

The Female Leadership Advantage – myth or fact?

In recent popular literature, there has been recognition of a 'feminine advantage' in leadership (Eagly and Carli, 2003; Vecchio, 2002; Yukl, 2002). An example of this is the *Business Week* article on the 'New gender gap' cited by Eagly and Carli, which declared that 'Men could become losers in a global economy that values mental power over might' (2003, p.808). Stereotypical gender effects attributed to females may suit popular modernist 'transformational' leadership styles which, tending to be androgynous, are arguably easily taken up by women in comparison with 'transactional' styles which some argue are more likely to be assumed by men (Eagly and Carli, 2003, p.816).

> Leadership is not so much about technique and methods as it is about opening the heart. Leadership is about inspiration – of oneself and of others. Great leadership is about human experiences, not processes. Leadership is not a formula or a program, it is a human activity that comes from the heart and considers the hearts of others.
>
> *Lance Secrean, Industry Week*

A relatively recent increase in women leaders at very senior levels internationally is noted by Eagly and Carli (2003) who comment that '43 of the 59 women who have ever served as presidents or prime ministers of nations came into office since 1990' (p.809). Vecchio (2002) also comments on this, saying that during the 'last forty years the number of women in top or senior political leader positions . . . has been increasing exponentially'. Leadership roles and styles focusing less on formal hierarchy and more on collaborative ways of working, empathetic understanding and people-focused leadership styles tend to be those more associated with female leaders.

The leadership and management survey carried out by the LSDA in 2002 (LSDA, 2003) analysed results from nearly 2,000 questionnaire responses from PCE leaders and managers. The survey reported that senior management in the post-compulsory sector was still predominantly 'white, middle-aged and male' in 2002 (LSDA, 2003, p.15). Although more than half the respondents were female, women managers were much more likely to be in supervisory or middle management positions than in executive or senior management (LSDA, 2003, p.2). Numbers of women managers in PCE remained at a relatively stable level between 1997 and 2002, the slight increase in women managers being concentrated in supervisory and middle management levels.

An earlier Further Education Development Agency (FEDA) 1997 survey sampled 3,000 managers in over 250 of the then 452 FE colleges in England and Wales (Stott and Lawson, 1997) and found that more women than men (554:410) were recruited into management positions during the period 1993–97. At the end of 1997, there were 81 women principals – 17% of principals compared to just 3% in 1990. This compares favourably with wider figures on women in employment that indicate just 4% of women in England and Wales reach senior executive positions and 5% in European Union countries (Davidson, 1997, p.10). Such figures also represent a challenge to men's historical numerical dominance in FE management (see Pritchard *et al.*, 1998, for a discussion). However, women continue to constitute the majority of the workforce in FE, as is the case in both primary and secondary education where men outnumber women in senior positions in a predominantly female workforce. In FE, it is also the case that women are found predominantly in the lower levels of middle management (4th tier and below) where they comprise 50–60% of this level of the workforce compared with under 20% at the very top (FEDA, 1997).

Deem *et al.* (2000) examined the extent to which gender was a factor in the management of further education, considering the radical organisational restructurings that had taken place in FE, and the extent to which there had been a 'feminisation' of management. Basing their work on two studies of women managers in FE, these researchers found that 'some social and cultural as well as demographic feminisation of FE management is taking place' (Deem *et al.*, 2000, p.233) but that this was more at middle management level than in senior management, in which men and predominantly more masculinist styles still predominated. The picture since 2000 has not changed that much. Women principals and chief executives, particularly those from ethnic minorities, are still vastly in the minority in PCE institutions. There remains a more masculinist culture, linked to the performativity and task-focused transactional management styles which pervade senior management teams across the sector.

> I have to get the most energy out of a man and have discovered that it cannot be done if he hates another man. Hate blocks his energy and he isn't up to par until he eliminates it and develops a friendly feeling ... (towards all his teammates).
>
> *Knute Rockne - Professional Football Coach*

Black and ethnic minority leadership

The Commission for Racial Equality recently called for greater attention to be paid to the lack of black and ethnic minority staff at top levels of management in further education colleges (Clancy, 2005). The Commission for Black Staff in Further Education has called for higher levels of appointment of people from black and ethnic minorities – for example, at Principal level, in which the representation is currently at around 2% across the UK as a whole (Commission for Black Staff in Further Education, 2002a, 2002b).

Challenging prejudices

Lumby *et al.* (2004) note that a black and ethnic minority interviewee reported that he always had a need 'to prove myself as a black man in this profession', having worked previously in an organisation which was 'not yet ready for a black manager' (p.139). Prejudices against black and ethnic minority appointments, at both principal and other senior management levels in the PCE sector still, apparently, abound, and need to be directly and systematically challenged.

The Centre for Excellence in Leadership (CEL) is tackling the difficulties of prejudice against and under-representation of black and ethnic minority leaders at a national level. CEL's second key priority is 'Improving the diversity profile of leaders at all levels' (CEL, 2004b, p.1). The report on *Challenging racism* by the Commission for Black Staff in Further Education (2002a) urges institutions at all levels to take responsibility swiftly to tackle the twin issues of racism and a lack of equal representation of black and ethnic minority staff at senior levels. This is a key issue that cannot be ignored, and one which needs to be systematically addressed at every level of senior and middle leadership and management in PCE.

Synergistic leadership theory

Addressing the predominance of masculine leadership styles they felt had dominated leadership theories of leadership for two decades, Irby *et al.* (2002) proposed the need for an additional 'synergistic leadership theory' (SLT) for educational organisations. SLT theory, these researchers propose, is the first major theory to embrace both feminist and postmodernist organisational principles, proposing a tetrahedron model comprising four different factors:

1. attitudes, beliefs and values
2. leadership behaviour
3. external forces
4. organisational structure

A variety of new aspects of leadership are outlined in this model, including an explicit involvement of female leaders and feminist leadership principles in its development. While feminist principles are particularly appropriate in its implementation, it is nevertheless also generally useful in terms of other diversity and inclusion issues in PCE.

Synergistic theory does not focus solely on either individuals or organisations, but on a complex interaction between the four factors operating within a particular situation and organisation with specific leaders. The theory can be used to examine the organisational 'fit' between a leader and a particular institution – for example, if tension exists between two of the factors, then there may not be an effective relationship operating between a particular leader and the organisation they work in.

The theory is therefore useful to diagnose, make more comprehensible and possibly to remedy problematic conflicts in leadership situations. For example, in a situation in which an inclusive participative democratic female senior manager does not 'fit' into a bureaucratic organisational culture based on autocratic top-down masculinist styles of leadership, the SLT model might be applied to demonstrate why this leader might need either (a) to attempt to change the culture or external forces operating; or (b) to accommodate the organisational style and adjust her behaviour to 'fit' more; or (c) to decide that the effort to adjust personal values and beliefs or other elements 'out of synch' with the organisation to fit in with the culture is too much, and leave.

Leadership for diversity and inclusion in providing for students

Synergistic theory may assist us in considering the development of leadership diversity and inclusion but, for a more rounded view of PCE leadership, we also need to consider these issues at the level of providing for, and welcoming, student diversity and inclusion. There are problematic issues regarding diversity and inclusion that need to be addressed at every level in PCE institutions. An example is provided from the interview with Anne Morahan at Dover Immigration Removal Centre (DIRC) (see Chapter 12). I asked Anne about the provision at Dover and her answers indicate the huge difficulties of providing effective education for refugees from many different countries:

> We haven't found a suitable initial assessment test. ESOL is lagging behind with the *Skills for Life* initiatives: we found the Initial Induction Tests were all very cultural. There were disadvantages in using them. We also found the detainees were very, very stressed when they came in to do induction. Many of them didn't have the written ability to do a test. We found that by doing initial tests we were actually

losing our students. We have a full-time induction co-ordinator and an education booklet translated into different languages. Gina actually goes out into houses, meets with the new receptions; she might have a game of table tennis with them, just to build up confidence, and then say, 'Why don't you come and have a look around education?' (Anne Morahan, interview, 2005)

Despite the difficulties of inappropriate assessment tests for ESOL and many other problems, Anne and her team have worked to provide inclusive learning effectively for an extremely diverse and transient population:

We have used the walls in the education department to inspire learners by using lots of picture-based information and translations. We carry out an informal induction, show them around, and show them into the classroom so they can see for themselves what we do there. Then we raise the front page of the Individual Learning Plan (ILP), which just gives a very general background to the student's ability before they go into the classrooms. Individual planning when they come and go so quickly is really, really difficult. We do have plans for the way they can progress through education but, with regards to an individual level, it's very, very difficult. Some people have never been to school in their own country, have not got a written language in their own country, so they are unable to express themselves. (Anne Morahan, interview, 2005)

Anne suggested what might help providers working to manage an inclusive education service. This would include fewer targets, less paperwork, to free up teaching time, and the provision of a 'skills for life' programme including good diet and exercise, notably for people with certain kinds of disabilities:

In the future, I would like to see a move away from bureaucracy. Teachers have become burdened with government targets, paperwork, record collecting. I would like to see teachers have a chance to spend more time teaching students, concentrating on what is important. We also have an obligation to build more rounded individuals. That is something that isn't happening generally: people are not developing the social skills they need to survive in society. I also think diet and exercise with education is important. Research is highlighting how diet and exercise are essential for brain development. The DDAT[i] (Dyslexia Dyspraxia Attention Treatment) Centre runs an exercise programme for people with dyslexia, dyspraxia and ADHD[ii] (Attention Deficit Hyperactivity Disorder) which is absolutely incredible – it's very successful. A different approach like that would be fantastic for prisoners with special needs. (Anne Morahan, interview, 2005)

Having considered briefly the issues of equality and diversity in PCE leadership – and their relevance and importance currently for future leadership in the sector – we now move to look at the issues of change and transformation in PCE.

Summary

In this chapter, we consider the roles of diversity and inclusion in relation to leadership in post-compulsory education. Having cited the findings of a recent LSRC report, we recognise the clear need for sustained measures to address the unequal representation of women, black and ethnic minority staff and people with disabilities in leadership. We consider whether women have a new leadership advantage, but recognise that there is still something of a 'glass ceiling' operating. We examine the under-representation of black and ethnic minority staff, and the need to challenge prejudices. We briefly examine synergistic leadership theory as a helpful new leadership theory embracing feminist principles. We then consider the role of leadership in providing for student diversity and inclusion, and cite some specific examples relating to this from Dover Immigration Removal Centre in terms of recommendations for the leadership of inclusive learning provision.

Notes

i There is advice relating to this neurological disorder at http://www.mentalhealth.org.uk/page.cfm?pagecode=PMAMAD, accessed 7 August 2005.

ii http://www.ddat.co.uk/, accessed 7 August 2005.

Equality and diversity perspectives

'It's all change!': Transformations in post-compulsory education

> ❝Leadership is an improvisational art. The game – hey, the rule book – keeps changing . . . so leaders need to change, to keep reinventing themselves.❞
> Tom Peters

Since the Further and Higher Education Act, 1992, and the resultant incorporation of colleges in 1993, massive changes have been imposed by government on the post-compulsory education sector. During the decade 1993–2003, the Further Education Funding Council (FEFC) was set up, managed the strategic operations of colleges and was disbanded, to be replaced by the Learning and Skills Council (LSC) with its 47 local arms. As many researchers and academic writers have noted (see Avis, 2002, 2003; Briggs, 2002; Cole, 2000; Deem *et al.*, 2000; Frearson, 2002; Harper, 2000; Leader, 2004; Lumby, 1997a, 1997b, 2000, 2002; Lumby and Tomlinson, 2000; Randle and Brady, 1997a, 1997b), significant challenges were placed on leaders and managers in the sector during this period by the numerous demands placed on colleges to manage their own budgets in the same way as corporate businesses operating competitively.

A culture of 'performativity' to externally set targets to meet the market-led funding system of the FEFC and LSC caused significant emphasis to be placed on the strategic planning process. Strategies and mission statements, operational plans, performance indicators, targets for performance, quality assurance systems, appraisal systems, and a range of financial control and monitoring systems became the norm for PCE institutions.

> Leaders don't force people to follow – they invite them on a journey.
> *Charles S. Lauer*

The creation of specialist management posts in FE (and some other parts of the PCE sector) during the incorporation era meant that certain functions that had hitherto been relatively alien to teaching-focused institutions (for example, the marketing, MIS, ICT and enterprise initiatives of FE colleges) were now taken on by new kinds of business-minded specialists with professional qualifications in the new incorporated functions. This created a business-driven approach which sometimes sat uncomfortably alongside the professional ethos of staff more experienced in and wedded to public service traditions of teaching, student support and administration.

The values of principals and senior management teams in the sector at this time were shaped increasingly by the demand for a 'tough' style of operating that tended to distance senior managers from middle management as well as teaching and support staff (Lumby and Tomlinson, 2003). As Shain (1999) and Lumby and Tomlinson (2003) have noted, the prevailing style in this era tended to be one which was frequently described and experienced by FE critics as 'boys' own' or 'real men', while other researchers described this kind of domineering style as 'chauvinistic', 'cowboy' or 'bullish'. The implication in all such descriptions is that the leadership and management style adopted during the post-incorporation era was primarily dominated by values labelled more 'masculine' than 'feminine', such as autocratic, aggressive, controlling, directing behaviours. By contrast, more 'feminine' types of behaviours might be labelled in this kind of definition as more democratic, yielding, negotiating and 'softer' in style.

We need to be aware that this is clearly a superficial division providing only a rough hypothesis. It is evident there are many women operating with predominantly or exclusively 'masculine' styles of leadership. In addition, many men often operate with 'democratic', 'negotiating' and 'softer' elements of leadership that are sometimes superficially labelled 'feminine'. The picture is therefore generally much more complex than any one single definition could capture: the concept of gender-specific styles is highly problematic.

However, both of the 'harder' and 'softer' leadership styles adopted during the post-incorporation period were labelled 'managerialist' in a number of works painting a highly critical portrait of the leadership of PCE post-incorporation (Leader, 2004; Randle and Brady, 1997). Simkins and Lumby (2002) proposed a more critical look at this question (Lumby, 2000; Simkins and Lumby, 2002), but in general most writers depict a leadership roundly criticised for many failings (see Chapters 1 and 3).

According to these critics, autocratic, controlling and hierarchical models of leadership prevailed in which power resided almost exclusively at the top of PCE organisations. The Principal, renamed a 'Chief Executive', with a small number of top managers, was often seen to hold the only

> Leadership should be more participative than directive, more enabling than performing.
>
> *Mary D. Poole*

loci of control, with students and lower echelons of staff rarely if ever being able to have a say in the running of the institution. The investment of greater levels of power at the top of institutions created a distancing effect from staff at other levels, with a concomitant clash between the values of teacher professionals and the more business-led focus of controlling senior managers (see Chapter 3).

This gap between senior and middle managers was described by Lumby *et al.* (2003, p.286) as 'the well-documented difference in perception of the middle manager role from the perspective of senior and middle managers' (Briggs, 2001a, 2001b). In general FE colleges, in particular, a form of managerialism developed which was distinguished from other levels of leadership in colleges (see Chapter 1). Lumby observed that 'the stretching of tasks over senior and middle management appears to have resulted in leadership where neither middle managers nor senior managers appear to be focused on learning' (Lumby *et al.*, 2003, p.288), reporting from the results of her research that this situation affecting general FE colleges was markedly different from the pedagogical distributed leadership culture characteristic of sixth form colleges, in which the whole of the leadership team tended to focus on learning. The changing cultures under the FEFC and LSC did not therefore necessarily affect all PCE institutions in the same way, and sixth form colleges tended sometimes to resist externally imposed changes, keeping strongly to their original mission, possessing a strong sense of self-identity. The changes that they had to make tended to be adjusted to suit the mission, so that the institution 'owned' the change.

Distinguishing between 'change' and 'transformation'

Distinguishing between unwanted externally imposed 'change' and voluntary, self-induced 'transformation' can be helpful. This is particularly in terms of transformational and quantum leadership, in which leaders invite and lead their organisations to change in radically positive ways. Relentless externally imposed changes can result in a situation in which organisations feel disempowered, frozen by their inability to cope and respond to external demands. One of the profound achievements of transformation and quantum leadership models, if well-achieved, is to accept the continuous changes being required by external agents and to work within this, embracing change in a self-empowered way and turning it into self-induced transformation.

In fact, one of the main qualities which seems to distinguish capable leaders is the capacity to cope with, learn from and adapt successfully to continuous challenges and changes arising within difficult and unpredictable circumstances. Leaders who can cope well with the unpredictably difficult situations lying around the corner of the future are often those most valued by institutions. Leaders unafraid to grapple with new demands, meeting challenges and criticisms with zest and enthusiasm, are often also those who can deal effectively in an entrepreneurial way when faced by changing business imperatives. As Lynne Sedgmore notes:

> Learning leaders will have the self-confidence and self esteem to risk and enjoy learning with all the joy, pain and challenge that growth brings . . . They will be leaders who will create living, authentic learning organisations and learners.
>
> (Sedgmore, 2002, p.10)

For those who are not learning leaders, capable of adjusting to change, however, difficulties can arise and failures can and do occur – we consider this situation in more detail in Chapter 6.

Summary

In this chapter, we consider the massive changes that have occurred in the PCE sector, including FE, since 1993, and the culture of performativity and 'tough' management that have developed. We then discuss controlling and hierarchical models of leadership, and note the gap that developed between 'senior' and 'middle' management, in PCE, especially in FE, as well as differences observed between FE and sixth form leadership. It is noted that some sixth form colleges held on to their mission and embraced changes in ways that served their purpose. This attitude of maintaining identity in the face of change is taken up in relation to the distinction between 'change' and 'transformation' in leadership. We observe that it seems more beneficial to accept continuous change in a self-empowered way, considering briefly the quantum and transformational theories of leadership, and noting the necessity for leaders to take on a 'learning' role to adjust to changes positively.

Leaders in trouble: the dark side

> ❝Nearly all men can stand adversity, but if you want
> to test a man's character, give him power.❞
> Abraham Lincoln

This chapter considers leadership in the context of failures and problematic ethics, suggesting some ways in which we can learn from mistakes that have occurred in leadership in a range of settings with direct relevance to PCE or in ways relevant to public sector organisations in general.

Leaders seldom if ever find themselves in a situation in which everything automatically operates correctly. Similarly, they rarely encounter situations in which there is complete power to build an organisation freely without constraints. Even the most effective leaders are required to deal with aspects of organisations or situations which are immoveable, perhaps facing also a problematic leadership legacy from other people. Diagnostic skills for analysing organisational development and problems within organisations can be useful (see Cummings and Worley, 2001).

> When enough people start to authentically examine their deepest hopes, and tell the truth about the problems that exist and their own part in creating those problems, the field starts to shift.
>
> *Joe Jaworski*

Among the challenges placed on leaders in PCE is the requirement to maintain a standard of personal ethics and integrity superseding the temptations of power. Many in leadership roles have succumbed to the temptations of power and have become, perhaps subtly or gradually, oppressors of other people reporting to them, whom they enjoy controlling. Such leaders forget that they are, in fact, equal to everyone else. As Paulo Freire wrote:

> Too bad that all the people who really know how to run the country are busy driving taxi cabs and cutting hair.
>
> *George Burns*

The pursuit of full humanity . . . cannot be carried out in isolation or individualism, but only in fellowship and solidarity; therefore, it cannot unfold in the antagonistic relations between oppressors and oppressed. No one can be authentically human while he prevents others from being so.   (Freire, 1972, p.58)

Good, bad and ugly leaders

I have met, in my time, a number of educational leaders who have systematic-ally demonstrated a lack of ethical awareness, a dearth of humanity and more or less appallingly insensitive levels of arrogance. Sometimes people grow to develop undesirable characteristics as a direct result of holding privileged posi-tions. Alvesson and Sveningsson (2003) describe three moral aspects of leader-ship. They characterise these in terms of the 'good, bad and ugly', indicating that leaders and managers can move between these states when facing the ambiguous and difficult challenges of the many demands of tricky situations requiring leadership.

The kind of drift that occurs in 'ethical fading' (Tenbrunsel and Messick, 2004) is a case in point. Researchers Tenbrunsel and Messick identify the impor-tant role of self-deception in unethical decision making. They analyse the pro-gressively deteriorating shifts in moral standards that can occur in unethical leadership situations. Helpfully, they state that it is hard to explain, otherwise, how intelligent people, presumably still regarding themselves as conscientious and worthwhile human beings, could succumb to such unethical practices. These researchers trace the self-interested slippage in moral standards that can occur in leaders who believe, on the one hand, that they are upholding moral principles, while simultaneously carrying out a range of unethical practices on the other (Tenbrunsel and Messick, 2004, pp.223–36). This formative concept – that leaders sometimes deceive themselves through a series of 'fading' ethical slippages, rationalising poor behaviour, greed and immoral actions, perhaps through arguments of economic necessity or the need for change – is extremely useful in explaining how corrupt practices can occur in formerly well-ordered institutions.

Institutions in trouble

The continuously changing difficult circumstances leaders in organisations may face around the corner of an unpredictable future can include the unforeseen impact of imposing organisational change, including the effect, for example, of institutional restructurings. In the PCE sector, organisational restructurings have often taken place in response to challenges placed on the institution by external demands. These demands include those from the market requirements

> ...And on the pedestal these words appear; 'My name is OZYMANDIAS, King of Kings.' Look on my works ye Mighty, and despair! Nothing beside remains. Round the decay Of that Colossal Wreck, boundless and bare, The lone and level sands stretch far away.
>
> *Percy Bysshe Shelley*

created by students and employers in an area (for example, demand for courses to train staff for a particular industry) or the necessity to achieve learning, quality and financial targets imposed both externally and internally by monitoring agencies within the post-compulsory education sector.

Numerous examples of failures in restructurings, as well as some successes, have been witnessed in the PCE sector during the past decade. Leadership failures – including some celebrated cases – have occurred particularly in the case of heads of institutions and departments faced with stringent externally imposed targets for student, business and financial success (see Chapter 1). These targets have often been imposed within a climate in which there have been, simultaneously, cuts in resource allocations and external threats to institutional survival, such as competition from other institutions. Some institutions faced with this predicament have found themselves operating in declining situations in terms of recruitment success, financial targets, retention and achievement.

'Organisational anorexia' and 'the cesspool syndrome'

Organisational development and management researchers Bedeian and Armenakis (1998) have observed that, when organisations are forced to restructure as a result of a decline in institutional fortunes and achievement, a direct result can be

> Though I speak with the tongues of men and of angels, and have not charity, I am become as sounding brass, or a tinkling cymbal.
>
> *I Corinthians*

that an increase in voluntary and involuntary staff redundancy occurs. The most talented and marketable staff will usually leave the institution first during a period of employment uncertainty created by restructuring. Such staff will frequently find it easier to obtain another appointment quickly. This early departure of the most able staff can lead to a more or less severe thinning out of the institutional workforce, so

> You do not lead by hitting people over the head – that's assault, not leadership.
>
> *Dwight D. Eisenhower*

that a kind of *organisational anorexia* sets in. In such cases, organisations lose people who are the most talented and skilled, retaining a thinned out staffing comprising those who cannot find jobs elsewhere, or those 'stuck' in institutions for family, community, or geographical area-related loyalties.

With a sad irony, therefore, an acceleration in the decline of failing institutions can be caused because the most talented people sometimes instantly leave, including those the institution can least afford to do without. By contrast, those whose lack of abilities caused the decline in the first place will often stay on and be reappointed to existing or even more senior posts, as in the 'Peter Principle' or Dilbertian concepts we discussed earlier in this book (see Chapter 1). Bedeian and Armenakis write:

> In contrast to successful organisations in which cream rises to the top, organisations falling victim to decline often suffer from the 'cesspool syndrome', wherein, figuratively speaking, dreck floats to the top. In declining organisations, the early departure of qualified employees will inhibit recovery and, if unchecked, can accelerate decline.
>
> (Bedeian and Armenakis, 1998)

Things that block achievement in PCE

To investigate interviewees' views about the problems that can affect leaders in PCE, I asked all the case study interviewees to tell me about things that block achievement in the post-compulsory education sector. Their replies reveal some of the reasons why some PCE organisations might have a hard time succeeding at the task of leadership in difficult times.

Lynne Sedgmore noted that:

> Things that block achievement in post-compulsory organisations include, firstly, culture clashes, a lack of coherent culture. Really it's about different ways of seeing it all, as in Senge's five disciplines. Secondly, very defensive and negative behaviours of key staff. You know, people who block information, de-power others, who sabotage, who say 'yes' but then don't do it, rather than being honest. That's at the heart of what blocks most things happening. Thirdly, insufficient resources. There's something about the post-compulsory sector never quite having resources. I've been one of those people – we've co-created miracles within limited resources. But it does draw your energy, it does deflect time, it does block some things, or slows it down and drains energy. Fourthly, poor communication: I'd love to find the organisation where everybody says, 'communication's fine and good' – where it really is poor, it hinders. Fifthly, staff insufficiently skilled for the task. You can always upskill and update people, but there are huge issues in the sector about insufficient investment for workforce development over many, many years.
>
> (Lynne Sedgmore, 2005, interview)

> Remember, no one can make you feel inferior without your consent.
>
> *Eleanor Roosevelt*

Daniel Khan observed:

> Things that block achievement include bureaucracy. Anything we have to do with government, despite what the agenda is, you always seem to have a lot of bureaucracy. If I had my way, I would just kill bureaucracy. I have killed it in the college, I have rewritten all our procedures because we had so many procedures and policies, I just wiped them out because I really feel that you just have to go out and get things done, and you have got to have some safeguards, but I think England as a nation has gone over-bureaucratic. I really think this is what interferes sometimes with enterprise. Other things that blocked achievement are petty rivalries, and the question of resources. We have been responsive, but it has been real hard management of our resources, cutting waste – that is where strong leadership comes. Salary levels are also a big hindrance. (Daniel Khan, 2005, interview)

> Let no one say he is a follower of Ghandi. It is enough that I should be my own follower. I know what an inadequate follower I am of myself, for I cannot live up to the convictions I stand for. You are no followers, but fellow students, fellow pilgrims, fellow seekers, fellow workers.
>
> *Mahatma Ghandi*

Bob Challis replied to my question about what had blocked achievement, saying:

> I would say the funding and audit regime. The stuff that's been addressed in *Trust in FE*, you know the George Sweeney task group, so that has been even more than we knew. It's just become crippling: there's hardly a day in the year when we haven't got an auditor of some sort in. And the funding regime, the fairly short notice in government policy and the lack of thinking through on that . . . I think it's some of the political absurdity of the structure of providers – the anomaly of setting up all sorts of post-16 or as it is now post-14 providers, funding them, getting them to compete and then saying, 'play nicely now, children, in the interests of the young people'. (Bob Challis, 2004, interview)

In terms of what blocks achievement, Wendy Moss said:

> I think what blocks where I would like to go, is targeted funding linked to very specific things, very tight control, a sort of obsession about certain types of outcomes which are 'in', as opposed to other sorts of outcomes that are 'out'. And how many times have we watched this go off you know, cycle after cycle after cycle, there's one phase 'in' and there's another phase 'out' you know, you keep shifting to try and meet whatever the new thing is. When you actually know what needs to be done and you just like to be celebrated for doing the things that you know need to be done as well.
>
> I don't mean that state organisation is wrong. I just think there's an awful lot of unintelligent leadership from higher up around education, which doesn't listen enough to what people need, what people want.

> It is a paradox that every dictator has climbed to power on the ladder of free speech. Immediately on attaining power each dictator has suppressed all free speech except his own.
>
> *Herbert Clark Hoover*

Things come in favour, things go out of favour, they throw money at things that don't need anything . . . don't give money to things that do. And I guess, given a decent income and free range on something we thought coherent, I'd be going for rather different things.

(Wendy Moss, 2005, interview)

Mistakes leaders make: top tips to avoid being a terrible leader

If I were to ask a range of 'followers' in the PCE sector to list the mistakes some leaders and managers routinely make, their responses would probably quickly add up to a sizeable number. For the moment, here are some ways in which leaders can avoid being terrible at the job, by avoiding behaviours that can very quickly alienate a wide range of staff. These have been developed from my 30 years' experience of PCE as a leader, manager, and team leader as well as follower (see Figure 6.1).

> When evil men plot, good men must plan . . . Where evil men would seek to perpetuate an unjust status quo, good men must seek to bring into being a real order of justice.
>
> *Martin Luther King Jr*

Support for leaders in trouble

Whether faced with problematic institutional situations, a legacy of others' failures, personal problems, difficult staff, over-demanding targets, family or health problems, leaders in trouble should seek help. Support can be provided by mentors, coaches, supervisors, peer group 'buddies', friends and family members. Sometimes just sharing the burden of difficulties can help to turn the corner towards solving the problem. The first, crucial step for leaders challenged with significant difficulties is to be honest about the real problems the institution faces, and to address them directly with a realistic series of action plans to overcome difficulties, in a progressive sequence of ongoing improvements. Significant resources and support from external partners may be available if leaders acknowledge problems and ask for help.

NEVER regard yourself as the only, most important person in the organisation.

DO NOT think everyone else is there to serve you and make sure you have a successful career.

DO NOT seek to ensure you have the best office, an exalted title, reserved car parking, and largest salary with increases every year. DO NOT butter up the Governors to achieve this.

DO NOT neglect to value your employees. Especially, DO NOT omit to remember employees' names, genuinely consult with them, or *really* listen to them.

DO NOT sideline the majority of staff efforts, hand-picking a tiny, elite, highly paid top leadership team of your cronies and buddies.

DO NOT ensure this top team acts in an autocratic, bullying, superior way, treating other staff with cool disdain. DO NOT think that the underlings are only there to service you.

DO NOT think you can have a glossy brochure with the mission and values of the institution on display whenever inspectors or local newspapers call, but forget about values at other times.

DO NOT seek to make it subtly clear to external agencies that you are the most brilliant person in the institution, who rescued it single-handedly from disaster. Instead, tell them about your staff.

DO NOT get rid of staff (see *Special note on restructuring*) just because they whinged/disagreed with you.

DO NOT restructure frequently, putting everyone's jobs on the line, to instil fear across the workforce. DO provide objective feedback with *real reasons* to those who don't get appointed.

DO NOT avoid communicating with staff except to boast about your successes. Don't think all success belongs to you and all failure belongs to lapdogs and underlings. DO learn humility, and avoid thinking of your staff as 'lapdogs and underlings'. They are worthwhile, unique human beings.

DO NOT threaten people directly in public if tasks you ordered are not swiftly achieved. Find out why, and use emotional intelligence to deal with failures sensitively.

DO NOT overload conscientious, clever but naïve workers with key areas of your own job, scapegoat others, or avoid showing *any* weakness ever!

DO NOT constantly bully and nag staff to perform better, especially just before weekends or holidays. DO always appreciate your staff, and enjoy good discussions and laughter with them frequently.

DO NOT be flattered by and surround yourself with staff who echo 'yes' to everything you say.

N.B – SPECIAL NOTE ON RESTRUCTURING – DO NOT undertake whole-institution restructuring lightly. Never, ever attempt to do it without planning well in advance, reading several volumes on change management, plus some Dilbert's cartoons and visiting several other institutions that have been through the mills of restructuring and come out alive. Never, ever, regard yourself as 'indispensable'. *Always* be prepared for multiple sudden changes. Plan effectively for your successors. But, in the meantime, relish the delights of working in a wonderful job!

Figure 6.1 Top tips to avoid being a terrible leader

Summary

In this chapter, we reflected on leadership in the context of problems and failures. We noted the requirement of leaders to maintain a sense of personal ethics and integrity without succumbing to temptations of power. We considered 'good, bad and ugly' leaders, noting the key issue of 'ethical fading' that can occur when leaders explain away poor behaviour by deceiving themselves. We discussed institutions in trouble in the context of 'organisational anorexia' and 'the cesspool syndrome' (Bedeian and Armenakis, 1998), and then looked at things that block achievement in PCE, citing extracts from interviews with leaders on this question. We then provided 'Top tips to avoid being a terrible leader' and finally rounded up the chapter with a recommendation that leaders in trouble should seek help, as significant support may be available to them if they have the conscientiousness and courage to ask.

New leaders on the move

❝The best thing about the future is that it comes only one day at a time.❞
Abraham Lincoln

Reflections on leadership

What have we learned from examining a range of issues and models of leadership in post-compulsory education? This chapter brings together the results of these theoretical discussions into a new theory and framework for post-compulsory education leadership, in preparation for Part Two, the interviews with case study leaders. I begin first by considering in more detail the *Leadership Qualities Framework* recently developed by the Centre for Excellence in Leadership (CEL).

CEL's Leadership Qualities Framework

> Good leaders develop through a never-ending process of self-study, education, training, and experience.
>
> *Manual on military leadership*

In November, 2004, the CEL published *The Leadership Qualities Framework*. This new framework was designed to provide support for leadership development for staff in the LSC sector (CEL, 2004). The framework aims to give 'a perspective on the core characteristics of executive leadership that can be influential in successfully leading within organisations'. The framework differentiates between management and leadership, but also links these:

Leadership and management are interlinked. The ideal top leader is one who combines leadership with the skills and knowledge which a general manager requires. Not all managers are leaders. The key tasks in management may revolve around planning, organising and directing with the achievement of acceptable compromise.

For leaders, the key tasks are defining purpose, creating shared vision and values and alignment with the organisation's purpose. (CEL, 2004)

The framework specifies a number of key characteristics for leadership behaviours, and is designed to be 'a reference point for individuals and organisations'. The *descriptors* for developing successful leadership behaviour are that such a nascent or developing leader can:

- Learn: performs with leadership skills in basic key actions, has significant development needs in key areas
- Assist: performs well in the core areas; needs some development in one or more areas or complex key actions
- Perform: strong performer in many but not all key actions; emerging talent – enhanced performance capabilities
- Guide: exceptional performer exhibiting core characteristics. (CEL, 2004)

Examining CEL's *Leadership Qualities Framework* in the context of the interviews

Within the framework, the four key characteristics of successful leaders are outlined as:

- focus to achieve
- mobilise to impact
- sustain momentum
- passion for excellence.

Focus to achieve

'Focus on achievement' is a key issue which was brought out in all the case study examples. Leaders interviewed for this book were very clear that their main focus was on learner achievement and success. The question of 'focus' is important, so that organisations do not stray from their intended goals. The ability of leadership to agree, and stick to, a clear focus for organisational aims and mission is an important component of success. The National Audit Office report on LSS strategic leadership notes that 'achieving a balance between different priorities is difficult' (NAO, 2005, p.22), and reports that 'better provision was in sixth-form colleges' though 'more of the general further education colleges were also well-managed including some outstanding in this respect'. The clear focus of high performing sixth forms, general FE colleges, adult training and prison providers who tailor their vision and mission assists staff and learners in these organisations to gain good results.

Table 7.1a The Leadership Qualities Framework.

Focus to achieve

Definition of Qualities		Descriptors
Shaping the future	Leaders within the sector often have to work with ambiguity, uncertainty and conflicting pressures. In making strategic decisions they need to take account of the present and yet be aware of future implications. They are motivated to achieve success for all. The improvement to the service often requires leaders to take calculated risks, to take radical actions, to be creative and challenging and to see change as an opportunity.	• Constantly stays close to customer perspectives and learner interests, to ensure improvement in service • Builds a shared and inspirational vision; helping others understand and feel how things will be different when the future vision is achieved. Champions appropriate change initiatives and motivates others to support them • Ensures corporate ethical and social responsibility in both strategic and operational aspects of service delivery • Uses networks and insights into the broad strategic direction of changes in the learning and skills sector, at local and national levels, to help shape the organisation and influence developments across the wider L&S context	**L.** Has some strategic understanding. Focuses on the present and operational detail. Aware of the need to consider the consequences of actions for the future. Aiming to develop a wider range of vision within organisation, locally or nationally. **A.** Makes the most of current opportunities to bring about incremental improvements in the service. Looks ahead within short term timescale. Uses own networks to gain information or communicate vision. Assists in shaping the future within the organisation. **P.** Has systematic ways of keeping in touch with developments through wider networks. Takes action to deliver an integrated service, the benefits of which should be realised in the medium term. Has a broad and appropriate vision that addresses and communicates the need for change. **G.** Thinks and acts with a long-term, futuristic perspective. Keeps abreast of national developments within the sector through active involvement in national networks. Understands the needs of the learning and skills sector at all levels, and uses this to deliver change. Is innovative and challenging in finding ways of developing service improvements. Articulates a compelling vision of the shape of things to come that others will understand and follow. Knows what is and what is not possible in a given local or national climate. Demonstrates high ethical, social and moral values.
Business acumen	Leaders in the sector operate in a complex national and local political context. They are astute in anticipating and interpreting policy direction, translating this into local action. Leaders recognise the significance of collaboration and the politics of the possible.	• Demonstrates broad organisational awareness by astutely perceiving political economic and social trends • Manages uncertainty in complex environments, balancing differing objectives/ priorities between national/regional/local • Understands and utilises econ/financial/sector data to accurately diagnose business strengths/key issues and future challenges. • Adds value through collaboration towards shared goals, partnerships and group synergy to deliver results	**L.** Recognises the complexity of the sector and is working towards greater analysis and sensing of major trends within and across the learning and skills sector. Seeking to make connections, to relate to wider context and to understand or work with networks to achieve synergy. Developing an approach less reliant on formal structures and processes. **A.** Understands the purpose of the data in informing the business strategy. Has some awareness of the impact of the external environment on organisational development. Is able to function in complex conditions and make a contribution to analysis of the issues facing the organisation. **P.** Invests effort in utilising knowledge of national/local trends to balance priorities. Sets the pace and challenges required to bring about local service improvements. Develops collaborative relationships to deliver results. **G.** Understands the political, social and historical factors that shape local and national realities of the L&S sector. Uses this understanding to move things forward at regional and/or national level. Ensures that the strategy for learner improvement is cohesive and integrated. Takes a strategic view of the business environment and is skilled in analysing management information to diagnose business issues and challenges. Maintains positive expectations of stakeholders and gives people a sense that change is achievable. Ensure ownership of the organisation's strategic goals and demonstrates the value of collaborative contribution and group synergy.
Action orientation	Those with vision are prepared to put it into action, challenge how things are done and to take others with them. Leaders fully understand what is achievable in a given context and set appropriately stretching targets for service improvement.	• Creates achievement-oriented environment understands that change may have to be radical to achieve learning improvement • Demonstrates strong judgement and discernment of self, others and situations • Establishes robust action planning to accomplish goals/ vision after analysing information, resources, constraints, organisational values and assumptions • Sets ambitious targets to deliver added value to the service, overcomes obstacles, accepts responsibility, focuses energy on what really makes a difference, rather than being constrained by previous methods	**L.** Reacts to current issues and problems decisively. Uses well tried methods to secure improvement. A number of targets and actions are achievable in the short term. Judgements and analytical skill is being developed. **A.** Anticipates and takes action to avoid an approaching problem that might affect service delivery. Will take lead from top on innovative ways to achieve learning improvement and will model action planning accordingly. Accepts responsibility for actions. **P.** Challenges the status quo and actions reform through accurate management information analysis, to realise service improvements over the next year or so. Looks beyond existing boundaries and identifies the implications and risks of actions. Sets challenging targets for future outcomes. Judgements and analysis are good and contribute to others following lead. **G.** Has an eye to the future when taking action in the present, driven by motivation to achieve ambitious targets for learning and skills improvement. High level judgement and analytical skill informs the strategic vision, allowing the taking of radical action which may be needed to modernise the sector and make it genuinely responsive to the needs of users. Understands the impact of context upon their decision-making and the importance of ensuring ownership of strategic goals and actions. Energises self, others and situations by creating a sense that change is achievable and that their contribution matters.
cultural sensitivity	Leadership is crucial in setting the organisational climate that will inspire people to make changes and in getting diverse stakeholders to work together. Motivated by a personal value about inclusiveness, effective leaders promote and model equality and openness in creating a positive climate for change.	• Understands the climate and culture of their own organisation and who the key influencers are and how to involve them • Understands and effectively adapts to fresh insights and perspectives from diverse sources; taking action to maximise the strengths of cultural diversity and using them as opportunities for growth • Creates and maintains an environment that enables all to contribute their full potential in pursuit of organisational objectives. • Demonstrates commitment to equality and fairness, within an inclusive approach	**L.** Recognises issues of climate, diversity and equality. Working towards demonstrating behaviours that are consistent to the core values of inclusiveness, openness and integrity. **A.** Models and promotes the organisational values and reacts positively to differing perspectives. **P.** Creates an environment of openness and inclusion, providing clarity of communication in setting the climate. Requires and expects others to do so also. Is aware of group norms and the way things have customarily been done; uses this to manage and influence change. **G.** Creates the climate that enables people from a diverse range of backgrounds, abilities and experiences to contribute their full potential. Knows who the key influencers are and how to go about involving them to shape and deliver change across the wider learning and skills sector. Ensures open access to information and that diversity is respected. Is pro-active in adapting to a variety of cultural perspectives and utilises these opportunities. Acts as role model for the involvement of all people, even when this results in challenges to how things are done.

Table 7.1b The Leadership Qualities Framework.

Mobilise to impact

Definition of Qualities		Descriptors

Organisational expertise

Leaders have the critical capacity to make sense of complex information and situations. They have the intellectual flexibility to ensure that resulting activity provides the best quality outcomes.

- Defines the organisation and processes to enable innovative thinking and successful partnership working to achieve excellence
- Possesses the ability to define key issues, secure information, overcome barriers, focus on achievable solutions
- Commits to action after identification of alternative courses of action that take into account resources, constraints, organisational values
- Prioritises, time and resource management opportunities consistent with goals; proactively negotiates and accesses resources outside of one's immediate domain

L. Sees the obvious and can on occasions make connection to the wider context. Requires greater awareness of complexity and diverse sources. Commits to course of action that offers one solution or approach. Prioritisation and resource management is often reactive.

A. Makes sense of disparate information; sees patterns and trends and takes these into account when devising action. Uses existing models to help integrate things into a whole.

P. Modifies own thinking and set of assumptions, to take account of wider picture and new/diverse perspectives, including those from different professional areas. Focuses on achievable solutions consistent with organisational goals. Is adept at moving between operational detail and the big picture. Creates structure and process to enable innovative thinking and effective partnership to take place.

G. Demonstrates the ability to move rapidly between strategic thinking and the significant detail of operation. Has the open-mindedness for creative and radical thinking, necessary to define and drive through change and reconfigure or reorganise services, so that they are more responsive to the needs of users. Consolidates key points from a diverse range of information and makes sense of complex situations. Proactively operates across domains to secure best possible solutions, partnership working and resource availability. Ensures that all people are aware of the organisation's purpose and their contribution to service improvement.

Distributed leadership

To affect lasting gains, leaders facilitate the contributions of others, share leadership, nurture capability and encourage people to take responsibility for changing and improving the learning and skills service. It is critical that as the L&S service partners with other agencies, that leaders provide clarity about individual and team roles.

- Uses appropriate delegation to create sense of ownership of higher-level organisational issues and encourages leaders to stretch beyond their current capabilities for organisational success
- Uses appropriate methods and interpersonal style to motivate and guide teams towards successful outcomes and attainment of objectives
- Knows when and how to attract, develop, reward and utilise teams to optimise achievement.
- Ensures that teams are aware of their contribution to the organisation as a whole

L. Working towards greater clarity and direction when leading others to achieve. Seeks to involve others in bringing about changes for improved service and is aware of the need to engage constructively with stakeholders so that common solutions can be agreed.

A. Expresses positive expectations of others and delegates responsibility, providing support to enable success. Acknowledges and respects the perspectives of others and uses mistakes/failures as an opportunity for learning.

P. Facilitates the effectiveness of leaders and groups by providing the right resource or information. Secures support or development for the benefit of both individuals and the team as a whole. Gets input from others with the intent of promoting the effectiveness of the process or the group. Explains the rationale for change and key priorities. Strives to create conditions for successful working partnerships.

G. Aligns effort and shares leadership to achieve the vision. Encourages others to drive forward change and enables teams to succeed in making changes. Mobilises people's energies and commitment both within the organisation and across the sector. Creates the conditions that enables collaborative working and a team to form at its best; gets the right people doing the right things. Acts to build team spirit so as to promote team effectiveness. Clarifies roles and responsibilities to effect change and encourages leaders to stretch beyond current capabilities. Allows freedom with accountability.

Influencing Relationships

Leaders need to be adept at sophisticated influencing to build support within and across the sector for continuous improvement. Collaborative working is crucial in delivering measurable and radical improvement in the L&S environment.

- Uses appropriate styles and methods to influence and build cohesive, collaborative and effective partnerships with stakeholders, community and others
- Expresses thoughts, feelings, ideas in a clear, succinct and compelling manner; adjusting language to capture attention and engagement
- Employs a range of influencing strategies to bring about change in the learning and skills sector
- Acts to build trust, to inspire sensitive and clear vision, to resolve conflicts and develop consensus in creating high performance teams

L. Is aware of differing styles of leadership. Relies on the force of their own impact and their side of the argument. Recognises that networks and coalitions across the sector have value. Uses informal influencing as a preferred influencing strategy.

A. Persuades using one or two well reasoned arguments. Uses direct logical persuasion, relying on facts and figures, costs and benefits to convince. Influences matters internally to bring different groups together to embrace new ways of working or other aspects of the change process. Identifies key people who can get things done.

P. Actively promotes the role of stakeholders and learners in shaping and influencing the service. Influences both directly and indirectly, taking time to build critical mass or support for position. Deliberately plans an approach that will be successful with a particular interest group or audience. Uses both subtle and direct influencing tactics in order to empower and create ownership of the change agenda.

G. Uses complex strategies that work in the immediate and longer term to bring about improvements. Understands the need to use informal persuasion and provision of information to influence others, over whom they have no formal authority. Builds and uses extended networks of influence, understanding the priorities of partners and responding appropriately to changes in their circumstances or issues. Ensures that the strategy is cohesive, integrated and representative of user needs. Shares power within the organisation across networks and develops constructive relationships which focus on consultation and involvement in decision-making.

Performance accountability

Leaders are accountable for standards of governance, for holding others and themselves accountable for the performance of the organisation and deliverable services.

- Creates a climate of support and accountability rather than a climate of control
- Holds people to account for what they have agreed to deliver
- Sets standards for performance and behaviours, ensuring support process in place to achieve
- Manages performance difficulties in objective and constructive manner

L. Supportive and caring. On occasions, allows performance drift through not identifying and/or addressing performance issues. Working towards greater consistency in challenging people about performance and in providing constructive and objective support. Leadership commentary is operational.

A. Assigns accountability. Ensures protocols are developed for coordination and governance of service. Provides others with clarity of direction and purpose, developing individual and team performance.

P. Sets boundaries for performance accountability. Ensures the processes are in place to support individuals in achieving standards and to learn from their mistakes. Is prepared to be held openly to account for own agreed goals.

G. Promotes a high performance culture. Holds self and others, both within and outside the organisation, accountable for delivering what has been agreed. Intervenes swiftly and consistently when performance is slipping, using appropriate processes. Challenges and confronts conflict, particularly where this impacts upon service delivery. Praises others for their achievements.

Centre for Excellence in Leadership

Mobilise to impact

The concept of 'mobilising to impact' relates to the kind of discussions John Guy and I had around the necessity for leaders not just to be self-driven, but to learn how to motivate and draw in other people through, for example, emotional intelligence training. This enables other staff to contribute to a shared institutional vision. Successful leaders energise and motivate others to accomplish significantly more than, under normal circumstances, they would. Lynne Sedgmore also talked explicitly about this need to delegate the task of leadership in terms of impact in a clear way, providing a balance between different dilemmas and requirements in colleges. David Collins' 'put your pictures on the wall' story (see Chapter 18) about motivating a whole college to share in the rescuing its failing fortunes, provides an extraordinarily effective model for the instant mobilisation of an entire workforce.

Sustain momentum

'Sustaining momentum' was particularly mentioned by Bob Challis as a key component of effective leadership in the longer term. Bob expressed strongly that there is a need just to 'hang on in there', even if things did not seem immediately to be working. John Guy discussed the role of leadership in sustaining continuous momentum for improvements in Farnborough Sixth Form College by specifying 'good enough is not good enough', and by devising the 'sigmoid curve' and systems of value-added analysis as mechanisms for whole-college inspiration towards generating renewable growth and improvement. PCE leaders in the future need to hold fast to high standards and have courage and determination to pursue these, despite setbacks.

Passion for excellence

A 'passion for excellence' was demonstrated strongly by all leaders, but perhaps nowhere more clearly than by John Guy, Ruth Silver, Wendy Moss and Daniel Khan, in relation to their particular institutions and areas of provision. Lynne Sedgmore, too, had a key focus on what Ruth called 'professional love' for the sector, and for the establishment and maintenance of quality at every level for the benefit of learners.

Having considered briefly this outline model, we can now examine the more detailed definitions of qualities in the *Framework*, which are elaborated as shown in Tables 7.1a–d.

Lessons for leaders of the future

Having briefly examined CEL's *Framework*, we now turn to some key issues derived from the interviews, giving locally variegated leadership suggestions deriving from these ten successful leaders. I asked all the case study interviewees what they would suggest leaders of the future will need to do to ensure success in their organisations. The replies from the interviews contain some very useful lessons for those planning to take on leadership positions in PCE. A selection of some of these statements follows.

Lynne Sedgmore noted, for leaders of the future, looking at new ways of doing things:

> *Collaborative working and the courage of that working and the interests of the bigger purpose* is important. If you've got egos in there fighting over who wins the collaborative partnership, it doesn't work. I really believe in the inter-dependence of collaboration: that's the kind of world we live in now. Leaders need to be *aware and skilled in enabling distributed leadership*. Leaders who do just want to lead from the top haven't really got a real understanding of empowering or creating empowered environments and enabling people at every level to step up, so the organisation doesn't survive.
>
> Leaders in our sector need to be more adept at *policy and its implementation and the bigger picture*, knowing how to bring policy into effective practice. Leaders also need to be *highly self-aware* and need to be able to *work across all the intelligences*, IQ or cognitive work, emotional intelligence, in terms of meta-cognitive *learning to learn*, really knowing about learning. We are professional leaders in our sector, so being 'a leader of learning', as well as of learners and staff, is very important. We need to be really skilled in 'how do people learn'. Leaders also need to be *resource magicians* and be effective in the *global economy, knowledge economy, knowledge environment* and *e-learning.*
>
> The most challenging issue for leaders is what goes on *inside you* as much as what goes on outside. If you get inner clarity, authority, understanding and skills, then, whatever situation you're in, you can deal with it. *What is your leadership identity?* Getting inner strength to know and live your values, be authentic, understand situations you're in, know how to get tasks achieved through effective processes, working in relationship with others. Because then it doesn't matter what kind of situation you're in, you're able to adapt. We developed *The Leadership Qualities Framework,* a set of skills, qualities and behaviours we think leaders need. It's getting some kind of understanding, a real sense of your own stage of development. It doesn't matter what framework people use. Find a very encompassing, inclusive framework model that helps you. Learn to get a balance of skills and qualities. Leadership is a constant challenge of people projecting things on to you, circumstances changing. You've got to find an equilibrium, live with that, not feel over-stressed, stay healthy and balanced.　　　(Lynne Sedgmore, 2005, interview)

Table 7.1c The Leadership Qualities Framework.

Sustain momentum

	Definition of Qualities		Descriptors
Driving for results	*The drive and energy of leaders created the momentum need for sector change and for meeting challenging targets.*	• Sets high goals for individual group accomplishment; using measure methods to benchmark progress • Tenaciously works towards meeting or exceeding goals and hold people accountable for service performance improvements • Enhances organisational achievements through beneficial networks and partnerships	**L.** Recognises the need for goals and benchmarking. Can on occasions "fire-fight" rather than applying learning from past situations. Seeks to develop sharp focus for priorities and effort. **A.** Shows determination to meet objectives set by others. Takes actions that lead to quantifiable improvements. Keeps track of and measures outcomes against own standards, over and above those set by others. Encourages others to find ways of delivering and sustaining services that meet needs of users. **P.** Sets and meets challenging goals. Takes the necessary steps to meet goals; tracks and quantifies achievement. Overcomes obstacles and uses failure as an opportunity to learn. **G.** Sustains focus. Tenaciously works towards achievement; resists any pressure to be deflected from this attainment. Challenges others and addresses poor performance where this impacts upon effective delivery of service. Takes calculated risks, based on learning and experience, to achieve longer term improvements. Uses networking and partnership to gain benefits for achieving goals. Delivers results through others.
Change management	*Strong and clear leadership is crucial in aspiring people, individually and in team roles, to deliver change. Leaders demonstrate adaptability and confidence when dealing with change issues.*	• Creates and manages changing environments and sector challenges. • Continuously seeks opportunities for different and innovative approaches to address organisational problems and opportunities • Motivates the team to deliver shared capacity and will energetically lead the change agenda • Values adaptability for purpose. Develops/improves existing and new systems that challenges the status quo	**L.** Acknowledges change and is developing greater clarity on how and why change is necessary. Works to help others see change as an opportunity and to positively manage change. Functions best in stable and routine conditions. **A.** Is able to function well under changing conditions. Conveys a positive image and motivates others to support through championing appropriate change initiatives. Demonstrates shared leadership and will develop appropriate leadership style and processes to support. **P.** Acknowledges and addresses the concerns of others about change; helps others to overcome their anxieties and understands how to overcome resistance. Anticipates the reasons why change is needed and the benefits it will bring. Is flexible and sees change as an opportunity, adapting systems and processes to deliver best value service. **G.** Communicates clearly the how and why change is necessary. Understands the process strategically and operationally and how best to sustain momentum in leading change. Is sensitive to organisational issues and politics. Uses both formal and informal systems for leading change and for recognition of people's efforts. Uses a range of leadership styles to encourage and motivate others. Works for shared understanding, tolerates ambiguity and maintains an open mind to differing viewpoints. Addresses concerns and reviews priorities to suit changing needs.
Building organisational capability	*Leaders with real vision take the time to develop a learning organisation and ensure that the vision has longevity and continues to re-energise.*	• Builds a learning organisation and models life-long learning, through encouraging staff to become enablers, facilitators and high-order learners themselves • Motivates, empowers, collaborates with and encourages others to feel ownership in what they do and continually improve the business • Through distributed leadership, re-energises and regenerates the organisation	**L.** Is self focused and refers to sharing in leadership development of others. Working to develop constructive support and recognition of opportunities for team and individual development. **A.** Helps to develop ideas and actions of others without taking credit for it. Involves expertise and knowledge of all members in order to build capacity for learning. Values development and opportunity for self and others, to sustain benefits of change. **P.** Uses leadership style to influence and motivate others. Recognises the creative efforts and ideas of others. Lets others take the credit and to lead, in order to grow their capability and benefit the organisation. Ensures that performance management and continuous professional development are the backbone of service improvement. Is a keen learner and models this behaviour to involve others. Adds value to the longevity of the service through spotting talent and encouraging others to seek new opportunities for their development. **G.** Values individuals and teams, as an asset to be nurtured and guided in the attainment of service improvement and collective leadership capability. Celebrates success and conveys a positive approach towards sharing leadership and championing others. Recognises and credits contributions from team members and supports the individuality of team members. Encourages an atmosphere where people can contribute ideas freely and fosters collaboration internally and externally. Sets example by modelling learning behaviours and places high priority on improving performance and spotting/growing talent potential, through providing opportunities that support the efforts of people to develop themselves. Ensures high morale through own actions and words, both within the organisation and across the sector, thereby regenerating enthusiasm for continual development.
Growing future talent	*Improving the talent pool is crucial to the long term success of the sector. Leaders recognise people as an asset, foster independence and accelerate the growth of the organisation through promoting the development of people.*	• Systematically plans for organisational succession and provides support to enable individuals to grow and develop, using positive action initiatives. • Provides timely coaching, mentoring, feedback and credit recognition to help others excel on the job, meet key accountabilities and create a leadership mind-set	**L.** Allows development of others on an ad hoc basis. Recognises the need to lead by example and make space for others to grow their talent or to contribute. **A.** Gives explicit encouragement and makes self available for support. Seeks dialogue as a means of learning. **P.** Lets others take the lead to grow their confidence and capability. Mentors, provides feedback and encouragement to accelerate the growth of others. Is pro-active in facilitating others' contribution and nurturing leadership potential. **G.** Spots talent and systematically provides support and opportunity to grow the capability of all leaders within the organisation. Coaches others, within and across the sector, challenging and asking questions to help them find solutions themselves. Provides space for others to be creative and to take risks, so they can develop their capabilities and approaches.

Table 7.1d The Leadership Qualities Framework.

Passion for excellence

	Definition of Qualities		Descriptors
Common purpose	In undertaking their leadership role, effective leaders demonstrate a strongly held sense of commitment to openness, trust, inclusiveness and high standards. Their integrity guides them and underpins their actions.	• Ensures high morale, through inspiring a common sense of purpose, belonging and action. • Shows passion and conviction to achieve excellence and about impact upon the organisation/sector. • Sets and models clear values and challenging performance standards • Engenders trust and respect through high integrity, ethical and social responsibility, transparency of decision-making, clarity of communication and accountability	**L.** Can on occasions of pressure stand up for own values and beliefs. Seeks to demonstrate commitment to core values of openness, integrity and inclusiveness. Demonstrates some understanding or working with the informal processes within the organisation. **A.** Behaves consistently with own stated values and beliefs. Deliver on what is promised. Uses internal networks to communicate and gain support. Is committed to the change agenda. **P.** Creates an environment in which transparency of decision making is prevalent; cuts through ambiguity to provide clarity in communication. Is aware of the relevant interest groups and uses this to get buy-in. Is highly committed to success for all. **G.** Acts as role model for involvement of all people in organisations. Supports others who act consistently with core values. Engenders trust and respect through a strongly held commitment to openness, inclusiveness and high standards in undertaking the leadership role. Operates with high moral, ethical and social values. Stands up for the common purpose, even when difficult to do so and when perhaps there may even be a personal cost in doing so. Is passionate about continuous improvement within the sector and creating a learning organisation.
Learning orientation	This quality provides the value base and drive for what leaders do to improve and transform the learning and skills service. Effective leaders are motivated by making real difference to people, through how learning is shaped and delivered.	• Demonstrates and encourages in others a zest for knowledge, experiences and challenges • Regularly creates and capitalises on learning opportunities • Recognises imaginative/creative ideas of others • Adapts leadership style to the current situation	**L.** Undertakes self earning and is working towards developing learning opportunities for self or team members in order to enhance the organisational benefits. Recognises creative approaches by others. Is aware of the need for flexibility in leadership style and effective impact upon transforming the service. **A.** Recognises the importance of being a learner themselves, as a motivator to others and a benefit to the quality of service delivered. Creates opportunities for others to capitalise on this and to make a difference through increased knowledge, skill and understanding. Is receptive to new ideas and adaptable in approach. **P.** Is a champion of learning and shared leadership. Encourages new ways of thinking and a wide range of leadership challenges in order to develop capacity and capability within the organisation. Uses a variety of approaches to motivate and lead the change process. Uses learning as a vehicle for improvement of the service. **G.** Is receptive to fresh insights and perspectives and encourages others to be likewise. Creates opportunities within and beyond the organisation for job challenges to develop the leadership strengths and potential of people, for the good of the sector. Demonstrated high level learning through encouraging imaginative and creative ideas and by sharing own learning challenges/outcomes with others. Uses a variety of leadership styles to suit changing contexts and to transform the service. Places high priority on developing high performance in leadership and encouraging the growth of talent within the sector.
Drive and Direction	To lead change within the sector requires staying power, stamina and resilience to manage the challenges of a complex leadership role. Self belief is necessary in a pressurised and rapidly changing environment.	• Demonstrates the emotional, mental and physical stamina to meet the challenges of developing and improving the service • Relishes challenge, takes calculated risks and encourages innovation. • Tenacious in driving for high performance • Exhibits high energy, self-belief and confidence; is optimistic and future orientated	**L.** Demonstrates emerging resilience and energy to manage the challenges of a complex leadership role and the drive for change. Aware of the need not to be overwhelmed by pace and scale of change, nor hesitant when faced with opposition. Influenced by need for personal recognition and aware of the need for achievement of corporate goals. **A.** Acts with confidence and has courage to make full use of the formal authority of the role. Relishes the challenge however difficult the task or confrontation. Draws on own relevant experience. Is optimist about achievement of goals. **P.** Rises to and relishes a range of challenges. Feels able to succeed and is prepared to be visible. Will involve others in support of a particular goal. Invests sustained effort and demonstrated stamina in meeting challenges. Sets achievable milestones and has expectations of self and others. Handles setbacks in a constructive manner and learns from them. **G.** Adopts positive approach to change. Is able to deal with pressure and still function well. Has a high level of stamina and resilience which underpins determination when dealing with key priorities. Has confidence to make tough decisions and keep going in face of adversity. Relishes very stretching challenges, takes appropriate risk and leads the pace and scale of change. Backs up position with evidence that the drive and direction is aimed at achieving service improvement. Is future orientated and seeks to leave a legacy of improved learner provision with enduring benefits for stakeholders.
Self awareness and growth	Leadership is increasingly about working across organisations and networks. Hence, leaders need to be able to share leadership with others and be aware of the impact they have on others. Effective leaders take account of their personal strengths and limitations.	• Willingness to reveal vulnerability, to learn from others. Awareness of own strengths and development needs, as well as impact of own behaviour on others • Prepared to be held to account by others. Actively seeks personal growth and improved awareness to deliver high performance • Advances own insight regarding sector issues and actively uses that knowledge to create best value services and opportunities	**L.** Has some self awareness; may be surprised by own emotions/ reactions to certain situations. Sets aside time for personal reflection. Has some recognition and/or acknowledgement of the impact of own behaviour on others. **A.** Registers own emotions and how challenges to personal values may impact on these. Manages own response when faced with demanding situations. Able to share leadership, to work in collaboration with others and be aware of impact of behaviour on others. Seeks personal growth in relation to improved performance. **P.** Has a clear focus on own direction. Is aware of, and sensitive to, the impact of their qualities upon others in a range of situations. Knows their own strengths and limitations in providing leadership that makes a difference to all. Learns from successes and mistakes and is able to absorb and deal with this constructively. Takes responsibility for self development. **G.** Understands emotions, strengths and limitations and the impact these have on performance and response of others. Takes conscious steps to develop qualities and learn from situations; willingness to reveal vulnerability and be held to account. Demonstrates high levels of self awareness which supports energy and resilience capability. Uses self knowledge to reflect upon contribution to organisational development and service delivery. Takes responsibility for own development and uses own contribution to creating best value services. Models the role of learner and shares leadership knowledge and development with others, in creating a learning organisation.

David Collins noted, in general, on leadership of the future:

Ideally, people share a vision about what they want to achieve. It is that sense of direction and movement that's essential to leadership, as distinct from the mechanics of management which is the best way of getting there and how you actually operate to get to where you are going. To do that, you've got to be able to free up people's thinking away from the day-to-day. This is where it flows into the time question. They've got to be thinking, not just how can I teach this group today, or how do I get through this year's budget but what is it that I'm doing today that's preparing the organisation for two, three, four years ahead? It's that ability to look ahead and think about what you're doing now and how it relates to what's going on in the future and the vision you've got for the future. So it's trying to make sure people don't operate in the present completely, because in the present you can't really have a vision because a vision is about the future.

For future leaders to be trained to cope, there is a need certainly for public sector leaders for a kind of pre-entry qualification before taking up the leadership of a major organisation. You do need specialist knowledge of how things operate and inter-relate. I think a qualification would help. I would make it compulsory for principals. (David Collins, 2005, interview)

Daniel Khan said, for leaders of the future:

What I would say about leadership, I think you have got to be positive. You must always be positive. You have difficult times, but try to be cheerful as well. The truth is we have just as much challenges, just as much difficulty, but being sullen does not solve them! Someone said they have never seen someone smile and still take such a tough decision. Because people sometimes believe if you are friendly and outgoing, then you can't take tough decisions, and that has been a surprise. Mix with your staff, mix with your students. When I joined in FE, I was told by someone, 'Keep your distance', as a senior manager. You don't have to; people will judge you by what you are.

If you are a good leader, a fair leader, always make decisions on facts, not on any prejudice. I have no baggage: everything is here on its merit. I try to press that throughout the organisation. One of the worst things the organisation could do is let people think there are favourites, the leadership is fanciful, things get back with no firm basis. You have got to explain your decisions. I always explain, to anyone who wants to ask, my decision. I have said to staff here, 'Don't be afraid to take chances, because if you try to do ten things and nine fail, and you succeed with one, that is probably the big break for you or your department'. I think generally in England, there is this fear of failure. It is a whole culture. All failure is a learning experience, just a further stepping stone to success. So I say to my staff, 'Try new things. Try new initiatives. If they do not work, we never hold it against you'. (Daniel Khan, 2005, interview)

Wendy Moss said, for leaders of the future:

> You will have to play a series of games at every point in your career. So you rewrap what you think is right, around whatever the current policy is. That's the bit of the game in being a leader. Just do what they say and get it out the way as fast as possible, so you can do your real job. Because in the end, the hassle of blocking is not worth it. If they ask for this, just churn it out. They just want numbers, just give it to them. You can waste a lot of energy complaining because you've got to do things, when it would take you much less time if you understood that actually there's a whole chain behind that request for something. Play the game for the small stuff and save your fights for the big stuff, that's what I'm saying. Nothing is life and death. It takes you a long time to realise that. Well, when they tell you the budget's going to fall apart next week unless you do something, actually, often it doesn't! There's a lot of drama goes on. Don't take responsibility for things that aren't your responsibility.   (Wendy Moss, 2005, interview)

Responding in more detail, David Collins recommended that these qualities be developed by leaders of the future:

> For leaders to ensure achievement and success, they need:

1. To be even more aware of the changing environment within which they work and to be able to change direction rapidly when the need arises. Certainly there is no sign of the pace of change decreasing. I don't know whether we'll hit a sort of optimum or that will change in the future, but certainly a leader has to be very aware of what's happening, the speed of what's happening and be able to adapt to it.

2. Given that awareness, to be able to create and maintain a flexible learning organisation based on *flowing structures and highly adaptable individuals*. The pace of change doesn't tend to go in staccato type leaps. Similarly, with structures – for example, in colleges, you frequently find colleges that do major restructures. Whereas, if it can be achieved, a more suitable model for today's world is a kind of flowing structure that evolves rather than creates a revolution every two or three years.

3. To be constantly seeking out best practice and ways to improve.

4. To be aware of the ways in which information technology can and will influence the education progress, and to stay at least one step ahead of the game.

5. To adopt a more business-like approach to educational management.

(David Collins, 2005, interview)

Talmud Bah said, for leaders of the future:

> In the future, the most important things for leaders in post-compulsory education will be to *know themselves* professionally and emotionally. Be aware of the climate, the climate you are going into, the structures which are in place so you don't feel

shell-shocked. Have a purpose. But the way you achieve that purpose needs to be flexible. Keep the needs of the learner at the heart of what you do. If the needs of the learners are at the heart of education in general, we would have a very different educational system. The key thing is to be aware. It's personal development. Know what your needs are, as a professional and as a person, and make a distinction. The problem is, when people have positions of authority and decision-making power, it's not led via the needs of the learners. It's led by ego. It becomes skewed. So, if you are in that role, you need to make a distinction. Separate yourself from your role. Look at training in interpersonal skills, how you communicate, the language you use, your body language. You need to be able to talk to people.

(Talmud Bah, 2005, interview)

I asked Bob Challis what was important for future leaders to do to achieve success:

> A man who dares to waste one hour of life has not discovered the value of life.
>
> Charles Darwin

Appoint good teachers and be intolerant of bad teaching. Ensure people in managerial posts or any kind of leadership post you fill are competent and are leading away consistently on what the college is trying to do. Focus on student success and find ways to ensure that that focus is apparent for all levels of the organisation. And follow through: so, focus and follow through. One of the big things is knowing what's important, knowing how to respond to some of the events outside, how to appraise and respond to a series of different stimuli from both government and the LSC. How to read the environment and make it a continuing cohesive narrative is really, really important. I think that's one of the biggest things new principals have trouble with. The worst thing is to find each new thing knocking the college off course, trying to steer towards the latest initiative. I think reading the environment is really hard. Maintaining a certain focus, finding ways to sustain the hope of the people in the organisation, that what they're doing is the right thing, and get them where they need to be. It's very fragile.

(Bob Challis, 2004, interview)

Ruth Silver said, about leadership challenges:

I think that the most challenging issue leaders have to face is loneliness, letting go of people when the time is right, taking up authority, not just power. Realising that leaders represent a concept-construct: they're not just a person with personal things. Leaders represent a construct about how the primary task is delivered or honoured. So training should, or development opportunities should, give a chance to experience that. I would train people in systems thinking.

(Ruth Silver, 2005, interview)

Creative Leadership Spaces – new model for leadership

Transforming Leadership Framework

The Transforming Leadership Spaces Inquiry builds on prior work written by the author with the *Creative Learning Network*, a pan-London network for widening participation in the arts for young people. This is based on an idea for youth arts learning spaces developed in partnership with Adrian Chappell, Director of the Arts Learning Partnership of London Metropolitan University, Phil Turner and Talmud Bah, as well as other colleagues from Second Wave Youth Arts in Deptford, London. A conference on *Creative Learning Spaces* was held at the University of Greenwich in 2005 to explore this and related work in an inquiry identifying a diagnostic model for creative learning spaces. These beneficially also demonstrate their usefulness for leadership situations according to the three themes outlined below in a new framework for transforming leadership.

Transforming Leadership Framework: head-hand-heart

Education and knowledge-driven spaces – intellectual leadership
'*Educational*' – *head*: knowledgeable educational leadership influences an excellent, shared understanding of the intellectual vision, awareness, strategic planning, decision making and academic standards necessary to enable high quality teaching and learning, and to facilitate successful learning leadership in a continuously improving educational environment. Institutional leadership is highly intelligent. Leaders are keenly and critically aware of national and local political and educational priorities. They recognise and meet their governance accountabilities. Institutional leadership is responsible, adept and flexible in responding to complex challenges, expertly using financial and sectoral data. Leaders effectively network to secure excellent positioning of the institution. They set challenging targets, measuring outcomes for progress against benchmarks. Leaders demonstrate outstandingly good judgement and decision making even in complex, ambiguous situations. Knowledge and skill are transferred effectively from senior leadership to make a beneficial impact on all parts of the organisation.

Enterprise/professional/entrepreneurial and physical leadership
'*Enterprise*' – *hand*: an excellent level of enterprising leadership fosters the right conditions for staff and students independently to develop beneficial skills, resources and professional expertise. Partnerships and entrepreneurial activities encourage creative resourcefulness in a healthy physical environment.

Distributed team leadership motivates people throughout the organisation in flexible ways to achieve high standards in making the most of professional, business and market opportunities. Activities involving funding bodies, external organisations, local industry and employers regenerate continuous growth within the institution. There is a sense of energy and purpose in the working environment. Resources, finances, estates management and facilities for learning and teaching are excellent.

Emotional and values-based leadership

'*Emotional*' – *heart*: emotionally intelligent leadership takes care of students and staff in a diverse, welcoming cultural environment. Leaders demonstrate a high degree of ethics, clear communication, mature understanding, optimism and sensitivity. Mutual respect is consistently shown to staff and students. A values-driven culture appropriately nurtures the positive development of personal confidence, teamwork and beneficial risk-taking. There is a creative, healthy working environment for staff and students. Institutional leadership encourages honesty, integrity, trust, inclusiveness, accountability and openness throughout the organisation. There is clear adherence to gender and racial equality, social and cultural diversity in the leadership. Leaders set high standards for personal behaviour, ethics and emotional maturity. A good atmosphere is immediately evident to visitors. It is clear to all that espoused values are continuously carried through and implemented in living leadership actions.

Mapping *transforming leadership spaces*

The Venn diagram with overlapping circles in Figure 7.1 illustrates the way in which leadership case study sites can be mapped according to an assessment of leadership capability. This is measured according to the tripartite 'head-hand-heart' model of qualities for leadership effectiveness using 'transformational leadership criteria' for staff and student intellectual, enterprise and emotional well-being.

In the model, each case study site is investigated using a range of methods. Learning leadership spaces case study sites are designated as appropriate, or not, for each theme, according to a notional 'pass mark' of acceptable performance in each area at 5, so that all marks in the range of 5–10 are deemed to have 'passed', with a ✓ symbol indicating this, ie 5–10 = ✓, whereas the ✗ symbol indicates unsatisfactory performance, ie 0–4 = ✗. The overall mark is allocated out of a total of 30, with the top range 27+ indicating very good to outstanding success levels, and the bottom range 15 and below indicating deficiencies in a number of qualities.

In this range of theoretical examples, the transforming leadership space at case study site 7 is the only one which 'passes' very well by all criteria. According to this model, the leadership space facilitated within case study site 7 immediately performs very well as a beneficial environment along all three indicators in the 'head-hand-heart' or 'educational-enterprise-emotional' model for measuring leadership spaces.

Diagnostic mediation process

This transforming leadership investigation also involves a mediated, collaboratively negotiated diagnostic process, whereby it is suggested that sites can beneficially develop along one or other of the three 'learning space' themes. For example, in the theoretical example shown in Figure 7.1, case study sites 1 and 2 can benefit from support and good practice examples in developing their sites across more than one theme simultaneously.

The 'hand-head-heart' model of leadership influence

Moving beyond the idea that any one person could ever be solely responsible for leadership in institutions, we consider the idea of classifying different kinds of leadership environments in the sector according to a tripartite 'hand-head-heart' model of leadership fields of influence. This maps out a range of attributes that can be identified. The model can be used to develop more positive spaces in our institutions, both in terms of relationships between people and in terms of learning and working environments. The mental, emotional and physical spaces within our institutions operate dynamically together in different 'leadership fields' that can be more positively or more negatively 'charged' with different kinds of energies and conditions affecting the atmospheres in which people function. If such leadership fields can be identified at different levels of 'fitness', to use analogics from both healthcare (relating to individuals) and environmental studies (relating to the 'small worlds' that are our institutions), so also 'illnesses' or 'weather conditions' can be diagnosed. From this concept of diagnosis, we can see that we can also identify ways in which to influence positively the organic 'wellness' of leadership fields.

The identification of different elements in the atmosphere of leadership spaces can improve 'wellness' factors within these fields of influence, and make for healthier and happier working environments for everyone in them. One of the benefits of this model is that it suggests not only that leadership is a phenomenon which goes beyond any one person, but also that different kinds of 'leaderships' are operating like continuously changing dynamic forces or weather systems functioning in multiple ways within the interactive spaces of

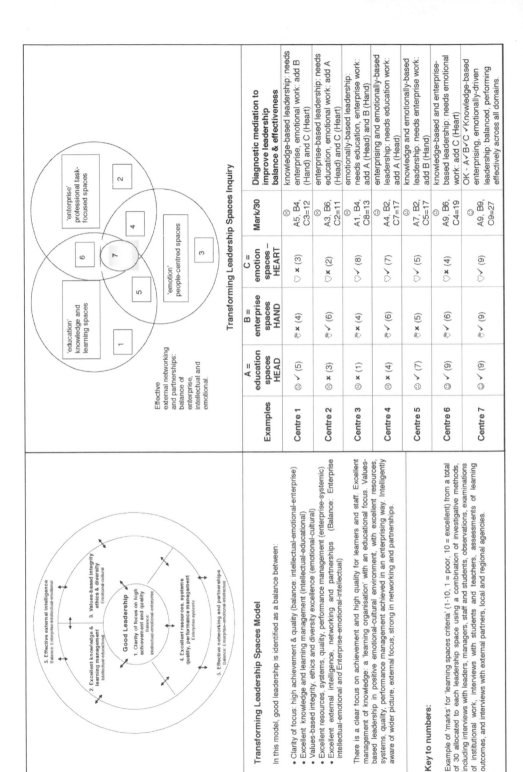

Transforming Leadership Spaces Model

In this model, good leadership is identified as a balance between:

- Clarity of focus: high achievement & quality (balance: intellectual-emotional-enterprise)
- Excellent knowledge and learning management (intellectual-educational)
- Values-based integrity, ethics and diversity excellence (emotional-cultural)
- Excellent resources, systems, quality, performance management (enterprise-systemic)
- Excellent external intelligence, networking and partnerships (Balance: Enterprise intellectual-emotional and Enterprise-emotional-intellectual)

There is a clear focus on achievement and high quality for learners and staff. Excellent management of knowledge: a 'learning organisation' with an educational focus. Values-based leadership in positive emotional-cultural environment, with excellent resources, systems, quality, performance management achieved in an enterprising way. Intelligently aware of wider picture, external focus, strong in networking and partnerships.

Key to numbers:

Example of 'marks' for 'learning spaces criteria' (1-10, 1 = poor, 10 = excellent) from a total of 30 allocated to each leadership space using a combination of investigative methods, including interviews with leaders, managers, staff and students, observations, examinations of institutional work, interviews with students and teachers, assessments of learning outcomes, and interviews with external partners, local and regional agencies.

Transforming Leadership Spaces Inquiry

Examples	A = education spaces – HEAD	B = enterprise spaces – HAND	C = emotion spaces – HEART	Mark/30	Diagnostic mediation to improve leadership balance & effectiveness
Centre 1	✓ (5)	✗ (4)	✗ (3)	A5, B4, C3=12	knowledge-based leadership: needs enterprise, emotional work: add B (Hand) and C (Heart)
Centre 2	✗ (3)	✓ (6)	✗ (2)	A3, B6, C2=11	enterprise-based leadership: needs education, emotional work: add A (Head) and C (Heart)
Centre 3	✗ (1)	✗ (4)	✓ (8)	A1, B4, C8=13	emotionally-based leadership: needs education, enterprise work: add A (Head) and B (Hand)
Centre 4	✗ (4)	✓ (6)	✓ (7)	A4, B2, C7=17	enterprising and emotionally-based leadership: needs education work: add A (Head)
Centre 5	✓ (7)	✗ (5)	✓ (5)	A7, B2, C5=17	knowledge and emotionally-based leadership: needs enterprise work: add B (Hand)
Centre 6	✓ (9)	✓ (6)	✗ (4)	A9, B6, C4=19	knowledge-based and enterprise-based leadership: needs emotional work: add C (Heart)
Centre 7	✓ (9)	✓ (9)	✓ (9)	A9, B9, C9=27	OK - A✓B✓C✓Knowledge-based enterprising, emotionally-driven leadership: balanced, performing effectively across all domains.

Transforming Leadership Spaces: Criteria for measuring effectiveness

'Head' – educational/intellectual leadership

- Effective, knowledgeable educational leadership prioritises learner achievement and maintains a clear organisational focus. Good leadership influences excellent, shared understanding of the intellectual vision, awareness, strategic planning, decision-making and academic standards necessary to enable high quality teaching and learning and to facilitate successful learning leadership in a continuously improving educational environment.

- Institutional leadership is intelligent, critically and keenly aware of national and local political and educational priorities. Leaders recognise governance accountabilities and are responsible, adept and flexible in responding to complex challenges, expertly using financial and sectoral data.

- Leaders effectively network to secure excellent positioning of the institution, setting challenging targets, demonstrating outstandingly good judgement and decision-making in complex situations.

'Hand': Enterprise professional/ entrepreneurial and physical leadership:

- An excellent level of enterprising leadership fosters the right conditions for staff and students independently to develop skills, resources, professional expertise, partnerships and entrepreneurial activities encouraging creative resourcefulness in a healthy physical environment.

- Distributed team leadership motivates people throughout the organisation in flexible ways to make the most of business and market opportunities.

- Activities involving local industry and employers generate continuous growth.

'Heart' - Emotional & values-based leadership:

- Emotionally intelligent leadership demonstrates a high degree of ethics, clear communication, mature understanding, optimism, and sensitivity. Mutual respect is shown to staff and students, and high standards for behaviour and emotional maturity are practised and expected across the institution.

- A values-driven culture appropriately supports positive development of personal confidence, positive teamwork and beneficial experimentation with risk-taking in a creative environment for staff and students. Institutional leadership encourages good levels of integrity, trust, inclusiveness and openness throughout the organisation.

- Leadership throughout the organisation proactively welcomes and supports cultural diversity, racial equality, gender equity and inclusion. Leadership is active in implementing equal opportunities and social justice.

Mapping collaborative leadership spaces

The venn diagram with overlapping circles in the figure above illustrates the way case study sites are mapped according to assessment in a leadership investigation for effectiveness by 'transforming leadership spaces criteria': organisational learning, enterprise and values-based emotional well-being. Each centre is investigated using a range of methods. Leadership sites are designated as effective, or not, according to a notional 'pass mark' of 5-10 =✓, 0-4 = ✗. In this example, the learning space at case study centre 7 is the only one which 'passes' by all criteria, immediately achieving an excellent balance of leadership effectiveness across all three domains. The Transforming Leadership Spaces Inquiry Framework builds on prior work done with The Creative Learning Network (see Ch 7). Effective transformational leadership spaces have a balance across the three domains of:

1) **Academic, learning, vocational, intellectual leadership: Head: 'educational' qualities:** effective educational leadership spaces which simultaneously liberate conventional teaching and learning dynamics and facilitate learning leadership with improved educational attainment.

2) **Enterprising, professional/ business, resources leadership: Hand: 'enterprise' qualities:** a useful level of 'enterprise' factors with the right conditions for staff and students to independently develop the necessary skills, expertise and enterprise to foster creative resourcefulness and focused proactivity;

3) **Values-based, emotionally intelligent, inclusive leadership: Heart - 'emotional' qualities:** a high degree of 'emotional' appropriacy in terms of positive characteristics for the development of personal confidence, positive teamwork and beneficial experimentation with risk-taking in a diverse, inclusive creative environment for staff and students;

The identification of these spaces are linked to more detailed criteria.

Diagnostic mediation process

The leadership investigation includes a mediated, collaboratively-negotiated diagnostic process, in which it is suggested that leadership can beneficially develop along one or other of the three 'leadership space' domains, in relation to the five principles outlined in the Transforming Leadership Spaces Model. In the theoretical examples in the tables from the leadership investigation above, case study sites 1-3 benefit from support and good practice examples to develop their sites across more than one domain simultaneously.

References

In the preparation of the above framework and models, the following work was consulted for good governance and leadership standards in public service:

Independent Commission on Good Governance in Public Services (2005) The Good Governance Standard for Public Services, publication by OPM and CIPFA, York: Joseph Rowntree Foundation.

Figure 7.1 Transforming Leadership Spaces Framework mapping 'emotional', 'enterprise' and 'educational' leadership spaces

relationships that occur all the time between people and their environments. To achieve an excellent balance between the attributes of 'educational', 'enterprise' and 'emotional' leadership is the aim.

Hence, one benefit of this kind of model is the idea that leadership fields of influence within the small worlds that are our institutions can *to an extent* be identified, diagnosed and therefore controlled. We can, in other words, 'take the temperature' of the leadership environmental influences operating in our institutions, in order to affect these for the better, and arrive at a healthy balance of good leadership qualities in institutions overall.

Summary

This chapter reflects on leadership for the future, drawing together some of the theories from Chapters 1–6 and considering these by examining CEL's *Leadership Qualities Framework*, with reference in particular to comments made by the interviewees. The four key characteristics of the *Framework* are examined in some detail. The chapter then moves on to consider lessons for future leaders, in preparation for the case study interviewee selections to be presented in Part Two. A new model for sectoral leadership is then suggested which builds on earlier work, and a *Transforming Leadership Framework* is put forward for the investigation of leadership spaces according to three main indicators. An explanation of the way in which this *Framework* could be used is provided, to reflect on the future possibility of developing more creative leadership spaces. The chapter then rounds off in preparation for Part Two.

PART 2

Models of
Post-compulsory Education
Leadership:
Current Leaders

Servant leadership: rounding up leadership roles

> ❝I just *love* the learning and skills sector or FE. I just love serving students. I love it. I never get tired of it and I have done it for 23 years. It's very much about that love, that passion, that commitment.❞
> Lynne Sedgmore

Rounding up leadership roles in PCE institutions – introduction

To provide an effective initial round-up of leadership roles in post-compulsory education, it is helpful to consider different 'layers' of positional leadership and management routinely found in the PCE sector. These include leadership roles in education and training relating to the areas below:

- international trends, policies, research, lifelong learning partnerships
- national education policy, government legislation, regulations, inspection
- regional and local policy and partnerships
- governance, senior and middle management of institutions
- business and community liaison
- department and classroom management, peer-group student management
- mentoring and coaching.

The extent to which leaders at different levels in PCE institutions are empowered to take up leadership roles in relation to the areas above will be determined in accordance with the situation, locality, culture, executive leadership and management ethos, resources, personnel, history, client groups, stakeholder links and investments, and a variety of other innumerable specific factors relating to people and circumstances within PCE institutions. Actual positional roles of individual members of staff (see Figure 8.1) interact more or less fluently with the sectoral and institutional requirements of the time.

The overall situation in PCE is extremely complex, individually variegated by circumstance. Generalities regarding institutions and roles are therefore somewhat limited. Each circumstance has a myriad of specific influencing factors operating in every situation. However, it is useful to consider briefly the following possible outline for leadership, management and administration in educational institutions, adapted for the PCE sector from an earlier model by Law and Glover (2000, p.16):

This table was originally drawn up mainly with school leadership in mind. I have adapted it to reflect the demands of PCE leadership. We can observe that,

---

Post-compulsory positional institutional roles can include the following:

Governance
Chairs of Governors, Clerks of Governing Bodies, Principals/Chief Executives, Senior Leadership Teams (SLT) or Senior Management Teams (SMT), Business and Parent Governors and Co-opted Governors.

Executive, senior leadership/senior management
Vice-Principals, Assistant Principals, Directors of Curriculum, Finance, Administration, Marketing, Human Resources/Personnel, Student Services, Registrars; other senior managerial posts.

Middle management
Assistant Directors (sometimes senior managers of a campus)
Heads of Schools or Departments and Heads of Administrative Departments.

Curriculum, Programme, Administrative and other 'first-line' management
Programme and Course Leaders, Administrative and other supervisory first-line managers, MIS/ICT leaders, Senior Technical staff, Personnel, Business and Community leaders, Chaplains, Counsellors, Guidance and Advisory staff, Staff Association/Union representative leaders, Nursery/Creche workers, Caretakers/Schoolkeeping and Estates staff.

Classroom and tutorial management
Lecturers and teachers, course tutors and personal tutors.

Technical staffing
Technicians, classroom technical assistants and other support staff at operational level.

Assistant Classroom management
Learning facilitators, learning support assistants, classroom assistants.

Student leadership
Student Association leaders, student course representatives.

All of these different 'layers' of leadership and management may have a part to play in PCET institutions.

Figure 8.1 Positional roles in PCET institutions which may have features of leadership

Table 8.1 Leadership, management and administration in educational organisations: a possible outline

	Principal/headteacher	**Subject leader/ co-ordinator**	**Class teacher/ course leader**
Focus	Whole school/college	Subject department	Curriculum delivery
Through	Institutional development plan	Departmental development plan	Schemes of work
Leadership	Vision Aims and objectives Strategy Team formation Organisational policies	Departmental aims Targets Resource bidding Team cohesion Subject policies	Classroom tone Subject mission Teaching and learning style
Management	Overall control of resource base Overall development of staff	Resource allocation Subject staff development Curriculum organisation Monitoring and evaluation Student progress	Materials development Resource use Curriculum tracking Student assessment
Administration	Responsible, but not active	Staff records Resource tracking Lists, lists, lists!	Student records Teaching and learning records

although it focuses on an academic model of an educational institution, it nevertheless usefully suggests a differentiation of tasks between different roles (at principal, subject leader and class leader levels) and also a split of tasks between leadership, management and administration.

The case study interviews

Having described briefly these potential roles for leaders in PCE, we can observe there is an important sectoral job to be done in developing staff in institutions across the PCE sector for future leadership roles. To situate this within specific circumstances, we now turn, in Part Two, to the ten case studies of leadership.

We consider, first, an interview with Lynne Sedgmore, as 'leader of leaders' in the learning and skills sector. Lynne has a national role across the sector for the development of leadership. She has a particular interest in the model of *servant leadership*. This concept of providing 'service' to others is based on a values-driven leadership particularly suitable to Lynne's background, interests and experience.

Servant leadership

The servant leadership model has been researched in a number of contexts. One of its most significant components is the ideal of '*stewardship*'. In education, the concept of '*stewardship*' translates into working in ethical service to address the needs of learners and staff. Servant leadership has been in development for some 40 years internationally in a number of organisations, including Harvard University Business School. Writers such as Robert Greenleaf (1904–1990), a retired leader from AT&T (the global networking giant, the American Telephone and Telegraphic Company) to whom is originally ascribed the term 'servant-leader' (see Greenleaf, 1970, 1977) and Peter Block (1993), have written about the concept of servant leadership, emphasising the role of the leader as a 'steward' of the resources of an organisation.

> A turning point in my career was learning to be *authentic and vulnerable*, while being *competent and adding value*, being really honest, clear and having a vision I shared with staff, and really knowing what I was doing. It wasn't easy – it was hard. It's being very authentic. My experience is that if you do that very honestly, it's amazing. It's almost like *people want the leader not to be perfect*.
>
> *Lynne Sedgmore, CBE*

In the servant leadership model, leaders avoid the hierarchical top-down autocratic style typical of over-controlling insecure managers, seeing themselves as serving others, while focusing strongly on the achievement of results to fulfil the values and mission of the organisation. Servant leadership aims to be collaborative, trusting of and empathetic towards 'followers', setting up teamworking structures and using power in an ethical way. A number of key personal characteristics are noted in prior literature as appropriate for servant leadership. Larry Spears, Chief Executive of the Greenleaf Center (*sic*) for Servant-Leadership, observes that he 'particularly like[s] Warren Bennis's short list as contained in his book, *On Becoming a Leader*, in which he identifies, "vision, inspiration, empathy and trustworthiness" as key characteristics of effective leaders. (p.140)' (Spears, 2005). Spears' (1998) work previously identified ten key characteristics of servant leadership as:

- listening
- empathy
- healing
- awareness
- persuasion
- conceptualisation
- foresight

- stewardship
- commitment
- community building.

To add to this, we note that Matteson and Irving (2005) distinguish 'servant' from 'self-sacrificial' leadership, identifying that

> Patterson's [2003] model of servant leadership includes the following dimensions as the essential characteristics of servant leadership: (a) agapáo love [ie divine love], (b) humility, (c) altruism, (d) vision, (e) trust, (f) empowerment, and (g) service.
>
> (Matteson and Irving, 2005)

Robert Greenleaf described servant leadership as follows:

> The servant-leader is servant first. It begins with the natural feeling that one wants to serve. Then conscious choice brings one to aspire to lead. The best test is: do those served grow as persons: do they, while being served, become healthier, wiser, freer, more autonomous, more likely themselves to become servants?
>
> (Greenleaf, 1970, cited by Spears, 2005, p.1)

The characteristics of servant leadership are described by Spears as:

1. listening
2. empathy
3. healing
4. awareness
5. persuasion
6. conceptualisation
7. foresight
8. stewardship
9. commitment to the growth of people
10. building community.

(Spears, 2005, pp.2–3)

Lynne outlines below her own concept of leadership in the post-compulsory education sector, and the way in which the servant leadership model can be included in that vision.

Case Study of National Leadership

Lynne Sedgmore, CBE, Chief Executive of the Centre for Excellence in Leadership

Deep blue water and 'the values lady'

I went to see Lynne Sedgmore at The Centre for Excellence and Leadership (CEL) in Liberty House, central London, meeting her twice in 2005 to discuss this book. I asked her about the role of the new leadership centre, and for her own views on leadership. CEL has only recently been set up. It is therefore still early days in the analysis of its contributions, but Lynne was happy to expand on envisaged developments for the Centre as well as some of the work already done. While she talked to me, Lynne was being 'work-shadowed' by a trainee future senior leader. Lynne revealed that she always loves having someone with whom to share her work. This ready support for others is demonstrably a familiar trait. An edited version of Lynne's replies to the questions I asked now follows.

How would you categorise the institution and client group of which you are a leader?

> The Centre for Excellence in Leadership has a specific role as a national agency funded by the Department for Education and Skills in the *Success for All* strategy. The Centre supports, develops and improves leaders and provider organisations in the LSC sector. It's a partnership national distributed organisation with three primary partners: Ashridge Business School, Lancaster University Management School and the Learning and Skills Development Agency (LSDA). CEL's mission is to improve the standard of leadership and the diversity and talent-pool of leaders in the learning and skills sector.

What, in your experience, is the distinction, if any, between leadership and management in post-compulsory education?

Lynne feels there are generic attributes, qualities and skills for both leadership and management, as well as specific contextual ones for PCE. She observed:

> Generically, leadership and management is a *spectrum* or continuum, with a leader more able, skilled, 'natural', even, perhaps, at visioning, engaging the commitment of others, co-creating and bringing about empowering environments. Fundamentally, a leader thinks, acts and impacts more in the 'meaning and purpose' realms. They win hearts and minds, generate followers, are highly relational, live 'distributed leadership', live 'learning'. They are in a constant inquiry, believe in leadership at all levels, and ensure the community, whatever it is, or that group that they work with, is doing the right things.

By contrast, managers need to be more focused on 'doing things right', such as systems, monitoring, operational realities and control of the environment. Effectively, leaders and managers need to carry out both roles, but not all are capable of this. The overlap comes in terms of strategy, though for managers this is 'more of a head thing', whereas 'leaders live, generate and live strategy'. Lynne went on to say:

> You have to have managerial operational excellence, strategic excellence, relational excellence, learning excellence, personal mastery, learning as a way of being. That's your outstanding leader, who's able to go across all of those. They might be a very ordinary leader, but at the same time they're skilled across that function. The essence of *educational* leadership and management requires a focus on *student outcomes and student learning*. It's about bringing generic leadership into the specific context of bringing everything to bear on the *success of students*. Then it's harnessing all the resources and people capacity of the organisation to put students at the heart of everything and ensure their success.

> You have to have managerial operational excellence, relational excellence, learning excellence, personal mastery, learning as a way of being. That's your outstanding leader, who's able to go across all of those.
>
> Lynne Sedgmore, CBE

> My model could sound like it's the heroic model, that what you need is a super-duper person who can actually function across all modes. That person does actually need to have some quite 'interesting', advanced qualities, but that can also be done in quite a quiet, ordinary way. Some of the most 'present and aware', enlightened beings you meet, they can also feel like they're the most ordinary, grounded, centred people. They're not big egos. They don't have huge charisma, necessarily, but what they have is a 'presence' or sense of being able to 'be aware'. Self-awareness and your awareness of your impact on others is a major element of leadership.

> But that can be quiet and very facilitative. I like the latest book, *Living Leadership* (Binney *et al.*, 2005), about ordinary heroes. It is a paradox. Really advanced, outstanding people don't need to tell everybody. They can do it in such a way that they're also very ordinary, very approachable, very accessible. It's that lovely paradox. They are quite outstanding, but also very ordinary, very real. So it's that mix. It's Jim Collins level 5, the new *living leadership* – parts of leadership are very mundane – you have to have the humility and the *service* to do whatever it takes.

Lynne responded to a query about the Lao Tse quotation, 'As for the best leaders, they are unnoticed by the people' by saying:

> There are people who happen to have big personalities as well, but it's where their ego sits, and who and what they're serving. If you're serving your ego, it doesn't matter if you're a quiet personality or a loud one. It's not the same as the servant leader, whatever shape or form their personality is, who is actually serving who they are there for. In our case, at the end of the day, it's about serving our students. I believe very strongly in the 'servant leadership' notion. My first aim is just to serve

student needs and their potential to achieve success in whatever shape or form that takes.

That is the *servant leadership model* – I'm not serving my own self-interest. I constantly guard that. I'm aware when that's coming in. I think people *know*. That's the essence. People want authenticity and to trust. They want people to help, facilitate and free up organisations. And to have a steer as well – to be visionary, to have creativity. It's a balance between setting direction in a consultative, co-creation way, being clear. People know when people are self-interested. It's what you're serving fundamentally, in your heart and your soul and your value system. People know that.

I've done a lot of work around 'values clarification'. *Integrity's* very important. Not just in terms of honesty and transparency: I also mean it in terms of 'integral' – seeing things holistically, systemically. It's about having a high level of self-awareness, congruence: that you actually 'walk your talk'. *Honesty* is very important. But it's more than that, it's in the Jungian sense 'being integral', coming to wholeness and being a healthy person. *Service* is very important – service to the highest good of the students and the staff, not serving self-interest. That notion of *stewardship* is very integral to servant leadership. Stewardship, guardianship: as a formal leader within hierarchies, you have a stronger responsibility around what stewardship is, to be very clear about that, able to articulate it. *Simplicity*. People make life far too complicated. Professionals love mystifying and making themselves feel important through it. It's something about simplicity, linked to humility. It is about trying to make things simple and straightforward, cutting to the chase, see it and move it as it is.

> Learning leaders will have the self-confidence and self esteem to risk and enjoy learning with all the joy, pain and challenge that growth brings. They will be leaders who will create living, authentic learning organisations and learners.
>
> *Lynne Sedgmore, CBE*

So integrity, service, simplicity and actually *love*. It's about tough love, not a sweetie sloppy thing. Having genuine regard and respect for others, but being prepared to challenge when necessary. It's about criticising or challenging behaviours, but always respect the person, and having real passion and love for what I do. I just *love* the learning and skills sector or FE. I just love serving students. I love it. I never get tired of it and I have done it for 23 years. It's very much about that love, that passion, that commitment.

Being a learner, being a constant enquirer just curious about everything all the time, being prepared to learn and grow is core to who I am. A learner, an enquirer, a constant curiosity that I just have. I love Peter Vaill's work, *Learning as a Way of Being*, and *Managing as a Performing Art*. All his work is about being a learner, being a beginner all the time and seeing the world fresh. That links very much in terms of spiritual traditions that are all about learning to be in the moment and everything being new and fresh and seeing it as it is and not bringing all your preconceptions and your messiness to it.

I have always been fascinated with self-awareness and growth. I did an MSC in 1990 in 'Change Agent Skills and Strategies', at the University of Surrey. I loved the work of Professor William R. Torbert, studied his work in depth, and how that related to whole organisational processes: the group, team, the systemic approach. Loved Senge's work around The *Learning Organisation*.

Responding to a query about distributed leadership, Lynne said:

Distributed leadership isn't just desirable and essential – it's a fact of life. I've just been reading *Deep Blue Water: Re-discovering The Source of Leadership*, in which there is the concept 'deep blue water'. It's a fascinating book looking at the source of where ideas of leadership come from and that notion that leadership isn't just the waves at the top, it's the whole deep blue sea. The waves are important too. So you need these leaders who step up and you need leaders in structured forms, but actually leadership is the deep blue sea: it's everywhere. But you need to create systems and environments that enable people to see that.

It's an essential, living reality that leadership is at all levels. Different shapes and forms of leadership, different functions, focus and responsibilities at different levels. The 21st century is about organisations that enable that through systems and processes and move us away from a hierarchical, patriarchal old-fashioned 19th century institutional shape and form of leadership.

'Students at the heart of everything'

I used to be known as '*the values lady*' in one college. Oh leave it to Lynne, she'll do 'the values'. In one college, we did a huge values clarification. Student achievements rose by 27% in four years. Fundamentally our vision statements narrowed down to '*students at the heart of everything we do*'. That became our by-line. By every measurement, staff satisfaction improved – we had an amazing perception survey in 2003 from stakeholders. We were living out that vision of *students at the heart of everything we do*, because that's what we were there for.

Things that helped me to achieve success have been *committed, aligned, high quality creative staff*. It's always, always worked when management and staff come together for the students. You forgive each other for an awful lot, work through a lot of tough things. If you have those staff, everything just flows. A *highly effective senior team* is also key. When you have really highly effective teams around you, it's just wonderful and makes all the difference. I've got the courage to build around me people who are better than me, people who kind of compensate for my weakness. I love to see people around me because I like to have people I'm learning from as well as hopefully their learning from me.

Reflective time is important. Making sure I think about what I'm doing in terms of reflective models of the effectiveness of my practice. *Having a coach*. Which is part of that: somewhere to go and talk it through. To ensure you have specific 'time out' for retreats and formal study, studying leadership, is important. So is a *reflective tool*. I've used the Enneagram, a particular approach I have been studying for 15 years. At one college, 50 staff engaged in it. It was quite remarkable what we saw happen: teams that were really struggling transformed. Communication is always an issue in organisations. It's about finding mechanisms to improve communication.

Lynne went on to explain that people wanted a leader to be *authentic*, not *perfect*:

> A turning point in my career was learning to be *authentic and vulnerable*, while being *competent and adding value*. That was a really big lesson. I learnt that by being really honest, being clear and having a vision I shared with staff, and really knowing what I was doing. It wasn't easy – it was hard. It's being very authentic. My experience is that if you do that very honestly, it's amazing. It's almost like *people want the leader not to be perfect*.
>
> You can't set that up, actually, you can't kind of go, 'I'll make a couple of mistakes and I'll go and apologise, then they'll all trust me or whatever'. These situations are very real. It's a form of – not weakness, but *vulnerability* and it's different. It took me a while to understand what that difference is.

When I asked what metaphors for her leadership style she'd use, Lynne said:

> The first metaphor of leadership that grabbed me was Peter Vaill's *Managing as a Performing Art*. I think of leadership as an art form. Leadership *is* my creative contribution in the world. I get really turned on and inspired by co-creating healthy organisations. That's my creative path. It's people's potentials. The core passion, for me, is 'how are you assisting?' They do it for themselves, but how do I liberate or enable someone to really get in touch with their potential, who they are? That to me is what leadership is about, at its best. It's a performing art or a creative art, as articulated by Max De Pree in *Leadership is an Art*.

> Leadership is my creative contribution in the world. I get really turned on and inspired by co-creating healthy organisations. That's my creative path: it's people's potentials.
>
> *Lynne Sedgmore*

> Leadership development is a long-term process. What CEL is trying to say to middle managers is, 'This is a journey you embark on. You never fully arrive, but really engage with a curiosity about what leadership means for you, about how you live that out as organisational practice as well as your own development'. Leaders need to be more effective in systemic approaches. The approach of *the learning organisation* is a good one for our sector, because learning is what we exist for. There are some quite interesting approaches within that we ought to get more savvy about.

Summary

A round-up of leadership and management roles in PCE, followed by a discussion of the principles of 'servant leadership', introduces the interview with Lynne Sedgmore, CEO of the CEL. Lynne sums up CEL's role as the leadership college for the LSC sector, discusses the 'servant leadership' model, her experience with values clarification, and stewardship of learning. She places students at the heart of everything, and asserts the values of authenticity, vulnerability, trust, honesty and integrity in leadership, placing a high priority also on reflective time, the use of reflective tools and informed theoretical models. She views leadership as a performing art and feels that Senge's idea of the 'learning organisation' is particularly appropriate for educational leaders.

Keywords

Leadership College, London-based national staff development and training role, servant leadership approach, learner-centred, economic efficiency.

Further reading and resources

Binney, G., Wilke, G. and Williams, C. (2005) *Living Leadership: A Practical Guide for Ordinary Heroes*. Harlow: Pearson Education.

CEL (Centre for Excellence in Leadership) (2004b) *Leading the Way 2004–06: Leadership for the Learning and Skills Sector*. London: CEL Standards Unit.

De Pree, M. (1989) *Leadership is an Art*. New York: Doubleday.

Greenleaf, R.K. (1977) *Servant Leadership: A Journey into the Nature of Legitimate Power and Greatness*. New York: Paulist.

Sedgmore, L. (2002) 'Learning excellence: towards a learning skilled age.' *People and Organisations*, 9, 3, pp.1–12.

Sedgmore, L. (2003) 'Transformational Leadership', in *Human Resources*.

Senge, P.M. (1990) *The Fifth Discipline: The Art and Practice of the Learning Organisation*. London: Random House Business Books.

Torbert, W.R. (1991) *Power of Balance: Transforming Self, Society and Scientific Inquiry*. London: Sage Publications.

Vaill, P.B. (1989) *Managing as a Performing Art: New Ideas for a World of Chaotic Change*. San Francisco, CA: Jossey-Bass.

Vaill, P.B. (1996) *Learning as a Way of Being*. San Francisco, CA: Jossey-Bass.

Guardians of knowledge: change agents

6 6Learning should be a voyage on a sea of ignorance to find islands of truth . . . you get a sort of *crystallisation. Suddenly it makes sense*. Those moments are quite special in learning.9 9
John Guy

Guardians of knowledge and change agents in leadership

The concept of 'guardianship' is a caring parental model, and one that is not afraid to be authoritative. It is conceptualised here as a variant of transformational educational leadership (Northouse, 2004, pp.169–99) particularly suitable for the 16–19 college age group. This model of leadership speaks with the authority of knowledge and experience about growing the next generation wisely, stewarding the future and shaping the character of young people by supporting them with a value system that is clear, firm, inspirational, skilled and safe.

The term 'change agent', by contrast, arises from language used in business organisational development, when we seek to make organisations fitter, leaner and more competitive. The convergence of these two leadership characteristics – guardianship of knowledge and change agency – seemed particularly appropriate in the context of the case study I now present of The Sixth Form College in Farnborough. In the College, the role of 'emotionally intelligent, authoritative but not authoritarian leadership' by the Principal, Dr John Guy, has been formative for some years in shaping the College to achieve high standards in an atmosphere of security for students. Yet at the same time, students are challenged with new tasks that take them 'beyond their comfort zones', to help them become fitter to go out into the world and to deal confidently with their new roles as young adults.

To act as a guardian effectively, a leader needs to make time for personal reflection and self-awareness. The role of emotional intelligence played by leaders is particularly important when handling students who are facing the multiple sensitivities of adolescence at sixth form level. The original meaning of the word 'mentor', in fact, comes from the guardian of Odysseus' young son, Telemachus, named Mentor, who shepherded his young subject well, with trust and care, over a long period of time (Blunt, 2001). Leaders who are guardians, who act 'in loco parentis' (in the place of parents), as in 16–19 education, have roles as teachers, guides, mentors, and exemplars. The 'guardian of knowledge and change agent' model therefore includes simultaneously a 'wise parenting' role, providing the scaffolding, care and support for safe, sustainable growth, and a catalytic, stimulating role that seeks to stretch the young person to achieve challenging new targets for self-development.

To carry out 'guardian of knowledge' and 'change agent' leadership roles effectively, Farnborough sets very high standards for both its staff and students. In my interview with him, Dr. Guy stated that he was unrelentingly self-driven, that he could countenance no excuses for providing an environment that was merely 'good enough'. He said, 'good enough is not good enough', emphasising the unending responsibility of the leader to provide 'distinguished provision' of the highest possible standards, in a situation in which young people crucially depend on the college during their short stay. The relatively rapid turnover of the client group in 16–19 provision means that every year there is a fresh cohort of young people coming into the college. Therefore, there is a continual need for the ethos and values of the college to be quickly and clearly explained and developed for every new group of students. A very clear mission and purpose is necessary for this.

The Sixth Form College in Farnborough provides an inspiring example of what it is possible to achieve in 16–19 provision. Dr John Guy, awarded an OBE for his services to education, has been the Principal of the College since 1992. Between 1992 and 2005, the College has achieved many outstanding successes for young people. John was recently described by Dr Kim Howells, Minister of State for Lifelong Learning, Further and Higher Education, as 'one of our most inspirational principals in the country – we need more like him to lead these important educational communities'.

In March, 2005, I took the short journey from London to Farnborough to have a chat with John about leadership in post-compulsory education, specifically for this book. I met John for a couple of hours, talking to him about his views on leadership, management and the features of these that were most important to the college. I was struck by the fact that the value-added system of internal quality management the college uses appears to be even more rigorous than Ofsted's. The inspectorate said they had not seen this kind of rigorous value-added system in operation in this way ever in any institution previously. An edited version of John's replies to the questions I asked is outlined below.

Case Study of Sixth Form Leadership

Dr John Guy, OBE, Principal of The Sixth Form College in Farnborough

Crystallisation, leadership and learning in Farnborough

How would you categorise the institution and client group of which you are a leader?

The College has around 2500 students from Hampshire, Surrey and Berkshire. Surrey and Berkshire schools are essentially 11–18, whereas in Hampshire they're essentially 11–16. Half the College's students come from Surrey and Berkshire. It is interesting, therefore, that students are opting to come to a post-16 centre. John speculated that this was probably because of the way the College helps them to achieve. The College strictly maintains that it is a College for 16–19 year olds, and that youngsters focus mainly on level 3 programmes. It would have been easy to let the mission drift into adult education, so one of the strengths of the College is the clarity of purpose it has managed to maintain. This is in spite of superficially attractive opportunities to bid for additional funds – the College management strictly examines all such potentials in the light of the College's mission and purpose.

The College management feels it has obtained 'the confidence of students, parents, local community leaders and local commerce and industry'. They have been 'delighted' to be awarded 'Beacon' college status. As Principal, John expressed an unrelenting desire to achieve the best possible results for all students, always, and to provide the highest standards of provision. Interestingly, he felt this aim was:

> . . . not about being 'best'. It's about a sort of feeling of irritation and, you know, curiosity, really, if somebody's doing it better. Well, 'What are they doing that we aren't doing?' That's what we say to parents and students: that business in the mission statement about 'the highest quality academic and vocational education', well, that is about 'doing as well as anybody is'. And if somebody else is doing it better than us, we want to know what they're doing, because, actually, well, we should be doing that.

This 'curiosity' and 'irritation' is mingled with a great sense of responsibility and guardianship of students. The fact that students in the 16–19 year old group are only at the college once means that there is a significant need to provide continual focus, discipline and clarity of purpose. This clarity of purpose has grown in recent years. Originally, the College had eight objectives. However, because they couldn't remember them all easily, John and his senior

> Our single corporate objective is 'improving students' achievements'. Not only do I memorise it, but it's embedded in the memory of all staff in the College. Clarity of purpose is the focus for discipline.
>
> *Dr John Guy*

leadership team decided some years ago to reduce these to one. He noted that now:

. . . Our single corporate objective is 'improving students' achievements'. Now, not only do I memorise it, but it's embedded in the memory of all staff in the College. So clarity of purpose is the focus for the discipline.

What, in your experience, is the distinction, if any, between leadership and management in post-compulsory education?

Differentiating between leadership and management, John observed that leadership was 'the vision thing', knowing what you want to do, where you want to go, and clearly articulating it. He expressed that his own style of leadership was that of 'authoritative leadership', *not* 'authoritarian' or 'autocratic'. He conceptualised this as 'vision based upon knowledge of the reality and the need'.

Hence, John quoted the familiar phrase that, if leadership is the vision thing, '*doing the right things*', then management is the way you do them: '*doing things right*' (see the distinction between leadership and management put forward by Bennis and Nanus, 1985, p.221). The single corporate objective that the College now has is encouraging greater focus on the potential for leadership to carry out change in a transformational way. John felt that 'the difference is that leadership is able to *transform* and the management thing is about *transaction*'.

Since students in the 16–19 phase are only there once, the College strongly believes they should have the best opportunities it is possible to provide. John noted that, if the college got it wrong during the year that students were there, it wasn't easy to repeat. Therefore, in sixth form provision, it's about 'getting it right first time, because good enough is not good enough'. A focus on 'high expectations' of both oneself and others therefore needed to be maintained all the time. But leaders could not fake high expectations – if you didn't do the work, John observed that you would be 'seen through'. Responsibility as a leader therefore meant you had to be prepared to do everything you expected others to do.

John felt that the values of leadership should be the same, no matter what sort of leadership role one had, and that the key values were respect for the people you worked with, combined with trust and integrity, focus and discipline. People wouldn't follow a leader if those qualities were not present, as they wouldn't feel 'secure', but being a coercive, democratic or affiliative leader wouldn't work either, as you needed to maintain a balance between 'people' awareness and values and task-centred standards. The senior management tries to follow the model of the sigmoid curve, a model used by Charles Handy in his book, *The Empty Raincoat*:

What we try to do is try and follow *the sigmoid curve*[i]. Things are going well. Then, if you don't change, they feel a bit tired and they begin to drop off, for all sorts of reasons. The trick is to understand when it's about to happen and introduce a change, an improvement, before it happens. Even though you must expect a dip when you introduce the change, the general forward movement can be maintained because the organisation is still being successful.

Figure 1: The Secret of Constant Growth is to Start a New Sigmoid Curve before the First One Peters Out (Point A). (Handy 1994)

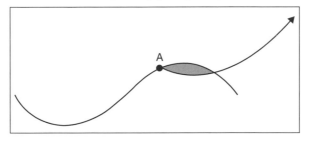

Figure 2: Real Energy for Change Comes when We are Looking at Overwhelming Evidence that Change must Take Place (Point B). (Handy, 1994)

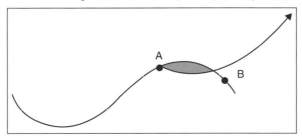

Figure 9.1 The sigmoid curve, as drawn by Dr John Guy

John feels that his role as the leader of the College is to challenge young people to try out new experiences, 'extending the comfort zone by going into discomfort.' He cited Bruner[ii] in observing that:

. . . *learning should be a voyage on a sea of ignorance to find islands of truth.* Learning is a bit like that. You're doing something and it doesn't always make sense. Then, all of a sudden, you get a sort of *crystallisation*. Suddenly, it makes sense. Those moments are quite special in learning. When you experience it, you think, 'Oh, how exciting!'

John said he felt that leadership in teaching was 'about journeying with students in this sea of ignorance'. If students felt 'at sea', the job of the leaders, as teachers, was 'about stopping people drowning', so they began to learn and understand, and did not drop out of college. Cherishing students, and demonstrating honestly that you believe in them, is very important both to John himself and to the College staff team. He quoted an incident from a previous college in which he had taken a high risk strategy to demonstrate his belief in the students. He said:

> There's a brilliant example of that in Marie Stubbs' book, *Ahead of the Class*, about her transformation of St George's School in London, where Philip Lawrence was murdered. What she took to the school – which seemed at the time to be an aggressive institution, children and teachers at loggerheads, it wasn't working – was belief in the kids. She told them she believed in them in her first assembly. 'This school belongs to you. The reason everybody's here, is because of you. *You're not here because of the school, the school's here because of you*'.

John not only clearly demonstrates to the students that he believes in them, he also lets them know that, in a sixth form college, they have now grown up and away from being school children. Since over half the population of the College changes every year, it is important to tell them explicitly, every year, what the mission and ethos of Farnborough is, so they understand their place, and know that 'the College belongs to them'. John stated that 'It's really, really important, therefore, that *we define the ethos of the College so everyone understands it*, rather than leave it to the kids, because the kids will bring with them what they've known before.'

So, even though the process of learning is dangerous, and students are faced with 'ignorances' they didn't know they had, the College team can help them avoid drowning in the sea of ignorance by helping them understand, and by providing solutions and life-saving devices. Some of those solutions could be about adopting a variety of learning styles and using formative assessment sensitively and sensibly, because in Bruner's terms, 'there's more than one way to the island where the student can feel secure'.

Faced with a Further Education Funding council (FEFC) funding crisis in 1997, the College re-engineered by improving the quality of its pastoral system and changing the way things were done, to achieve them more economically. John observed that, with maturity, leaders can 'become braver' about weighing risks, trusting that things were going to be OK, and having both 'commitment' and 'awareness of others'. These kinds of abilities were in particular developed, he felt, during a Principals' leadership course, organised by Hay McBer[iii] about *emotional intelligence*. He commented:

> That was really powerful. It was another one of those occasions when *crystallisation* occurred. You're in the sea of ignorance, hoping you're doing the right thing, not

ever so certain. And all of a sudden the emotional intelligence stuff provided an island you could sit on. It felt quite secure because it made sense of self-awareness, awareness of others, self-motivation, motivating others. It's about *security*, understanding your own self-awareness, understanding of others, *empathy*, it's about being motivated.

The Hay McBer training in emotional intelligence was so successful that John introduced it not only for his senior staff, but also for students, to increase self-awareness and awareness of others as learning tools throughout the College. The senior leadership team are excited by the new vision this has invigorated in the College because:

Colleagues will say out there that it has been transformational for some students because the blockage in their learning has not been about their ability to understand. It's been more about their willingness to allow themselves to reach that soft sand and walk up the beach because they think the only way up is the cliff face . . . and then they turn off. So, when they begin to drown, you fling a raft in as another way of doing it, you offer the chance of an alternative learning style, for instance.

The analysis of John's leadership style by Hay McBer revealed that he is *predominantly authoritative* (though not autocratic) followed by the sub-styles *democratic, coercive and coaching*. Both openness and knowledge within the Principalship were, he felt, respected in the College, as was the fact that the senior team have high expectations. But John felt that people would only follow if they respected the leader and understood the direction. To genuinely motivate staff, you need to work hard yourself:

There's all sorts of ways in which I would understand 'following'. At a transactional level, it's about working hard. You can't demand people to work hard if you don't do it yourself. In managerial-speak, it's about getting *discretionary effort* out of people. You won't get discretionary effort, going the extra mile, if you're not obviously doing that yourself. And if you're not, you'll get found out. So, it's the *motivating others* bit of leadership: not everybody is motivated, so you've got to find ways of doing it.

The Principalship at Farnborough has also worked on increasing rewards to achieve motivation and discretionary effort. An initiative to reward the staff just before the last inspection worked well – so successfully, in fact, that it created a 'good secret' within the organisation, a kind of island of community, coherence and safety of the kind that Walker and Adelman wrote about in *Classrooms Observed*:

Those are precious bits of community, important. It happens in families, all over the place: you get these *secrets*, which we understand but nobody else does. And getting those into organisations is a good thing, really. *Islands of coherence, community, and safety*. I think I've used this term *crystallisation* a few times, because I spent my life trying to make crystals.

John said that the College mission was a 'shared' one, as it was written together by staff in 1992. The mission aims to develop both excellence and the caring ethos of the College, in order to help young people go out into the world equipped to deal with their lives in the future. The College's aims are ambitious. The mission states, 'We want to develop as a distinguished major provider of the highest quality'. Therefore, 'good enough is not good enough'. The mission is deliberately intended to be continuously stretching, never able to be achieved, because not only is there a new cohort of students every year, there is also a changing world every year, so complacency is never an option.

In terms of continuously stretching and challenging performance, the sigmoid curve had been applied in terms of the embedding of emotional intelligence work into the College. This has recently had an effect, which is demonstrable in terms of 'value-added' analysis. John observed that the College is 'very strong about ALI's value-added data'. They have measured value-added achievement for every department each year, during the period 1996 to 2004. High achievement at two standard deviations above the norm gets a green colour, but under-achievement gets red. Having the latter means that the youngsters who've done that subject this year have done significantly less well than all other youngsters in the country with the same average GCSE score. The College rigorously applies this analysis objectively, and has very successfully turned around failing performance. John noted that he thought the College was 'more rigorous internally than Ofsted is externally'. The value-added analysis of data was 'a very good management technique, because it's transparent'.

John therefore felt that external factors should not drive an institution but, rather, 'leadership ought to drive achievement'. Leaders needed to be authentic and committed in taking ownership of responsibility, even in the face of turbulence created by external acts. Even though, 'as Macmillan[iv] said, *events* crop up'. The job of leadership was therefore to have:

the *antennae* up . . . so you know things, can see them coming. You've got to be aware . . . that your organisation will be in its own comfort zone, looking inward, comfortably. So the role of a leader is up on the deck, having a look to see what's coming, having the nose to realise there's an iceberg over there. That's what leaders do: they don't get stuck on the rocks. It's about *manipulating external things to suit the needs of your institution*, turning external changes to the good of the institution, so you're in control of it, rather than at its mercy. That's really important . . . you see what's coming and predispose the institution to deal with it.

> The role of a leader is up on the deck, having a look to see what's coming, having the nose to realise there's an iceberg over there. That's what leaders do – they don't get stuck on the rocks.
>
> *Dr John Guy*

John therefore saw his role as a kind of guardian in the face of continuously changing challenges buffeting the College from external events.

Summary

A discussion of the 'guardian of knowledge' and 'change agent' concept for sixth form college education introduces the interview with Dr John Guy, Principal of The Sixth Form College, Farnborough. John places students absolutely at the heart of the College, asserting a high priority in excellence of achievements, and sense of irritation and curiosity if he discovers that things could be better. Strong values of authenticity, vulnerability, trust, honesty and integrity in leadership are supported in the use of the sigmoid curve and value-added tools for improvement. Emotional leadership has recently been introduced across the College for all students. The achievements of the College have been excellent and its leadership is judged by Ofsted to be outstanding: one of the best sixth form colleges in the country.

Keywords

Sixth Form College, South East, guardianship and change agency in leadership approach, 16–19 focus, learner-centred, high quality, economic efficiency, Beacon college.

Further reading and resources

Bennis, W.G. and Nanus, B. (1985) *Leaders: The strategies for taking charge*. New York: Harper & Row.

Bruner, J.S. (1986) *Actual Minds, Possible Worlds*. Cambridge, MA: Harvard University Press.

Bruner, J. (1996) *The Culture of Education*. Cambridge, MA: Harvard University Press.

Handy, C. (1994) *The Empty Raincoat: Making Sense of the Future*. London: Hutchinson.

Hay McBer (2000a) *Models of Excellence for School Leadership: Raising Achievement in Our Schools: Models of Excellence for Headteachers in Different Settings, Parts 1 and 2*: Hay Group for the National College for School Leadership. Available online at: http://www.ncsl.org.uk/the_knowledge_pool/foundations/kpool-foundations-index.cfm *Part 3*: Hay Group for the National College for School Leadership. Available online at: http://www.ncsl.org.uk/media/F7B/52/kpool-hay-models-of-excellence-part-3.pdf Accessed 9 September 2005.

Hay McBer (2000b) *Research into Teacher Effectiveness: A Model of Teacher Effectiveness* (DfEE Research Report 216). London: DfEE. Available online at http://www.teachernet.gov.uk/teachinginengland/detail.cfm?id-521 Accessed 9 September 2005.

Northouse, P.G. (2004) Leadership: *Theory and Practice* (third edition). London: Sage Publications.

Walker, R. and Adelman, C. (1975), *A Guide to Classroom Observation*. London: Methuen.

Notes

i   For further discussion on the implications of the *sigmoid curve* applied to leadership and management studies, see also Charles Handy (1994) *The Empty Raincoat* (see References).

ii Jerome Bruner, distinguished educational psychologist and leading theorist in cognitive growth, intuitive and analytical thinking, the process and cultures of education (see References).

iii Hay McBer Management Consultants developed The Hay/McBer *Emotional Competence Inventory* (ECI), compiling management profile information via 360 degree feedback and comparisons of self-reported characteristics with those attributed by others – for example, managers, peers and subordinates (see Howells, 2000, Team Management Profile and Emotional Intelligence: More than the sum of their parts, http://www.tms.com/au/tms12-1s.html).

iv Harold Macmillan (1894–1986), British politician, Prime Minister January 1957–October 1963.

Transforming colleges: quantum leadership

❝It's a fantastic career – you change lives for the better – if you did this once in a lifetime it would be an achievement. But to do it so many times in so many years, what more reward could there be?❞
David Collins, CBE

What is quantum leadership?

Quantum leadership highlights the potential for individuals significantly to change and improve educational provision in response to a world which seems to be continuously changing at warp speed. This model of leadership conceives that institutional situations are always in flux and responds positively to opportunities for leadership to adapt to and encompass change. Having an understanding of the inevitability of change (as Heraclitus said, 'You cannot step into the same river twice') means recognising the need to transform situations with continuous improvements, high levels of responsibility and awareness.

Quantum leadership is a relatively new concept in leadership studies, linked with servant and transformational leadership and with the field of quantum mechanics. Quantum leadership tends to be strongly differentiated from reactive, mechanistic management styles and from *transactional* leadership, a task-focused style some find more appropriate to management than leadership (Downton, 1973; Northouse, 2004 – see also Chapter 2). Frearson (2003) notes that:

> . . . in the public sector, where all services are seeking ways to improve provision within constrained resources, there is a growing interest in the transformational role of leaders in improving organisations and the services they provide.
>
> (Frearson, 2003, p.7)

We could regard quantum leadership as an advanced, flexible and adaptable form of transformational leadership, linked to the 'New Leadership' concept put forward by Brymann (1996) which focuses more on whole organisation, organic, emotional and charismatic aspects of leadership than, for example, transactional styles (Northouse, 2004, p.169). Quantum leadership begins to move us towards that 'three dimensional moving hologram, as opposed to oil painting' that Lumby observes the learning and skills sector needs to conceptualise for leadership now (Lumby *et al.*, 2004).

If the process of transformational leadership is explicitly intended to raise followers' hopes, and to achieve change or 'transformation' in people and organisations, the role of quantum leadership is to do this in ways futuristically suited to the development of new 21st century organisations.

Transformational leadership is addressed at the 'whole' person within the organisation, including their emotions, thoughts, motives, values and longer term ideals and plans. The definition of quantum leadership moves beyond this and also encompasses more advanced elements of transformational capacity including, specifically, the ability to cope proactively and creatively with paradox and ambiguity. Shelton and Darling (2001, p.264) note that the following characteristics apply to quantum leadership: *quantum seeing, thinking, feeling, knowing, acting, trusting and being*. These qualities comprise, respectively, the ability to 'see intentionally', 'think paradoxically', 'feel vitally alive', 'know intuitively', 'act responsibly', 'trust life's process'; and 'be in relationship'. (Shelton and Darling, 2001, p.264). As defining features of a particular leadership style, these characteristics can do with further examination and refinement. Warren Blank (1995), Margaret Wheatley (1999) and Alexander Dawoody (2003) are among those who have explored the characteristics of quantum leadership more fully (see References).

Quantum leadership, like transformational leadership, encourages followers to achieve significantly more than they ordinarily would. The transformational model has been criticised for its relative ambiguity and vagueness, as well as the difficulty of precisely measuring its effects (Northouse, 2004, p.185). However, we could also argue that there is benefit in the 'futures proactivity' opportunities in this for new leaders to advance their own localised, differentiated models of leadership in multiple new ways potentially enabled by such relative openness. The quantum leadership model is at present still relatively open to new definitions, and thereby has perhaps even more potential for us to determine new ways of being for leadership in PCE adapted to particular situations and demands. The model has all the values of transformational leadership, but moves beyond them as well, specifying a conception of a learning organisation that is fluid, highly adaptable, capable of continuously self-generating improvements and technological advancements for the 21st century. The quantum leadership model is explored more fully in later work (see Jameson and McNay, 2006), as this chapter is dedicated to the description of an outstanding example of leadership that I have chosen to link to the quantum leadership model.

I have selected the case study of Dr David Collins at South Cheshire College to match the quantum model because the College's outstanding successes indicate an extraordinary level of organisational adaptability and 'fitness' for change. If the quantum model is a futures-centred organisational concept as yet not fully defined and understood in leadership studies, there is within it some *space* to listen to and learn from organisations such as South Cheshire, currently achieving excellent results. The holistic characteristics of the College leadership in terms of advanced capabilities of 'seeing intentionally', 'thinking paradoxically', 'feeling vitally alive', 'knowing intuitively', 'acting responsibly', 'trusting life's process' and 'being in relationship' (Shelton and Darling, 2001, p.264) fit the model. As Shelton *et al.* (2002) note:

> Quantum leaders use an inspirational purpose and timeless values to create strong, cohesive organisational cultures that transcend diversity. These quantum leaders . . . deploy innovative organisational development processes that enable other members . . . to make a similar quantum leap. Working together, they discover shared values and a shared purpose that transcend their differences and . . . create quantum organisations where behavioural style diversity, job/person fit and cultural cohesion simultaneously exist. (Shelton *et al.*, 2002, p.375)

The significantly beneficial organisational transformation of South Cheshire College during the past 12 years has resulted in the highest achievements under Ofsted and other inspectorates' measurements of quality indicators for any UK college. The values-based culture established by David and his team in 1993 has undoubtedly played an essential role in this, as has the strong, flexible model of leadership flowing through the College. Results at South Cheshire have been outstanding – what can the sector learn from this?

I went to see David at the College in Crewe in April, taking the journey by train from Euston. A bright, welcoming College entrance and friendly receptionist quickly put me at ease and David came down himself to greet me. David's responses follow the questions I asked below.

Case study of Further Education Leadership

Dr David Collins, CBE, Principal, South Cheshire College

Transforming colleges in triple time: quantum leadership

How would you categorise the institution and client group of which you are a leader?

South Cheshire College is a large tertiary college based primarily in Crewe, but with outreach posts in Sandbach, Congleton, Middlewich and a number of schools in the area. Crewe itself has five 11–16 schools but as you go outside the town the incidence of 11–18 schools increases and in total the College draws its full time 16–19 population from 43 schools in Cheshire and its surroundings. We have about 3000 full time students of whom 2200 are aged 16–19, and 800 of whom are more mature adults, and approximately 10,000 part time students. We cover the whole range of Ofsted curriculum areas, apart from agriculture, including construction, engineering, social and community care, a range of AS- and A-levels, travel and tourism, and catering. We have topped the inspection tables not only for 1994 but also for 2004, the last time we were inspected, and we have money in the bank. Overall we are considered to be one of the country's more successful institutions.

What, in your experience, is the distinction, if any, between leadership and management in post-compulsory education?

> Leadership for me is about creating a vision, and more than a vision, a set of underpinning values that can be understood and embraced by members of the organisation as they contribute to the achievement of that organisations' mission.
>
> *Dr David Collins, CBE*

Leadership for me is about creating a vision, and more than a vision, a set of underpinning values that can be understood and embraced by members of the organisation as they contribute to the achievement of that organisation's mission. It's about establishing a clarity of purpose, a direction for the organisation and a culture within which individuals feel willing and able to make their own personal contribution to the greater whole.

I think it's really a context for management. Although the two are linked, management, for me, is more concerned with efficiency and effectiveness, and the operations of the structure's policies, procedures and actions that help deliver the vision.

Of course, in the better institutions, neither leadership nor management exist solely at the top. Within a college, pretty well all individuals will have or can have elements of both management and leadership within their role. The designated leader, however, has the responsibility to ensure that both leadership and management exist in sufficient quantity and quality to allow the organisation to prosper. So, although both might be 'distributed', the responsibility for and extent of that distribution always remains with the leader.

Replying to my question about his main defining aims as a leader, David said:

I suppose I'm a bit of a perfectionist. I've always had a driving ambition to be the best. As a principal of a college, that's an aim that can only really be achieved by leading the country's best college. For me that means ensuring the widest possible appropriate educational opportunities are made available for potential students, that individuals have the support and environment to achieve over and beyond what they might have thought possible, that the staff feel they are making a significant contribution to a successful institution, and everyone agrees that no matter how good they are, they can always be better.

I also believe that you also have to accept the concept of *continuous improvement*, no matter how good you happen to be. These aims are then set in a context of a personal, strong commitment to public service, a belief in the transparency of operations and making it clear to everybody, not just what you're doing, but why you're doing it, equity and fairness and *social justice*.

David went on to explain the need for a clear and accepted values-based culture:

I'd like to go back to a time before I was Principal back in the late 80s, when I went to a number of community colleges in America and for the first time I came across a college that had spent some time defining its values. I was very much struck by how 'different' that organisation felt from the others that I had visited and it made me much more aware of the importance of successful organisations having a clear and accepted values-based culture. So when I became a principal in 1993, one of the first things I did was to draft a set of values for the College that reflected what I believed in. These were then discussed . . . and with relatively minor modifications became the agreed values on which the new incorporated organisation would be based. Every year since then, as part of our planning process, we review the values, but in essence they've remained unchanged for the past 12 years.

I asked David to talk to us about these values, and he said:

They're encapsulated in ten fairly simple statements:

1.   South Cheshire College exists to serve its community; each member is a valued asset.

2.   Everyone will be treated with care and consideration as an individual whose contribution to the College is recognised.

3.   Management is more concerned with guidance and support than with regulation and control.

4.   All members of the College are partners in the success or failure of the organisation; each one is accountable for results.

5.   Quality is at the heart of all we do; in our pursuit of excellence we recognise that individually and collectively we can always improve.

6.   The willingness to contribute to and respond to change is fundamental to our success.

7.   Within the College, integrity and commitment are as highly valued as enterprise and creativity.

8.   Clarity and openness of communication are considered essential to both our stability and our success.

9.   Co-operation is preferred to competition and partnerships will be encouraged with both education or location providers to develop our provision.

10. Perhaps the most important of all – equality of opportunity is a commitment which all members of the College will actively pursue.

We've been comfortable in operating with this list for over a decade. It's designed to create a corporate approach as to *how* we do things rather than what we do. I think a values-driven culture is absolutely essential to an institution's success. I don't know of any organisation that really succeeds without having implicit or explicit values that people hold in common. Without them you are invariably going to get tensions with people operating in ways they're not comfortable with or railing against ways in which things are supposed to be done.

David said it was essential to 'live' the values, that it was 'very important for a leader that they demonstrate *values in action*'. One of the first things he did as a principal was to get rid of reserved parking places, to send a 'very different' message to staff and students. He said:

I think in general as a principal, or leader, you have to be able to show that your words and your actions have a *congruence* and that you are setting the example for others to follow. There's perhaps no better way to doing this than by showing values in action.

. . . I'll give you an example. We produced, following our inspection, a publicity brochure showing various quotes we were particularly proud of from the inspection report, ending up with a photograph of the South Cheshire College team. Now, where do you think the senior management team are in the picture? The answer is not obvious and certainly not in the front row. The point is that there was an opportunity for the SMT deliberately not to be seen as having contributed any more to the inspection outcome than anyone else. I would suggest that in probably nine colleges out of ten, the senior management would have been closest to the camera! The point I'm making is there are sometimes relatively easy opportunities to make points about values. It's important to recognise them and use them when they occur. The position of the SMT in the photograph wasn't by accident, it was by design.

I've also learned to appreciate the importance of Maslow's hierarchy of needs in running any organisation. I've always worked hard to ensure that as far as possible the basic physiological, safety and, to a certain extent, social needs of the staff, are met. So even in situations when there have been huge savings to be made, I've never made anybody compulsorily redundant. You have to create a degree of security and a feeling that individuals are not under threat to enable people to perform at the level you want them to perform at.

I recognise too the importance of high levels of visibility. I've become much more aware that good communication doesn't actually happen by accident. It happens by design. We have a whole range of communication channels and methods within the College which enable people to know what's going on. It's something that's very important for leaders to work on.

David went on to explain how he felt that decisions should flow naturally from good policies:

I believe very much in (this is going to sound strange first of all), but I believe very much in *not making decisions*. If you've got clear values, very good policies and well worked out systems and procedures and systems, then the decisions will flow from them. People throughout the organisation will usually be able to take the decisions they need themselves because they will know they fit within the overall scheme of things. Only when there is some doubt or potential conflict will they need to ask.

I therefore think that the real role of a leader is to maintain the integrity of the mission, vision, values, structures, policies, systems, procedures, actions etc. so that the organisation functions as a coherent, purposeful and successful unit. It is that *tying it all together* element which is key to a leader. Otherwise, you won't get the organisation moving in a particular direction or the vision being achieved, because there'll be too many pieces pulling in different directions.

> I think that the real role of a leader is to maintain the integrity of the mission, vision values, structures, policies, systems, procedures and actions, so that the organisation functions as a coherent, purposeful and successful unit.
>
> *Dr David Collins, CBE*

Asked if a metaphor would describe this style of leadership, David said:

This requires different emphases at different times, the ability to see what aspect of the organisation's operation needs a particular focus or input. If I had to choose a metaphor, it would be *the music hall novelty act* where the skill was to keep as many plates spinning on a stick in motion at the same time. To be successful in doing this act, you always had to be aware of the one plate that was wobbling more than the rest, get to it quickly and give it an extra flick of the wrist or some extra attention. The added complication we seem to face in the real world is that nowadays the environment is constantly changing. It's as if in that music hall act the stage is also moving and the audience wants to see constant changes in the act. You're not just spinning the plates, but you're spinning them in a very dynamic environment. To be a successful leader, therefore, you've got to ensure that not only all the component parts of the organisation are moving as they should, but that all these extraneous movements are properly assessed and accommodated.

Another model that attracts me is one from Keith Grint at the University of Lancaster . . . the idea of the leader as a wheelwright. The expertise lies in knowing the relationship between the spaces and the spokes and if the spaces are too wide and the spokes are too few, the wheel will collapse as soon as pressure is applied.

Asked if he felt leadership should be distributed, David said:

I'm definitely a firm believer in distributed leadership, although in my opinion the overall responsibility for leadership can never be delegated. For real empowerment to occur, there has got to be a recognition that power, skills and responsibility, wherever they lie, must match; otherwise, all that is likely to be distributed in my view is stress and confusion. This points to the need for personal skills development at all levels in a learning organisation. What's more, without some form of distributed leadership, the institution is very vulnerable to being too dependent on an individual or small group for its survival and progress.

I asked if David felt the College mission had been achieved and what had helped:

We have enjoyed a lot of success. In 11 of the past 12 years we've grown. We're now over twice the size we were at the time of incorporation. The staying on rate in Crewe and Nantwich has gone from 60% to 74%. The College has gone from a financial deficit and being recognised as one of the poorest 30 colleges in the country to one that now has five years of grade 'A' financial status, and 10% of our £20m turnover (£2m or thereabouts) in the bank. We've consistently performed well at inspection in the top 25% or so in 1994 to the number one position for FE in tertiary colleges in 1999 under the FEFC, and the number one position overall in 2004 under Ofsted.

We have been awarded 'Beacon' status by both the FEFC and LSC and we've got a number of quality awards including Investors in People, Investors in Career and ISO9000. We've also built up a reputation for being consistently innovative.

The key thing is to make sure we are continually improving, looking all the time for ways in which we can do things better. In fact, we have a target of having one major improvement a week – 50 a year is our target, which we can say we've achieved since 1993. We also expect all staff to do at least two things better each year, so with approaching 400 staff that gives you 800 improvements annually! It works on Tom Peters' principle of using large numbers: it's easier to do a thousand things one percent better than one thing a thousand percent better. The principal's role is making sure that everyone in the organisation is constantly trying to improve, and encouraging and supporting their efforts.

Things that helped us to achieve success include a very talented and dedicated senior management team. They're absolutely fantastic. We've also got a really supportive staff who have worked their socks off to achieve what we've achieved. It is quite interesting, for example, when people ask how we have managed to do so remarkably well in inspection. The answer is quite simple. There were 26 of them, and 400 of us – the odds were stacked in our favour! I think it really was a case where people would have died rather than let the side down.

'Sufficient grit in the oyster for a pearl, not an irritated oyster'

The most challenging issues leaders face are:

- the need to maintain a high skill base and high level of radar so that they're able to understand the complexities of their organisation and the environment in which they operate
- finding and learning from best practice
- recognising and being able to respond to change as the new steady state. We will never get stability, it doesn't exist

- being able to create and maintain the necessary momentum and direction to achieve the organisation's objectives through harnessing the talents of individuals. It's introducing just sufficient grit into the oyster to make a pearl rather than an irritated oyster. It's to get people in a position where they *want* to change so that the organisation can move forward.

> It's introducing just sufficient grit into the oyster to make a pearl rather than an irritated oyster.
>
> *Dr David Collins, CBE*

David emphasised the importance of looking in three time frames at the same time:

> Lastly, in terms of the skills level issues, it's having the ability to work in what I suppose I could refer to as *three inter-related time zones simultaneously*. You've got to be able to examine and learn from the past, deliver excellence in the present, and have a clear view as to not only where the College needs to be in the future, but also what needs to be done now to allow that to happen. Sometimes you feel you're working in three time frames at the same time. Marrying those in a coherent way can be challenging!

'Leadership and followership should be fun'

A college is very much a social organisation. The social needs of both staff and students are very important. You can be very successful, highly professional and still enjoy yourself: it's not actually a crime to do so! I can't actually think of a day where I haven't spent a good part of it laughing. Some college leaders need to lighten up a little bit and enjoy what is a wonderful opportunity and a wonderful job. Leadership and 'followership' should be fun!

I've been very lucky, I've worked with some marvellous people who have taught me a lot and I've worked in some excellent places. It's a fantastic career because, whether you're a lecturer or a head of department, you change lives for the better. And if you did this once in a lifetime it would be an achievement, but the fact that you do it, not quite daily, but you do it so many times in so many years, what more reward could there be?

Summary

A discussion of quantum leadership theory introduces the interview with Dr David Collins, Principal of South Cheshire College. David describes the College and its many successes as the highest performing college in UK inspections in 1999 and 2004. For David, leadership is about creating a vision, a set of underpinning values, clarity of purpose, direction and culture. Following a formative visit to US community colleges which convinced him of the importance of a values-driven culture, David established ten college values which are lived by the leadership as *values in action*. Ofsted has judged the leadership of the College to be outstanding.

Keywords

College of FE, North West England, quantum leadership approach, learner-centred, economic efficiency, Beacon college, highest performing college Ofsted 1999, 2004.

Further reading and resources

Bennis, W.G., and Nanus, B. (1985) *Leaders: The Strategies for Taking Charge*. New York: Harper & Row.

Blank, W. (1995) *The Nine Natural Laws of Leadership*. New York: AMACOM, American Management Association.

Dawoody, A. (2003) *The Matriarch as a Leader and the Metaphors of Chaos and Quantum Theories*. Bloomington, IN: 1st Books.

Handy, C. (1995) *The Age of Paradox*. Cambridge, MA: Harvard Business School Press.

Jameson, J. and McNay, I. (forthcoming) *The Ultimate FE Leadership and Management Handbook*, Book No. 9 in *The Essential FE Toolkit Series* for senior and middle managers, Series editor: Jill Jameson. London: Continuum.

Kilmann, R.H. (2001) *Quantum Organizations: A New Paradigm for Achieving Organizational Success and Personal Meaning*. Palo Alto, CA: Davies-Black.

Shelton, C.D., McKenna, M.K. and Darling, J.R. (2002) 'Leading in the age of paradox: optimizing behavioural style, job fit and cultural cohesion.' *Leadership and Organization Development Journal*, 23, 7, pp. 372–79.

Wheatley, M.J. (1999) *Leadership and the New Science: Discovering Order in a Chaotic World* (second edition). San Francisco, CA: Berrett-Koehler.

Women at the helm: systemic leadership

> **❝One of my main defining aims is a belief that we can change people's lives: a belief that further education is a fabulous place to be, in this community.❞**
> Ruth Silver

Systemic leadership theory

The systemic approach to leadership focuses on the unity and coherence of organisations as systems, existing both internally and within the external environment. The 'systems model' assumes there is a boundary between the system itself and the outer environment which is more or less permeable, depending on whether the organisation adopts a closed or open systems model. Peter Senge's revolutionary organisational leadership and management work, *The Fifth Discipline: The Art and Practice of the Learning Organisation* (1990) stimulated considerable interest in 'systems thinking' for the generation of creative and adaptable leadership solutions within organisations. In his formative work, Senge discussed blockages in complex problem-solving resulting from 'the learning disabilities' of organisations. Discussing the difficulties of this inability to learn, he cites colleague Chris Argyris, who 'argues that most managers find collective inquiry inherently threatening. School trains us never to admit that we do not know the answer' (Senge, 1990, p.25).

Educational institutions such as colleges, dependent on public funding, are more likely to have an 'open systems' approach, with more or less reliance on and interaction or interdependence with funding and regulatory bodies, public agencies and partner organisations in the wider environment. When Ruth Silver discusses the role of Lewisham College within the environment, she conceptualises the College as 'a corridor between worlds', part of what she calls 'the adaptive layer of FE', indicating that, at one level, she clearly sees the College as an 'open systems' organisation needing to provide responsive curricula to cater for the needs of partner agencies.

I selected the case study of Ruth Silver of Lewisham College for this chapter on systemic leadership because Ruth provides an outstanding example of a female principal, whose definition of 'the systemic approach' is highly advanced. She also focuses on the 'fit' between the organisation and the leader, in resonance, for example, with synergistic theories outlined elsewhere in this book. An edited version of Ruth's replies to the questions I asked now follows.

Case Study of Inner City FE Leadership

Ruth Silver, CBE, Principal of Lewisham College

The love of the task: winning hearts, changing lives

How would you categorise the institution and client group of which you are a leader?

> Lewisham College is a large inner city college in a very deprived area, a general FE college with a hefty vocational focus. Ruth noted that the description was 'strategic and intentional, because communities like ours, we know the power of the vocational impulse for learning, so we're deliberately staying with that kind of characterisation of ourself.
>
> The average age of Lewisham's students is 31, 63% are on benefit, there are 2500 16–19 year olds and about 500 14–16 year olds. There are 47% women and 53% men. The college serves the 16th most needy community in England, and there is a real problem with teenage health, pregnancies, sexually transmitted disease.

So, Ruth says that she thinks the college represents:

> a *corridor between worlds* for those communities. From school to work, from school to university, from home back into learning when children start school. We are *a first day place*: people come here on the first day of being unemployed, first day of your child going to school, people come here. *We're a second chance institution.*
>
> So, if people didn't get it right first time, even though they're only 14, if something went wrong somewhere else, something's been switched off, we are a second chance for switching on. And we've always worked – forgive the phrase – *in the third way* with partners: with universities as our partners, with employers as our partners, with schools as our partners. For my money, it is the most exciting part of the education service. Further education colleges are the 'adaptive' layer in the UK education system, so we are continually changing, as the economic and social context changes. That's just the most challenging and creative place to be.
>
> Colleges absolutely have to deliver a curriculum desired by other people, so this notion of a 'corridor between worlds'. Our job is to get people ready for those destinations, whether it's university, employment, a further course of study, or preparation

for retirement. We are continually designing learning for destinations that are not about us, and not just about the learner. Colleges would not survive if we were closed systems, simply because of this notion of 'readiness': you know, 'learner readiness' for progression. There's a Scottish notion, by Brunswick, called 'the vocational impulse' in which they say, actually, quite often learners who'd been turned off doing reading, writing, arithmetic, can be 're-turned on' by doing, getting ready to do, nursing or carpentry. The vocational impulse is very motivating, when the educational impulse alone has been turned off. And we use that here. So we take that as presenting an intention to be respected when learners say, 'This is what we want to do'.

We have 130 nationalities in this College: our College has the world in it. Age, you know, gender, nationality, learning need, social need, aspirations. This is a poor community and we still cannot keep up with their aspirations. People don't want to have the lives they have here, so it's a delightful way to serve. If I took the 'readiness' curriculum, very much a Lewisham notion, we found a way of thinking collectively about how we absolutely serve our learners, by talking about people who come to the college being one or more of these things. We need to be 'classroom ready', 'learning ready', 'work ready', 'job ready', 'university ready' and 'success ready'. One of our key beliefs here, because of where we are, is that 'fit for purpose' for us is a definition of quality, but equality we see as being 'fit for context'. So hence the notion of being *more than a college offering more than a qualification* because our learners have less than they need and have a right to expect from our society.

What, in your experience, is the distinction, if any, between leadership and management in post-compulsory education?

I absolutely believe that 'management is doing the thing right' and 'leadership is doing the right thing'. At Lewisham, we have a collective way of thinking about this. So we define 'management' as 'getting things done through, with, and by others' and 'leadership' is 'having the capacity to win hearts'. Our belief is that you cannot buy a heart, you cannot instruct a heart – that actually you really do have to *win hearts*, for the primary purpose of the organisation, for the decorum, the professional decorum you want to see in there. And, of course the need for *reputation* in an area like this, where people know we are successful.

Ruth described her belief in the need to instil 'the love of the task':

'Winning hearts' is what leadership has to do. I think you can buy brains. And we do. That's called 'being a worker, an employee'. You can instruct hands, because that's part of the job description detail. You know, people sell their labour, but you cannot instruct a heart, and you can't buy a heart. One of the notions I really believe in – and I think it's the task of leadership to breed this – is a kind of 'professional love'. We don't talk enough of that. We talk about interpersonal love – but actually there is a *love of the task*, of the organisation. That *is* in the hands of leadership.

Ruth went on to explain how the animation of ideas is where you start to 'win the heart':

People always say when you walk in through the door at Lewisham, you can feel a difference. And I think that's what they feel. The animation of ideas that is absolutely the leadership's task is where you start to win the heart. So this College is about serving this community: absolutely honest public service, in its old sense, not the managerial kind taken at so many places. We have as you know, 'Beacon' status, excellent performance reviews, financial grade 'A' status. We have all of those dimensions. So management is kind of the least of our concerns. But hanging together, around this very needy and quite often difficult community, I think takes real work. It takes working with threads, and with the seams, of the many parts of this organisation, the breeding of 'the spirit of the enterprise' that is this institution.

> We talk about, you know, interpersonal love – but actually there is a *love of the task*, of the organisation. That is in the hands of leadership.
>
> *Ruth Silver, CBE*

I differentiate between institutions and organisations. We're both of those things, of course. We are three, we're an organisation and we are well organised and very successfully running that and we're an institution and for my purpose for me that means that we have a social purpose. So organisations have a business and a task purpose, institutions have a social purpose. And enterprise is much more. The word that comes to mind is 'spiritual', but it's a kind of a 'spiritual-political wholeness'. So the spirit of the enterprise that's Lewisham is 'We want to change people's lives', mainly because their lives are intolerable in the 130 nationalities, newly arrived people from dreadful circumstances, people here, more indigenous communities, who have terrible circumstances as well. That almost sounds missionary, but I don't mean it to be that. It really is about seeing, in areas like this, that the importance of education is absolutely transparent. In more prosperous areas, that may not be the case. But it's not only about the 'spirit of the enterprise'. I want that to be seen as 'spirited'. Energetic, spirited, challenging. There's quite a lot of defiance – the defiant mindset that says 'no, we're not having this, we *can* make life better' and the defiance that allows us to publish our argumentative pamphlets and reports.

We're here to make our students fit for the world and the world fit for our students. So it is my expectation that every colleague that joins us will find themselves on a national committee, because actually the world needs to change, and the fit isn't right at the end of it either. So I absolutely encourage my colleagues to sit on national committees, to argue for change.

I then talked to Ruth about her aims as an educational leader:

One of my main defining aims is a belief that we can change people's lives. A belief that further education is a fabulous place to be, in this community. That's kind of the social purpose. I'm very interested in the animation of ideas and devising learning. I am, first and foremost, a teacher. How you change things is an abiding interest, but really that notion of 21st century public service, too. I'm a socialist, not particularly a Christian socialist, but that absolutely is the route for other kinds of values – inclusiveness, service, respect and excellence. By now (I've been here a long time) it's in the fabric of the organisation. It is there in the job descriptions we write and person specifications for joining Lewisham College. It's there because the strategic plan and development plans all have those values inside them. It's there because of the kind of people who are on the governing body, and their values.

For me, it's a political root, but for some of the governing body and for some of my colleagues, it would be a faith root to their being. For others, it would be, you know, a kind of cultural root. So whatever the source is in us as human beings working in this College, people can associate with those from different value perspectives. I think those are the values of a civilised society. And, given that I grew up in Scotland in the mining community, you can see the kind of political start I experienced.

What I want for my students is what I want for my child. *I want them to be all that they can be*, through self-discovery and the building of wisdom. Not just 'knowledge' and not just 'developing intelligences' but what we need in the world is a wisdom, *a wisdom that knows how to be in the world*, imperfect as it is, but to be in the world in a creative and proactive way, so that breaking of the victim cycle. We see a lot of that in communities like ours: a sense that *the future is not a place you go to, it's a place you make.* You have to be careful that you don't make promises that you can't keep. But that breeding of independence, independence of thought, independence of action, is the first step towards an interdependence of the community.

I see a thread in my life, which almost feels ancestral, which has been 'Actually, it needn't be like this, it has to be better'. I have to make my contribution to that. As I became a principal, I brought to this task a toolkit in which, as a psychologist, I learned to wonder about people's behaviour; as a professional, I had seen the wonderful value of imagery in people's life; as a parent, I knew the importance of connectedness; as a political person, I knew how systems worked and how the world should be. And of course as a principal, I've learned to look at places of leverage and change.

Probably the most important source is my upbringing in a Scottish mining village, just after the war, where people had to pull together and, when my father died and I had a place at grammar school, the NUM came and knocked on our door and said to my mother, 'We hear she's a clever lassie, well we won't walk away from her' and they paid for my university education. So when you've been brought up like that, to hold together, and to make a contribution, to take responsibility for things, I believe you take that forward with you for the rest of your life. And it's in me still, you know: I still stand up on the buses for old ladies, forgetting that I am nearly one. It's just intuitive and instinctive, shaped around the sense of community: a community where everybody had their difficulties. I think that world is inside me. Actually that's my interior and that's what I take wherever I go. That and key people in my life even though they no longer exist. So those traditions, the people who fold into us as we grow in our humanity, you know, it's what you take with you. Interior worlds don't develop in a lovely pink and fluffy way. Learning the hard way is quite often the only way to learn in some situations. Wisdom comes, I think, from having the opportunity to reflect with others.

'Obstacles are our teachers'

> I don't believe in leaders. I absolutely do not believe in leaders, but I do believe in leadership and leading.
>
> *Ruth Silver, CBE*

I have a systemic approach to leadership. I don't believe in leaders. I absolutely do not believe in leaders, but I do believe in leadership and in leading. To personalise that, it's about a systemic approach to running an enterprise. The biggest changes in me came on the whole from the changing world. You remember that lovely Buddhist phrase, 'obstacles are our teachers'. So all of those are the tools of sculpture, I think, to take the idealised version of yourself and make it real, authentic and useful. So from a view of kind of 'hands off' leadership I may have started with, to find myself a year later with my sleeves up brushing the steps. And so I've learned that *leadership is about doing what has to be done, but in an ethical and related way.*

I'm very delighted with the layers underneath me. We've never had it so good. I'm really trying to nurture them as much as we can and nurture by challenge quite often. I have such a belief that organisations talk to you, they send you signals all the time on what is to be done. I have enough sense to say, I wonder what does that mean, what does this behaviour mean in this organisation? And that keeps you beautifully grounded. In terms of a creative and positive mindset.

There are clear characteristics to my leadership style, but it's pretty eclectic. I will do what has to be done in order to serve this organisation and its mission and its values. Other people tell me I 'grow things'. The whole time we're 'growing it', we're talking what's not working, growing it, trying to make that better. So I would describe myself as eclectic, organic, passionate – I think the passionate others would share. You have to watch that passion doesn't turn into hubris, so even coming up to my 14th year, I still, every six weeks, go for supervision, because it's a lonely thing, leadership. No, being a leader is lonely – and so I need somebody outside my world who will keep an eye on me, help me think, and help me reflect on how things are.

> I believe in leadership and leading. I think that's a dimension of absolutely everybody's role ... that notion of leadership as winning hearts, as the animation of ideas, as ethical, holding a value system, and that notion of creativity. All of that, I think, are dimensions of everybody's role in College.
>
> *Ruth Silver, CBE*

I believe in leadership and leading. I think that's a dimension of absolutely everybody's role. But I think I'm slightly sceptical about this notion of 'distributed leadership' because there is only one person held accountable for this organisation, by way of law. So I'm into 'everybody taking up that leadership dimension on their role', but think in the end it's one person whose head will roll. And there's no place to go with that: you just live with it. But that notion of leadership as winning hearts, as the animation of ideas, as ethical, holding a value system, and that notion of creativity. All of that, I think, are dimensions of everybody's role in College. What varies, and what's not distributed across the College, is *discretion*. The *deployment of discretion* is really what makes creativity thrive. To mobilise creativity, you have to make sure the basics are done. I also am clear that you cannot be a good leader without being a good manager. So we develop leader-managers and teacher-managers and teacher-leaders, you know we really: it is a dimension of another role.

Leadership's real skill is the *joy of the fit* which in an organisation is its social purpose, primary task and the world it finds itself in. We welcome change here and it's seen as a good. It's the aliveness of the institution. When I say 'fit', it is the optimising and maximising of all of those things for students' success, students' progression. We have very strong management practices of reviewing, monitoring, allocating, inspecting. All of those go on apace here by very excellent managers. I'm very clear that we stand, I stand, on the shoulders of giants in this College. There is a community of professionals here that are just remarkable. So I really, like a parent, try to get for my staff the best for them for whatever it is that they need. So this thing about being a good manager is a platform for really excellent leadership. That, and *the love of the task*.

You will remember our organisational chart is a dahlia. In a flower, a petal can drop off without destroying the rest of the flower. So the petal drops off so another one can grow in its place. And if you don't have that sense of organisational life, then you have to completely restructure things and actually disturb the soil and neglect the offshoots. But in that version of a dahlia, a leaf or a petal falls off and a new leaf will grow, depending on the changes in the environment, but it all remains the same. And Lewisham's organisational chart has got learner services at its heart at the centre and then all the petals come off.

In terms of drivers for achievement, there are critical drivers outside of our responsibility, like funding and national targets. They're critical because they are delivered from government and I am a public servant through and through so I can live with those, but my own sense of what's critical has a much more interior sense: 'breeding new leaders' by developing their hearing and their spirit as well as their skills and their brains. I'd like to see a more academic approach to the development of leaders. Leadership is a bit more than a set of interpersonal skills for managing people or a bag of techniques. There are a lot of unknown dimensions to leadership. And so my reading list would have something like *The Ragged Trousered Philanthropists, Sons and Lovers* and *An Intimate History of Humanity*, so that they'd be well educated, used to reflection, to developing creativity. But I think the real critical drivers are too often seen as funding and league tables and targets and competitive bidding. I suspect it's one of the dimensions of 21st-century life: the 2000s are the age of responsibility: the adaptive layer will have to deal with being seen and examined as to how responsible they've been by way of league tables, funding and so on. And of course Lewisham never ever fails to meet its targets, has got great achievement rates. Those are the givens: they are the outcomes of something much more systemic and collaborative and collective.

'Where *you* are, a place arises'

The root of my experience, the ancestry I talk about, is a political literacy. There's a lovely line in Rilke's poetry, the *Duino Elegies*. He says in that, 'Where you are, a place arises'. This is true of all of us. The leader has to remember that. So – develop a consciousness around the place that will arise where you are, and steward it well, with as much matching the level of care as with creativity. It's that notion of 'Where *you* are, a place arises'. I don't think you know that in advance, by the way. I think that's the thing about 'the fit of the organisation and the leader', if I can use that phrase. I have been known to say 'where the place is that *you arise* is'. That fit, the fit between the relationship between the place and the person is crucial.

Summary

A discussion of the principles of systemic leadership introduces the interview with Ruth Silver, Principal of Lewisham College. Ruth discusses leadership within the College in a wide-ranging interview describing the multiple challenges and joys of working in the 'adaptive layer' of further education in Lewisham College. Ruth refers to 'systemic leadership', capturing for us attributes defining the connected, distinctive emotional intelligences guiding the exterior and interior worlds of the College. She outlines her own unique conception of 'professional love', describing the College as a 'first day place', and 'a second chance institution' for the vulnerable client group in Lewisham. Ruth places a high priority on student success and asserts the values of 'winning hearts', 'the love of the task', uniqueness, authenticity, vulnerability, trust, honesty and integrity in leadership, placing a high priority on excellent organisational systems, and on 'reading' the College as a psychologist – she says that 'organisations speak to you'. Ruth feels that leaders need to discover that 'where you are, a place arises'. There is a place for leaders in which, fortuitously, 'the joy of the fit' arises, when organisations and individuals, working well together, discover deeper truths about themselves within each other. Ruth views leadership organically and feels further education in Lewisham is 'a fabulous place to be'. Ruth recorded an outstandingly inspiring interview, for the benefit of future leaders.

Keywords

College of FE, Inner City London South East, systemic leadership approach, 'the fit' of good leadership, learner-centred, economic efficiency, excellent leadership, quality assurance and management, Beacon college.

Further reading and resources

Lawrence, D.H. (1970 [1913]) *Sons and Lovers*. Harmondsworth: Penguin Books.

Northouse, P.G. (2004) *Leadership Theory and Practice*. London: Sage Publications.

Rilke, R.M. (1939) *Duino Elegies*. (trans. J.B. Leishman and S. Spender). New York: W.W. Norton.

Senge, P.M. (1990) *The Fifth Discipline: The Art and Practice of The Learning Organisation*. London: Random House Business Books.

Tressell, R. (1971) *The Ragged Trousered Philanthropist*. London: Lawrence & Wishart.

Zeldin, T. (1998) *An Intimate History of Humanity*. New York: Vintage Books.

CHAPTER 12

Diversity in post-compulsory education: inclusive leadership

> **"I think it is very important to value the students, and try to fit everything else we are asked to do around the needs of the students."**
> Anne Morahan

Leading inclusive and diverse educational provision

In her report on *Inclusive Leadership*, Kugelmass (2003) reports from three international case studies of inclusive leadership in schools. She identifies that 'inclusive education' has sometimes been associated with integrating children with disabilities into schools, but that 'internationally, "inclusive education"' has 'broader aims . . . as a reform that supports and welcomes diversity among all learners' (Kugelmass, 2003, p.3).

'Dear All the ESOL Teachers,
Thank you very much.
You are all gold, from my heart.
I was in Dover, very interesting.'

Postcard from Turkish student to Anne's staff in Dover IRC

Kugelmass's comparative analysis of three 'inclusive' schools revealed that although the institutions selected were superficially different from one another, common themes relating to leadership emerged. Key among these were:

- A strong and 'uncompromising' set of principles for inclusive education shared by both positional and functional leaders across the organisation, enabling a culture of genuine equity in terms of valuing the active participation of all students

- A collaborative culture within a distributed leadership structure, with participative decision-making. Kugelmass notes that this is not necessarily easily achieved:

Responding to student diversity requires . . . staff to move beyond established practices, that . . . . demands a process of learning about new practices and a willingness to struggle. These processes take place most effectively within a collaborative context. (Kugelmass, 2003, p.19)

The need to foster a strong collaborative determination to enable inclusivity applies particularly to adult and prison education. Achieving an inclusive culture in heterogeneous educational settings is by no means easy. It is particularly challenging when the client group is diverse, transitory and faced with exceptional difficulties. Such a case occurs in an Immigration and Removals Centre. To give such clients a useful educational experience, you need a dedicated collaborative team performing to high standards, such as the one at Dover Immigration Removal Centre (DIRC).

I went along by train from London on a grey, misty day in early April to Dover IRC to talk to the IRC Education Manager, Anne Morahan, about her role as an educational leader managing extremely short-term educational provision for a diverse client group facing daily personal challenges of potential deportation. Anne has recently (2004) been awarded a national STAR award for Outstanding Management of Learning, sponsored by the Centre for Excellence in Leadership (CEL), for her work.

> We must use time creatively – and forever realise that the time is always hope to do great things.
> *Martin Luther King, Jr.*

Anne greeted me at the IRC gates and we walked up to the Education centre, chatting about leadership and education in an IRC. An edited version of Anne's replies to the questions I asked now follows.

Case Study of Prison Education Leadership

Anne Morahan, Education Manager, HMP Dover Immigration Removal Centre

Inclusive leadership when there is no tomorrow, but only today, at Dover

How would you categorise overall the organisation/group, and client group in which you are currently a leader?

Dover Immigration Removal Centre is the centre for failed asylum seekers. However, some of them are still fighting their case, some actually do get to stay, but the majority are deported. We are a small education department in comparison with the colleges. The Education Department is run by Kent Adult Education Service. I have 14 members of staff: 6 full time teachers, 7 part time, and one admin assistant. The centre holds up to 316 adult males, aged 18+. At one stage we had 70 different nationalities on the roll on one day. The average length of stay varies but is under a month, so the students are coming and going at quite a rate of knots, really. We run a varied programme within a drop-in centre: detainees can drop-in to education at any time during free flow. The priorities for the detainees are their cases. They might be talking to Immigration, dealing with solicitors, making phone calls or having a visit. After that, if they are not too stressed out, then they'll come to education. Within 'free flow movement', detainees are free to leave the houses, and can wander around the Centre, Education is open 9–11.30 am, 1:45–4:15 pm, and four evenings a week, 6.30–8.00.

Our core subjects are mainly English for speakers of other languages (ESOL) and IT, which we run as a daily programme. We also run Art, Music, Relaxation, Woodcraft classes and short courses such as Food Hygiene, Manual Handling and Heart Start. Short courses are very popular, as people stay long enough to actually complete them. Stress levels and language barriers are the main issues that affect attendance. However many students attend classes regularly and are very keen to learn.

What, in your experience, is the distinction, if any, between leadership and management in post-compulsory education?

Management is the day-to-day running of the department, all the usual things such as data collection, staff management, dealing with problems, speaking to detainees. Leadership is about vision, energy behind the running of the department: strategic direction and vision for the future. The key for me is communication: you have got to be able to communicate. In a centre like this, diversity is also a big issue. You have got to be able to look at the diverse needs of the population.

DIRC is very different from Adult and Prison Education. We have had to change quite a bit since we re-roled, and to look very closely at equality of opportunity to cater for up to 70 different nationalities at one time. Another big issue we have had to look at is motivation to get students in to education. When we were a prison, we would have a set number of students brought to us for the duration and it was 'set out' what they had to do. With Immigration Removal Centres, there is very little structure to the day. Immigration is not interested whether we gain any accreditation, as long as we provide purposeful activity to keep them busy. It's a very different kind of world.

I asked Anne what her overall aims as a leader were:

The first aim was to make the change from the Young Offenders Unit to an IRC. I wanted to raise the profile of Dover Immigration Removal Centre in the local town, because at the time, asylum seekers were getting very bad publicity within the press. We have put events on in the town, had an art display in the local Adult Education Centre, and organised an art sale for the Tsunami Fund. Despite this, we are very isolated at DIRC.

Another aim is to raise the standards in our Education Department and promote equality of opportunity for everyone here. Team building has also been important. I've tried to build a good team, and tried to be fair to my staff. You have got to build up trust within your team. I think it is essential to have got a good team that works together. I also believe it is very important to value the students, and to try to fit everything else we are asked to do around the needs of the students. Rather than stating, *'The Common Inspection* says: You must do this', or *'Skills for Life* says: You must do that', we have tried to look at student need, pick out relevant guidelines for them, and then work backwards. I am quite enthusiastic.

I asked if Anne's values had changed. She said that with asylum seekers, motivation continues to be key. Standards of education, drive and enthusiasm to raise standards are always important priorities. Commenting on challenges to leadership, Anne said:

One problem is that we don't fit in anywhere; we are out on a limb, really, in an Immigration and Removal Centre. We are funded from Prisons, so we still obviously have to provide a safe, secure environment, but, with the move from Immigration, they have tried to lessen the regime. It is very much more laid back than prisons as detainees are free to move around the Centre and don't have a set programme. It is also very different from adult education centres as students have access to other facilities to support learning and are more settled within the community and have some idea where they will be living in the future.

Students were very motivated, however. They came to education because they 'wanted to', not because they 'had to'. Anne described the students:

They are very, very polite, incredibly keen to learn and sometimes it is difficult to keep up with all the work that they produce. The detainees haven't had the same education background as English students, they are from different countries and cultures where education is organised differently. They are used to teachers telling them what to do. They find it very difficult when we ask them what they want to do as part of their learning journey, for example when creating ILPs (Individual Learning Plans). Language barriers are another big problem: the ESOL (English as a Second or Other Language) teachers do very, very well, but teaching and managing detainees is very different.

I have had to change a lot. I have had to adopt a different style of leadership which is a much more relaxed kind of style. There was a lot of training before we re-roled covering issues involving detainees and the problems that they face. Sometimes the teachers are more like social workers. Sometimes that becomes more important really, because detainees desperately need someone to talk to. We have to try to reduce the stress levels of our students in order for them to even contemplate learning.

We recently had a full ALI (Adult Learning Inspectorate) inspection and were found to be satisfactory in all areas despite the huge constraints of being a removal centre. Inspection really makes you look at things in a different manner. We were really trying to fit into a 'one size fits all' style of inspection and even the inspectors agreed that we were trying to fit a round peg in a square hole. I found the process of inspection demoralised good teachers, whereas the idea was to raise standards.

The process of inspection was very challenging but the final report was fair and really helped us. It helped to raise standards, and to make changes; it's good to have got fresh pairs of eyes coming in and looking at the situation.

Being a nominee was very challenging, probably the most challenging thing I have had to do; I do think it changes you, makes you look at things differently. It was a worthwhile experience for me. I learned a lot from it. I learned to look at the bigger picture. That was something I wasn't really aware of previously. Take class-room observations, for example: when I go into a classroom, I am looking at what is going on in the classroom with the teacher and the students I was not looking at how the big picture affects what is happening at the lower level. It is unfair however to penalise teachers for things that are out of their control and are really leadership and management issues.

The teachers always ask, 'How can you plan, when you don't even know which students you have got coming in the door tomorrow, because the turnover is so fast?' I have seen teachers spend an hour going through a dictionary, trying to do a very basic ILP with their student, only to find that they are gone the next day. The inspectors were not aware of the problems of running detention centres as we were a pilot inspection, the first IRC to be inspected by ALI, and they could not relate us to anywhere else.

I asked Anne how she would describe her leadership style:

I saw an article on leadership styles talking about change. It said, 'Great idea, let's try it.' I think that's what we do here. We work as a team. I am definitely a relation-ship-builder, I like a hands-on approach; I am not a paper person. I am told I am quite good at problem-solving, and also quite tactful. I think emotional intelligence is quite important for leadership. I asked a teacher to describe my style. She said, 'You work informally as part of a team . . . you explain the end result of what you want to achieve, and then we work together to get to those goals.' So that's how we try to work. We are quite a close-knit team. I am definitely not one of those people who can sit in an office, develop plans and then say, 'Right, this is what we are going to do. Off you go and do it!' That's not me at all.

Anne noted that leadership has to be distributed in a team and you needed an effective blend of skills:

We have a good team at Dover, a really good mix. Everybody puts something in: they are all committed in one way or the other. Distributed leadership is important, but ultimately you have to take the responsibility don't you? If things go wrong, I take the responsibility, but it doesn't mean to say I have to do everything.

I asked Anne about her mission and vision and if she felt these had been achieved:

Did you see that we have our statement on the gate when you come in? The mission statement is to treat the detainees humanely with respect and value their cultural and diverse needs, whilst providing purposeful activity. So it is quite a nice statement for what we are trying to achieve here, and education is a part of it. I have a lovely letter here from a detainee from Turkey we received this morning. He said:

> Dear All the ESOL Teachers,
> Thank you very much.
> You are all gold, from my heart.
> I was in Dover, very interesting.

We do a very good job here. We have a postcard system so we can forward certificates. Education is very important; the students get a very good education. I think we have improved a great deal. We have done well. We can't measure ourselves by accreditation, but we can look at how many people have finished separate units. The short length of stay affects achievement. If people stayed longer, we would get a lot more accreditations: that's obvious really.

The Education Department was very run down when we took over, so the first thing we did was redecorate it to try to make the environment here the same as any adult education centre; we removed the bars from the fronts of the windows. We have an open door policy, so people can literally come and go: it is very welcoming. We have different types of music up on the landing from different cultures, and we've tried to make it a relaxed educational environment.

I have got a very loyal, hard-working, qualified workforce. I am very lucky to have a well-qualified and experienced workforce; it really has made a difference. We have quite a low staff turnover; the average length of service here is six years, which is quite good.

However, Anne went on to describe the major problem of turnover among students:

Retention. It is a massive problem: *there is no tomorrow at Dover.* That makes planning really impossible. You can do a lesson plan for a group of students you had in today, only to find you have got a completely different group at different levels come in tomorrow morning. A massive problem. I wish I had the answer to it, but I don't. It is difficult. The issue is with the continual changeover and the constant change in student need, which is the reason why Immigration do not push us to gain accreditation, or set key performance targets.

> Retention ... is a massive problem. There is no tomorrow at Dover.
>
> *Anne Morahan*

We are merely asked to provide 'purposeful activity'. We haven't done only that. We could have just sat back and said, 'OK, we'll just do that, and we won't worry about standards or anything', but at the same time Kent Adult Education, the OLSU[i] (Offenders' Learning and Skills Unit) and ALI all demand good standards.

Detainees go off to court, so they may suddenly hear their pager ringing, and are gone. The detainees are all fighting their cases, so there is no continuity. Yet some people get stuck here, if they come in on forged passports or something, and they are waiting to get new documents from their country of origin, then they can be here quite a while, but – you don't *know*, that's the problem.

Anne described how, during an inspection, a third of the students changed over in the week:

When we had the inspection, a third of the Centre stayed for less than seven days during that week. So, literally, a third of the Centre changed over in a week. It can become quite stressful. If they stay for a while, you get to know them, and then you don't know where they've gone. We get quite a lot of letters from detainees after they've gone, saying what they are doing, how they are getting on.

The detainees are really keen to learn and work really hard. They are a pleasure to teach. So you do get rewards. We also get some colourful characters coming through. The teachers *are* coping with the massive turnover, although sometimes it does get to them. Sometimes you wonder what exactly happens to detainees. They tell you about their personal situations, which are heartbreaking, and they suddenly disappear. You don't know what happened. That can be difficult.

I asked Anne about critical drivers of achievement relating to Dover:

> We are probably the only place in the country that doesn't have key performance targets. They are set at zero.
>
> *Anne Morahan*

Targets? I would just like to say we don't have any here. This is probably the only place in the country that doesn't have key performance targets! They are set at zero. It was agreed when they were re-enrolling, because of the short length of stay, and a variety of other factors, that we wouldn't have any targets. We have however set our own internal targets as part of our quality assurance process and they are quite challenging.

Cultural diversity and the need for 'incredible flexibility'

Dover is one of the most culturally diverse centres there is. We have got people from literally everywhere across the world coming into education for a short period

> Dover is one of the most culturally diverse centres that there is.
>
> *Anne Morahan*

of time, people of all levels, people with degrees down to people who have not even got a written language in their own country, so it is very diverse. You need to be a special type of teacher to work here. You must be incredibly flexible, be able to think on your feet and have a range of things at your fingertips that you can pull out at the drop of a hat.

Lesson planning is very difficult. You can have all the plans you like, but I do not think I have ever sat through one teaching observation where it has gone to plan. Once in a blue moon you may get to do the lesson you planned for the students but it is very rare because of continual disruptions throughout lessons. Sometimes detainees have medical appointments or are called to see Immigration. Because of stress levels religious needs are also heightened, so in the middle of a lesson they will say, 'We are just going to the mosque to do our prayers' and come back 20 minutes later. That makes the planning of education very difficult.

In a day we could have between 70 to 110 students. We are busier in the afternoons than the mornings as detainees can sleep in. One of our big problems is identifying students with dyslexia or other special needs. We have a special needs teacher with a diploma in Specific Learning Difficulties. We purchased a range of equipment to support special needs students and have the facility to provide one-to-one support. With non-English speaking students, it's very difficult to pick out whether they don't understand, because 'they don't understand', or because 'they don't understand because they have special needs'.

> Kind words can be short and easy to speak, but their echoes are truly endless.
>
> *Mother Teresa*

When I go into classes, I see that we offer good support to individual learners. The tutors are really good with the students. There are good relationships being forged. Student feedback is always good. We devised a very simple survey that has been translated. We give the students the opportunity to write their own comments, in their own language, at the bottom; we then spend the next month trying to translate it! Some of the comments are really good: 'Good teachers, new skills, I learn a lot'. I thought that was quite nice.

Anne explained the need to stand back to measure achievement:

Sometimes you get bogged down with the sheer turnover of it all. You have to stand back and say, 'What have we achieved?' If you can't measure it in qualifications, you can measure it in other ways. How do you measure success? What are you looking for? Sometimes, the fact that they come here, and are concentrating on their lessons, instead of sitting in their rooms being really depressed, is an achievement, you know. We encourage students to get involved despite high stress levels within the Centre. We have a lot of student work displayed around in the Centre, especially in the care suites and are continually trying to reduce stress levels around the Centre. We have a relaxation class on a Wednesday to help detainees cope with their problems.

> Sometimes the fact that they come here and are concentrating on their lessons instead of sitting in their rooms being really depressed is an achievement.
>
> *Anne Morahan*

Anne said she had introduced a 'Quality calendar' following the launch of these at the OLSU. This had been very successful, as had a range of other measures:

I've kept it very simple, Quality assurance is mapped out through the year and provides a structure that has helped us raise standards. The Quality Improvement group meets regularly to monitor and plan improvements. We used our student surveys to find out whether detainees would like to have structured lessons, or whether they preferred to be able to drop in. The detainees like our internal certificates. They are especially for students who complete work but do not stay long enough to gain a formal certificate. They look quite nice and are quite colourful. We also have a 'Student of the Month Award'. Every month we nominate a student, put their photograph on the board and pay them a small reward. Simple things like this really help to motivate students and encourage participation.

Summary

A brief discussion of some aspects of 'inclusive leadership' introduces the interview with Anne Morahan, Education Manager at Dover Immigration Removal Centre. Anne and her team are working hard to ensure detainees have very good support in education, but the situation is difficult in terms of the temporary and diverse nature of the client group. The team is achieving much, and has set up a number of schemes to motivate and reward students while they pass through the Centre. Detainees have expressed appreciation and are willing to learn, but teaching is difficult: there are no performance targets because 'there is no tomorrow at Dover'. Anne's team do the best they can in these difficult circumstances.

Keywords

HMP Immigration and Removals Centre, South East England, inclusive leadership, extremely diverse client group, no targets, quality model for supporting diversity.

Further reading and resources

Blank, W. (1995) *The Nine Natural Laws of Leadership*. New York: American Management Association.

Kugelmass, J.W. (2003) *Inclusive Leadership; Leadership for Inclusion, International Practitioner Inquiry Report*. London: National College for School Leadership.

Ryan, J. (2006) *Inclusive Leadership*, Jossey-Bass Leadership Library Set. San Francisco, CA: Jossey-Bass.

Wilson, A. (2003) *Inclusive Leadership*. Berkhamsted: Ashridge Centre for Business and Society. Available at http://www.ashridge.org.uk/www/ACBAS.nsf/web/Publications/$file/InclusiveLeadership.pdf

Note

i See http://www.dfes.gov.uk/offenderlearning/, accessed 7 August 2005.

Movers and shakers: skills empowerment leadership

> **❝ I have a really evangelistic fervour that education can make a big difference in your life, and I am passionate about that: I believe it. ❞**
> Daniel Khan

The skills empowerment approach

The skills approach to leadership does not concentrate on innate personality, but speaks to us of the equal potential of every human being to grow leadership characteristics (Northouse, 2004, p.35), and the empowerment to individual people's lives that can come from that. It is a businesslike people-focused approach also inclusive of multiple community perspectives. The skills approach was one of the first leadership models to stress the importance of the acquisition of 'leadership competencies' in terms of skills which could be taught. It therefore radically opens out the potential for leadership training to everyone, regardless of background.

Professor Daniel Khan's absolute insistence on equality, diversity and high quality provision in his leadership as Principal of The Grimsby Institute of Further and Higher Education is a way of seeing leadership that is to me reminiscent of the skills approach. Daniel describes himself as 'evangelistic' in his desire to help people change their lives through education. Having grown up in the Caribbean from a family in which his father could not afford to leave the children much money, he remembers his father saying, 'What I will leave you all is an education'. Empowered with this education, all his children made a success of their lives, achieving advanced skills that have served them well throughout life.

The skills leadership model was initially conceptualised by Katz (1955) as a three-skill model including technical skill, human skill and conceptual skill, all of which were variously distributed at different levels in the hierarchy of organisations. It was further elaborated by Mumford *et al.* (2000), who developed a more complex capability model looking at the relationship between leadership capabilities and performance. The skills approach emphasises the capabilities of leaders that make good leadership possible, rather than focusing on what leaders do (for example, transformational leadership, the style approach).

> If you come here and get a skill and get trained, you could make your way in life. Don't waste your life!
>
> *Professor Daniel Khan*

To carry out the skills approach well, there is a need to ensure that 'human skill' is equally represented at all hierarchical levels. When I interviewed him in Grimsby, Daniel stressed the importance of teamworking at every level of the College. He said that he wanted staff to take responsibility for resolving petty disputes harmoniously, and to find solutions to problems that they raised with him. When staff came to see him about a problem, he stressed the importance of not whinging about this uselessly, but asked staff to find solutions to their own problems, so that problem-solving capabilities – leadership outcomes of the skills model – were achieved. Essentially, the skills approach is about empowering people in proactive and positive ways to live the best lives they can achieve. As Daniel put it:

> The passion for education, empowering people so they can actually make something of their lives, has been the overall driver.

The skills approach is also particularly appropriate for the Grimsby Institute of Further and Higher Education in view of the large amount of work-based training, many successful links with employers, partner educational providers and community agencies the College has, and its important role serving local communities in the region. My case study notes and interview with Daniel, recorded here, demonstrate this in more detail. An edited version of Daniel's replies to the questions I asked now follows:

Case Study of Business and Community Leadership

Professor Daniel Khan, Principal and CEO, The Grimsby Institute of Further and Higher Education

'What I will leave you all is an education'

How would you categorise overall the institution and client group of which you are currently a leader?

> We have had significant growth over four years. We take anyone who comes to us, with qualifications, or without: it does not matter. Whatever the person's level, we

try to find a programme for them. We have an amazing range of courses. When I joined here in 2000, we had about 800 courses. We now have around 1500. We have from 12 year old excluded children to Master's degree students and over 5000 employees. We teach in factories and businesses through our Workforce Development Unit to well over five to six hundred companies. The range is unbelievable. That's what I find most exciting about the job, that we could provide such a vast range of programmes, and cover such wide age groups. Last year, we had an adult learner at 84 years of age who learned to surf the net. So, from 12 years excluded to 84 year old grandma, and all ages in between, all ranges, all levels. So we try to be all things to all people in terms of education, within the sphere of our influence and ability: it really is *an open access institution.*

What, in your experience, is the distinction, if any, between leadership and management in post-compulsory education?

In terms of the leadership role in the College, Daniel said this had to be a role with 'vision and strategic overview, that sets an example, is the driving force in business development, taking decisions as to the positioning of the institution'. By contrast, Daniel noted, 'Management is very much more about managing the affairs of the institution, resources, courses: looking at issues for retention and achievement; managing budgets, making sure of quality'. He went on to say:

> We all have a vision that means we help quality, but you have got to really manage that to make sure teaching quality is good, the resource quality for students is good. That is very much a management role. Leadership can, actually, look at the strategic issues, set mission statements, but the truth is the entire institution has to deliver the management of it. Because management is so complex, it's not just about people in senior positions, it's about everybody, a lecturer in his class managing lessons plans, delivery, to make sure it meets that overall objective of being good quality and a good interface with students. Managing the learning process is crucial. The people who do that are the lecturers. I see leadership as *facilitating* the management of learning programmes.
>
> My main aim is that we must have quality provision. I will not accept substandard provision. Quality is my main driver. So quality is first and foremost, but you can only have that with excellent staff. We really believe in good physical resources, a good physical environment. We believe partnership with local companies, showing them what we could do to help them, is important, but so is partnership with the local authority, the local schools. We want to be known as a good quality provider that is responsive. I am an accountant by training, but finance is only a tool of the means to the learning process. We adopt the 'five loaves and two fishes principle' here. We try to stretch resources as much as possible with the results we get.

David explained his belief that education can change people's lives:

I spoke about my belief that education can actually change people's lives, improve the quality of their lives. I spoke to the local bishop and his vicars and said, 'I believe our businesses are very similar, because through spiritual realm and religion they hope to change people's lives, in terms of happiness and satisfaction. In terms of education, I hope we achieve the same, make people happy, with better prospects, higher quality of life.' When I finished, the Bishop of Grimsby said, 'I wish my vicars had the evangelistic fervour you have.' I have a really evangelistic fervour, that education can make a big difference in your life, and I am passionate about that; I believe it, so that whenever I speak people come up and say that it just shows through.

'What I will leave you all is an education'

I grew up in the Caribbean. My Dad always said to me, because we were not very wealthy, we just made ends meet, he said to me, 'I can never leave you lots of money, but what I will leave you all is an education, and that will make sure you all have a good quality life'. And I never forget that. And so today I have my brothers – one is a doctor – I have two sisters who are teachers, and I have another brother who runs his own business, and that's come from Dad, and Mum, that if you just give a child an education they can make their way in life. I have captured that passionately, that philosophy, not just for my kids, but for all kids.

Daniel described how he urges his students to make the most of their opportunities:

If you come here and get a skill and get trained, you could make your way in life. Don't waste your life! The passion for education, empowering people so they can actually make something of their lives, has been the overall driver. It's the real valuing of students, as learners, as 'customers'. Another aim is valuing staff, because staff have to help us deliver that objective. If you don't have good quality staff, you can be the most inspirational leader in the world; you can inspire people who won't do a very good job. You have got to be followed up with good staff. I believe in trust and integrity in all that we do is important as well.

Daniel told me about his efforts to ensure that there was no discrimination in his institution:

We must produce equal opportunities for all. We will have no discrimination here. Grimsby is 99.4% white, and yet, in the sector, we were shortlisted last year for our work on equality and diversity. We promote the diversity agenda tremendously: that is another issue of our growing international side. It is a very inclusive agenda. It is challenging because, when you are trying to work in an organisation like this, with over 20,000 students, and say *everybody* must have an opportunity: we expect excellence in some, but we expect people who have never progressed to be able to learn and at least progress; then it is such a challenge.

I started off a career in education on the finance side, but as you go up the ladder, and especially when you become Chief Executive and Principal, you realise every aspect of the organisation has to be working. The overriding interest has to be learners and the achievement of their outcomes, and that they feel they have bene-fited by coming to the Institute. I am very much people-focused. I mix with the stu-dents a lot, talk to them, find out what difficulties they have, how do they find the Institute, what they think we can do better, how they are finding their learning. I am very conscious that if employers write to me on any issue, I right away act on it. I am very much focused on students.

I have really seen how a local institution could make a significant contribution to local economy, the skills base and the local education agenda. That is why I am so excited about this job; I really believe we can make a difference to the people around, who live within the vicinity of this institution.

I am very open in my leadership style. My style is very encouraging and support-ive. It is very innovative. I don't care if it hasn't been done before, if that's what we feel we should be doing, we will do it. It is risk-taking, at times, but not in a stupid sense, in terms of a balanced judgement. So that is my leadership style, very expan-sive. When I joined this Institute, they planned to reduce it by about 20%; we have increased it by about 70%, which shows we have virtually doubled the size of what was planned. That is because I always look at new things, new developments, new ways of experimenting and with learning. So we do a lot of support, but the leader-ship style is quite a strong leader who does not accept poor performance because quality is paramount, and who is not afraid to take hard decisions. So it is a nice sup-portive environment but there is an underlying toughness and strength in that we know where we are going, we know what we are setting out to do, and we will ensure those aims and objectives are achieved. I will intervene if things are not working, but if they are working well I am very much hands off; 'you develop it, because I have lots of other things I want to do, but we won't deter from intervening if I feel and hear a division is not performing'.

We have no kind of politicking. If someone has a complaint about someone else, I bring them together. At the end of the day we are here for the learners, we are not here to fill out forms and have grievances. So if someone comes to me and says, 'I have got a problem,' I say, 'Well, tell me some of the solutions you think we could implement.' It is empowering people to think for themselves and not thinking that solutions just drop out of the air. That helps people develop their own selves, and in their own

> If someone comes to me and says, 'I have got a problem,' I say, 'Well, tell me some of the solutions you think we could implement.' It is empowering people to think for themselves ...
>
> *Professor Daniel Khan*

personal lives, so that if you have got a problem, well there is a solution, because to everything in life there is a solution.

In religion you could have a charismatic leader and he could have a big congre-gation, and his charisma keeps that institution going, but education is not like that. *One* individual cannot keep it going and even one individual, in religion, if he does the whole thing. If it is not built on a sound basis, it falls apart. Education leaders should be charismatic, without a doubt, in terms of being able to really encourage people on, but the actual *leadership role*, and that is the difference between a 'leader' and a 'leadership role', because the leadership role has to be throughout the whole organisation. So I have a strategic management team, and they are invaluable because each of them have strengths that they bring that completes what I regard as the leadership in terms of a strategic management team.

I have 21,000 learners, and everyone is a different individual. We have 1200 staff, but staff are highly skilled, very intelligent and professionals in their own right. Empowering them, but also making them feel and believe, because it's true that they have just as much role in the success of an organisation as you, as the principal or chief executive, is one of the big challenges. The other big challenge is making sure students are fully committed to their programmes and remain focused. The job is challenging, which is why it is so exciting. If it was dull and boring with no challenge, I wouldn't be here.

Our main overall vision is really about being first class, customer focused and dynamic, to be a 'dynamic provider for education and skills'. We aim to be first class, and will not tolerate or accept sub-standard qualities at work. And we must be dynamic.

Our penetration is unbelievable: the population around here is 160,000, and with the villages about 200,000, so you can see with 1300 staff and 20,000 students, how this Institute is one of the focuses of the local community. If you are successful, people want to be part of that story.

We have achieved our mission and vision, and have external evidence to prove this. In terms of quality, we had an Ofsted inspection last year which was very good. For leadership and management they had some very kind words, generally in most of our areas, gradings were very encouraging, very good quality grades; we have had a higher education QAA – all inspections have been good. We also have four centres of vocational excellence. We have also won Beacon Awards; every year for the last three years we have won a Beacon Award from the Association of Colleges. We are a Grade A college, financially, and for the last four years since I have been here we have had surpluses.

Things that helped me to achieve success include the good quality team we have. I talk a lot about the quality of teaching, but quality of facilities and staff as well is important. That is number one, our success with our staff. We have also had a very supportive board of governors. Another area of success is because we have addressed customer needs. If that is what the customer wants, then we need to provide it. We have been particularly successful in workforce development.

The most critical drivers of achievement in post-compulsory education are effective understanding of the needs of the learners/customers: right products, horses for courses. Don't have a standard provision. Our relationship with learners is critical: we must be excellent in delivery. Exploiting the resources we have, we must be really good in supporting learners, not just with resources, but with learning support. Excellence in delivery in the quality of the programme, but also very good detail supporting learners' needs. An open access policy, being very flexible, open access, being an inclusive college, making everybody feel welcome: I am very strong on that. I have said to my staff, 'What I want from you is loyalty to the learners and the Institute, in that we share the vision of what they come here for, what we are trying to give them, and you actually are sold on that vision, and parity of esteem of any element of training we do'.

I stop, I talk to them all. I say this at all my graduation speeches, and all presentation speeches to my students: 'Don't let society limit you, don't let peer pressure limit you. You decide what you want for your life. We are here to help you realise that. I commit this Institution, and its staff and its resources, to that purpose. You have got to respect. We will tolerate no discrimination, no sexism, no ageism. All have to be treated the same. I will not tolerate disrespect to anyone, from students or staff. I have told the staff as well that they have got to respect the students. Respecting the dignity of every human being and the dignity of where you live and work, it is just respect for everything. It is all about mutual trust and respect. I believe respect for each other is crucial. Sometimes people think you cannot tell people off. That is a load of rubbish. I will respect you but I will tell you what I think. That is what openness, trust, integrity is all about.

I believe the most important thing for a leader in any education establishment is a passion for learners, for learning, a real passion. Not from educational, theoretical and philosophical points of view, but a real passion that education can change lives, and enable people to have a higher quality of living. I think that is fundamental. You have got to believe in the product, you have got to really believe that education makes a difference. I think that is the most important character.

> I believe the most important thing for a leader in any education establishment is a passion for learners, for learning, a real passion. Not from an educational, theoretical and philosophical point of view, but a real passion that education can change lives and enable people to have a higher quality of living.
>
> *Professor Daniel Khan*

You have got to respond to local needs and respect your learners. You have got to have quality as your driver. You have got to make sure your resources are balanced with the aims and objectives. You could be a visionary, and have all the vision in the world; it's no point if you can't deliver it. You *must* make sure you are able to deliver your vision. I never say anything to the staff, the students or the public if I believe we can't deliver it. Whatever we say publicly, we deliver it.

I think also you must work as a team. You cannot ever have success or achievement in an organisation if the entire organisation doesn't work together as a team. I *really* believe in that. I think that is sometimes missing in the public sector. It is only with that 'togetherness' can we actually focus on our vision and mission.

'Every learner matters'

I think one of our most biggest challenges is to make sure our staff believe in the learners. Don't limit your learners, don't have preconceived conceptions. We must always believe any individual we have has that human potential to develop, not only to achieve something in their life, but they can also change the world with their achievements if we work with them, nurture them and get the best out of them. One of the skills of leadership is actually being able to inculcate that belief in their staff, that *every learner matters*, and *every learner is our responsibility, individually and collectively*. So they have that vision.

We try to be very positive, I try to be in my attitude and always say we are going for it, we will do it, we will achieve it and, when you hit the problems, you think it through, life has hurdles, otherwise how will you ever develop if you do not have some challenges and hurdles, and you do not give up, you keep plugging on.

But what you do is you do it in a positive light, in a positive approach. Life is too short to be depressed. Get on with the business of delivering and moving forward, see how we can improve people's lives, because we have only one life here, and it is not for long. I really have no time for bickering. I just cut it, slash it. I just say there is an issue, let us sit down, let's discuss it, make a decision and move on. What we say here is, forget those small grudges, look at the big picture; we could provide people who could change this world, if we have the right positive attitude, and get rid of all the niggling nonsense that people spend half their lives worrying about, which everyone should realise isn't important.

Summary

A discussion of the skills empowerment approach in leadership introduces the interview with Professor Daniel Khan, Principal and CEO of the Grimsby Institute of Further and Higher Education. Daniel discusses his approach to leadership, and experience with values clarification and empowerment in learning. He places students at the heart of everything, believing strongly that 'every learner matters', and asserts the values of authenticity, vulnerability, trust, honesty and integrity in leadership, placing a high priority also on economic efficiency. Deriving from the Caribbean, Daniel's missionary zeal to educate students for empowerment was inspired by his father, who said to all the children that for his legacy, 'What I will give you all is an education'.

Keywords

College of FE/HE, North East England, skills empowerment approach, learner-centred, economic efficiency, Beacon college.

Further reading and resources

Block, P. (1987) *The Empowered Manager: Positive Political Skills at Work.* San Francisco, CA: Jossey-Bass.

Bolman, L.G. and Deal, T.E. (1995) *Leading With Soul: An Uncommon Journey of Spirit.* San Francisco, CA: Jossey-Bass.

Covey, S.R. (1991) *Principle-Centered Leadership.* New York: Summit Books.

Northouse, P.G. (2004) *Leadership Theory and Practice* (third edition). London: SAGE Publications Ltd.

14

Guiding lights: ethical leadership

66What I have always tried to assert is quality and student success. I feel very strongly when students come here, they enter into a kind of understanding with the college. There's a strong moral dimension to this.99
Bob Challis

Ethical leadership

Rubenstein (2004, p.1) observes in relation to ethical leadership that there is a problem with the multicultural definition of ethics – what some cultures consider ethical, others don't. So there is no *one* universally adequate definition of ethics, nor could there be. Nevertheless, there are, despite this, generally upheld standards of human behaviour which most cultures and peoples internationally would agree could be termed 'ethical'. There is a greater danger in being ethically neutral or indeterminate than in upholding moral relativism or ethical neutrality for the want of agreement on finer points of multicultural differences. It is critically important for leadership to establish generally publicly acceptable good principles, values and standards of behaviour to ensure the well-being of the institutions and followers under their influence.

Rubenstein notes that conceptions of 'ethical leadership' have mainly been envisaged from a negative perspective – for example, in business school courses about the dangers of unethical leader behaviour. Putting forward a new definition of ethical leadership emphasising the importance of long-term, reliable, repeatable standards of beneficial actions, Rubenstein (2004, p.2) pro-

> Leadership is the creation and fulfilment of worthwhile opportunities by honourable means.
> *Herb Rubenstein*

poses that ethical leadership can be summed up in the statement: 'Leadership is the creation and fulfilment of worthwhile opportunities by honourable means'.

Useful as this definition is, it lacks detailed information on wider principles and practices appropriate to ethical issues in leadership, as outlined, for example, by Northouse (2004, pp.301–29). Northouse puts forward five principles of ethical leadership: 'respect, service, justice, honesty and community', discussing the centrality of ethics to leadership and considering the approaches of Heifetz (1994), Burns (1978) and Greenleaf (1970, 1977) to ethical leadership. Linking ethics and leadership back to the work of Aristotle, Northouse provides a useful commentary on ethics in leadership which outlines the following standards of behaviour: Ethical leaders:

- respect others
- serve others
- are just
- are honest
- build community.

Northouse then observes:

> . . . leadership is not an amoral phenomenon. Leadership is a process of influencing others; it has a moral dimension that distinguishes it from other types of influence, such as coercion or despotic control. Leadership . . . is not a process that can be demonstrated without showing our values. When we influence, we have an effect on others – and that means we need to pay attention to our values and our ethics.
>
> (Northouse, 2004, p.317)

Selection of case study: Bob Challis from Abingdon and Whitney College

I selected the case study interview with Bob Challis, for many years Principal of Abingdon and Whitney College prior to his recent retirement, to exemplify ethical leadership because the interview with Bob indicated a strong moral dimension to leadership, focused on student success. This was combined with interest in coaching for leadership development, demonstrating the value of 'building community', not only in the College, but in the communities of leaders present and future.

Scrutinising moral value systems to avoid 'bad faith'

An example of the way in which Bob has scrutinised moral actions on the part of the leadership of his College is his statement:

> If the College doesn't believe sincerely that they can achieve that goal and that they the College can help them and make sure it happens, then there is serious bad faith in there somewhere.

Bob felt strongly that the College must treat students properly and appropriately throughout their studies and that was a key 'mission' of all the provision. Providing particular support to those who have formerly had least access to education – the key purpose of a moral dimension in provision through widening participation following the Kennedy report, *Learning Works*, in 1987 is another of his criteria for an inclusive, responsive agenda for the College. Bob also expressed particular scepticism with 'heroic leadership'. I interviewed Bob at the College just prior to his retirement from many successful years as a principal. An edited version of his replies to the questions I asked now follows.

Case Study of Rural/Market Town FE Leadership

Bob Challis, Retired Principal of Abingdon and Whitney College

Believing sincerely in quality and student success at Abingdon and Whitney

How would you categorise the institution and client group of which you are currently a leader?

I would say that the College in a nutshell is a general further education college focused on principally southern and western Oxfordshire for some of our work, the whole county for some of our work, beyond that, of course, the region and further, in certain areas of expertise. The college has 3500 FTE students, 600 staff, and a budget of £14.5m. It owns or leases six major sites, including two farms, and runs courses in 40 more. Student success rates are high. We have a student body which is 93% white British: of those 7%, probably about 3% are international students; the population around here is about 1.2% minority ethnic group; we've got about 4% minority ethnic group in the full time student population plus international students. The college sets out to be 'a source of learning of undisputed quality for towns and rural communities in Oxfordshire.'

I'd say the College's particular *strengths* are the quality of what we do, judged by the success of our students, by the usual indicators, which I fully support: I'm in very strong favour of standard, benchmarked indicators for student success. We are the only general FE college in the South East to have achieved accredited status under the FEFC. I think our ability to respond to our locality is also strong. I think our ability to work with other providers and other partners in a way that makes them feel confident that we are getting somewhere is another strength, too. So I would say we are a general FE college, but with certain particular distinctive features.

What, in your experience, is the distinction, if any, between leadership and management in post-compulsory education?

There is a growing distinction in common usage between leadership and management, that 'management' is the task-centred, and that 'leadership' is the more fundamental, the more far-reaching, the more process-orientated, the longer term timescale, etc. If that's the way the usage is going, I can live with it, because it's the English language, but there is also a very strong political slant to much of this.

I don't believe that anybody really spoke of *leadership* until about seven or eight years ago in this kind of public sector. And even if you consider the old *FEFC Inspection Framework*, it was 'management', not 'management and leadership'. One of my concerns is that this very persuasive definition of leadership has now come in which is very much the distinctive, potentially heroic, leader who, if not telling people what to do, because that is so 'last century', nevertheless inspires them to want to do it anyway, and without them. And so if it's a success, then ultimately the glory comes back to the leader from whom it originated and if it's not, the leader must go.

I find that model of how organisations work very dubious and I have got concerns. So this present government, I would say, does use that model of leadership extensively and uses the term to designate that kind of model, so I recognise the common usage, but I do reject the slant our politicians have given it.

It's got beyond telling people what to do – that obviously is not at all in tune with the times, quite rightly – but has become now the role of *inspiring others to do what you want them to do and to the extent that you're successful, it's because you've inspired them not just to work hard and not just to work skilfully, but in the service of the goals you have shared with them*. The whole language and concept of 'the leader develops a vision and shares it with the people', I don't feel is a very effective way of looking at how organisations ought to be led or managed in the future. It's the hijacking of the term I find a little tricky.

Bob explained the College's priorities of quality and student success:

What I have always tried to assert, first of all, is quality and student success, particularly student success. I feel very strongly that when students come here, they are entering into a kind of understanding with the College. There's a strong moral dimension to this.

It's not a 'generating the cash' or 'achievement and funding' issue: it's the moral issue that if a student for any particular purpose joins the College to achieve some particular goal, if the College doesn't believe sincerely that the student can achieve that goal, and that they, the College, can help them and make sure it happens, then there's serious bad faith in there somewhere. Any areas where students tend not to succeed need very close looking at. The first priority for the College has to be the proper growth and success of the students who join us. I'd say the outcomes, benefits and

> The first priority for the college has to be the proper growth and success of the students who join us.
>
> *Bob Challis*

results for students are the highest priority for the College. Every student is entitled to succeed. If they don't, it's failure for us. Even if it isn't our fault, it's a failure for us.

Bob explained his belief in the need for unremitting effort to achieve quality and student success:

It's unremitting, the effort needed at any level to achieve quality and student success. At course level, at school level, or at college level, for there to be high student success rates . . . it is absolutely day in, day out and it's everybody. This is why I think a college that takes seriously how can we *really* be an outstanding college for our students has a much, much more complicated and much harder task I think than sometimes is presented.

Bob offered some suggestions for avoiding a drift towards expediency:

There can be a drift away from student success towards expediency, a drift towards 'bums on seats', because one of the hardest things is to get consistency in messages. To balance recruitment demands with the quality message is quite difficult. This comes on to the business of *focus*. How do you focus on what's really important? How do you identify what's really important? Is it agreed by others that it's really important? It took me a while, I think, to realise that certain things were very simple. It's much clearer to me now what the Principal's role can be.

'The importance of values is undeniable'

The 'values bit' is really important. Yes, I would say that, though I'm not sure about the logic of it, the importance of values is undeniable. I've come to realise the depth, or the importance and the profundity of some of these things, which I wouldn't have realised before.

I would say if there's been a change over the years, it's been towards the belief that you can be a lot simpler in terms of the values you assert. I've certainly changed in that I've been increasingly, over the years, realising that you can start putting student success much more centrally, in terms of people's lives, and that one mustn't be diverted from that. Before that, I saw it as more complicated than I do now, as an issue; I was probably more open to 'trophies' than I think I am now.

> The 'values bit' is really important . . . the importance of values is undeniable. I've come to realise the depth, or the importance and profundity of some of these things, which I wouldn't have realised before.
>
> *Bob Challis*

'Don't stop short' – the difficulty of implementation

So I believe I've got a more serious understanding of what these things actually mean than I had in the past. I think the question that comes in is – *don't stop short* – the huge importance and the difficulty of implementation. I think the shift comes in knowing how to make these things stick throughout the organisation. It's seeing how some of those things work in reality, I think, that change over the years: the values become simultaneously more complex and more straightforward.

'Reaching "the hard to reach" – the joy of learning'

The next College priority is *finding ways of reaching people who otherwise may not engage in learning.* I get very passionate about the *joy of learning* and about the importance of it – the emancipatory, liberating effects of learning. Although I'm interested obviously in the economic skills aspects of learning, the immediate and visible aspects of learning that you have in a college are the individual ones. The publication of Kennedy's report, *Learning Works*, on widening participation in 1997 was in my view still one of the seminal moments in FE history. People still haven't quite realised the implications of the Kennedy report. Certainly it's not this year's fashion. 'Social inclusion' is not the same thing, though it's a pretty good thing, and certainly not skills strategy stuff. I'd say that's the second priority: trying to find ways of doing widening participation, social justice.

> I get very passionate about the joy of learning and about the importance of it – the emancipatory, liberating effects of learning.
>
> *Bob Challis*

The question of defining what counts as student success in this context is tricky. There are lots of busy words talked about this. These can result in excuses to ourselves for not following through in terms of widening participation. It's very easy to drift away from widening participation. Because the immediate imperatives now are the quality issues, which of course don't encourage you to go looking for the people who might be harder to bring in. There's no difference between recruiting 'the hard to find' and recruiting 'the easy to find', for any of the indicators that we're working on. Assuming that you don't take the route of only offering the courses that people can do well in, of course, which is one way to become outstanding, as we know.

Bob stressed the importance of College values – openness, respect, fairness, honesty and trust:

The third priority comes down to the people *who work in an institution and how they ought to be treated and feel about it.* This gets increasingly difficult the bigger the institution is. The values are about openness, an *active openness for the community* – always behave to everybody, all students, all potential students, everybody in the community and each other in the college, the staff, with proper respect for them as individuals and members of the same species. There's something here about *fairness*, which I feel quite strongly about, in terms of fairness-come-justice, I mean both about how people are treated, but also particularly about how we bear ourselves in relation to people in the community.

I can go with trust. I can go with honesty. Honesty is part of that. I subscribe to the truth and nothing but the truth. I don't subscribe to the *whole truth*, because I don't think that's always possible. I suppose the most important values would be *doing right by our students and doing right by the people in the communities outside that need what we have to offer* – get on your bike and make sure people who come get from us what they need.

Another thing that changed views about leadership was round about the time of the '98 inspection, when we ran on from that for a couple of years and got accredited status. What came up in thinking about running up to inspection is that management finds a way, leaders find a way, to be seen to be putting ourselves and our own self-esteem at risk. It's subjecting yourself to the same exposure and risk as other staff. It can appear to be bad faith to be urging people to take risks themselves and say it's worth it, but not taking any yourself, not exposing yourself to any risk in terms of the opportunity of public failure.

Bob identified the problems of leadership when faced with ambiguity, uncertainty and the 'unknowable':

Leading or managing where the situation is ambiguous and highly uncertain and highly complex, is often *not enjoyable*. Uncertainty and ambiguity in this case is not simply about not knowing enough. It's about it being *unknowable*. I think what it comes down to is that working in those sorts of situations it's the real *texture* of that experience for everybody, where you realise where you cannot be absolutely certain about the benefits of what you are doing, nor can you therefore rationally convince people.

When we announced the merger, the memory I was left with was how good the staff were about it, about why they should have to drive up and down the road to do teaching in different campuses three times a day. Suddenly out of the blue as far as almost every member of staff was concerned, they were going to merge with this College, and bad things happen from mergers as we know. So what I think became apparent after that for these people having to lead it through was, it's a bit like going through a tunnel, in smoke with multiple entrances and exits and that working in that kind of uncertainty, you don't arrive at certainty, you just arrive at a conclusion.

'An investment in trust'

We had a very strong case of a supportive senior team here and the Heads of Study at that time were also very strong. You realise that the quiet years, well not the quiet – there are no quiet years – but the years where you do what you say you are going to do, are a kind of investment. And then when it comes to a time when it's not clear that what you're going to be doing is the right thing, people will go with you if you seem to be acting in good faith and your record shows that you generally meant well and can be trusted. Trust needs continual reinvestment in this way.

I asked Bob about his leadership style:

I try to assert a fairly participative style, a fairly open style, to which people can contribute and have a share in the decisions, often a very strong share in the decisions, but at the same time is recognising the way FE is generally set up and the nature of the environment, so there is still a hierarchy, there's a lot of authority. But with the hyper-importance of those values we talked about, which is the trust, commitment to doing things right to our presence within the communities and the fairness and the quality aspects.

Bob touched on the different roles of enabling and coaching:

Enabling other people to do well what they do and allowing people to get on is important. And there is a fair amount of *coaching* going on, I've coached more and more open over the years. We do a lot of consultation here. Most anybody who has an interest in how the place works can actually join in and take a lot of decisions.

I asked Bob what had helped the College to achieve success:

I'd say the presence in the staff body of outstanding people, and the large number of very, very dedicated people. There is a disposition among the staff here to do what is needed and the next step after that. I think there have been, and are, really very, very good people here who have been able to take on really very challenging tasks. I personally have felt hugely supported by this, and by the quality and the commitment of the senior team. There has also been a very good network and support locally outside the College. The fact that I am constitutionally a fairly optimistic person helps. Another thing that's really been helpful is some understanding of how organisations work. Knowing some of the literature and the theories [on leadership and management] is hugely helpful.

In response to my question about the critical drivers for PCE, Bob said:

My own personal driver is a moral one. I believe it's a moral issue to do with students and entitlement once we've taken them on. What are the drivers outside the institution? It's everything ranging from the fear of Ofsted, reputation in the local communities, and the wish for staff to do well by their students. Staff love seeing students succeed, they love them coming back, they love hearing how well they've done. One of the problems sometimes is that, if teachers haven't experienced success for their students, they don't they won't know what it is and they won't know how good it feels.

Bob expressed the view that more coaching in leadership was needed:

There should be a lot more shadowing and coaching going on. There's very little opening up still between people in senior posts, so I think it would be quite reasonable for there to be internships and somebody to spend two weeks in a college as a kind of 'principal intern'.

Summary

A discussion of ethical leadership introduces the interview with Bob Challis, Principal of Abingdon and Whitney College until September, 2004. Bob placed a very high priority on student success, and on the moral dimension of supporting students to achieve what they came into the College to learn. Bob valued the importance of coaching to encourage and develop staff. He recognised the enormous contribution made by his senior team, and by many talented individuals in the College who helped to achieve success. Wary of 'heroic leadership' models, Bob emphasised strong values, including honesty, integrity and trust. He said he would like to see 'principal internships' being set up for the coaching and support of new leaders. Bob pointed out the many strengths of Abingdon and Whitney College, which achieved Grade 1 for governance in inspection during 1997/8 and was the only college in the South East to achieve accredited status under the FEFC.

Keywords

General FE College, South Oxfordshire-based rural and market town, ethical and coaching leadership approach, learner-centred, economic efficiency.

Further reading and resources

Bennis, W.G. and Nanus, B. (1985) *Leaders: The Strategies for Taking Charge*. New York: Harper & Row.

Burns, J.M. (1978) *Leadership*. New York: Harper & Row.

Greenleaf, R.K. (1970) *The Servant as Leader*. Newton Centre, MA: The Robert K. Greenleaf Center.

Greenleaf, R.K. (1977) *Servant Leadership*. New York: Paulist Press.

Heifetz, R.A. (1994) *Leadership without Easy Answers*. Cambridge, MA: Harvard University Press.

Kennedy, H. (1997) *Learning Works: Widening Participation in FE*. Coventry: FEFC.

Northouse, P.G. (2004) *Leadership: Theory and Practice* (third edition). Thousand Oaks, CA: Sage Publications.

Rubenstein, H. (2004) *Ethical Leadership: The State of the Art*. Article in the CEO Refresher Archives, Toronto: Refresher Publications Inc. Available at: http://www.refresher.com/!hrrethical.html

Roots and all: networked and evidence-based research leadership

> 66Things really can be good, you can overcome obstacles, you really can have excitement, quality and enrichment.99
>
> Andrew Morris

Network leadership

Network leadership is the bringing together of collaborative actions by many people into a fluctuating, decentralised series of team processes and actions linked, sometimes loosely, to a central initiative. The network may be a relatively self-forming system, self-managing and constantly in flux. More or less fragmentary power structures may serve the network, and allegiances between groups and individuals may change rapidly, although there will be some underlying self-interested power structures.

Leadership of a network with a centralised focal point of influence may be through a series of communications initiatives pointing out the advantages of group collaboration, putting forward a vision in which the network strives to participate. The leader or leaders of the network may quickly be in touch with localised parts within a decentralised structure, although the central unit may be relatively weak in coercive terms. Leaders may have energetically created the entire network, but the way in which this has been done may not be directly evident to localised membership, who may regard the network as a free-standing system, not observing any obvious power-structures.

There are a range of different kinds of networks – the 'network' metaphor is of course predominantly used in relation to computing. The Internet is sometimes cited as an example of decentralised power structures in which each part is potentially able to link with many others, yet no one part can be regarded as 'the centre'. The negotiatory power of this kind of network of equals with a central structure that is one of influence rather than positional power (or alternatively with multiple decentralised points of influence) is reliant on trust and self-determinacy: leadership may reside in and stem from any part.

An example of an influential national network which was set up over a number of years is the Learning and Skills Research Network (LSRN), (Hillier and Jameson, 2003). This has regional research networks across the UK, which regularly meet to discuss educational research in PCE. The original architect of this network was Dr Andrew Morris, Director of the National Educational Research Forum (NERF). In his role as a research manager at the Learning and Skills Development Agency 1997–2004, Andrew proposed and set up the LSRN network, with the involvement of multiple colleagues from public sector institutions, including leaders and practitioners from adult education, FE colleges, universities, work-based training agencies, employers' and staff organisations, research groups and representatives from the LSDA and LSC.

A community of practice in research

On account of his energetic and visionary work setting up this research network in the learning and skills sector, I selected the case study interview with Andrew to exemplify this brief portrait of networked leadership. The history of the formation of the LSRN network as a phenomenon has been traced in a number of articles, including in the *Learning and Skills Research Journal* series of research papers collected together and edited by Andrew, originally under the title *College Research*, since 1998 (Hillier and Jameson, 2003). The voluntary nature of this kind of *community of practice*, and its energy, vision and collegiate support to many people created a new movement for educational research in the sector during the period 1997 to 2005, particularly around the concept of 'evidence-based practice', and the way in which this could positively influence performance in colleges. I met with Andrew at NERF in the Sanctuary Building of DfES to discuss some of his ideas on leadership.

> Besides the noble art of getting things done, there is the noble art of leaving things undone.
> The wisdom of life consists in the elimination of non-essentials.
>
> *Lin Yutang*

Case Study of Network Leadership in Educational Research

Dr Andrew Morris, Director, National Educational Research Forum (NERF)

Designing and growing learning: systemic solutions through NERF

Dr Andrew Morris works at NERF in the DfES buildings in Sanctuary Buildings, London. I went to see Andrew there and chatted to him about his role leading educational research. An edited version of Andrew's replies to the questions I asked now follows.

We were talking about leadership research – can you expand on that?

In social science research, one of the weakest areas for evidence base is leadership and management. I know education is relatively weak, but apparently the base in management and leadership is also particularly weak. Serious thinkers in management and leadership can get good, well-paid jobs in industry, so it is difficult to sustain a strong research base in university and the public sector. I wonder if that relates to the tradition of 'gurus' publishing pulp paperbacks about 'ten tips for being a good manager'. I dislike this approach: there's a kind of 'finger pointing' attitude. It puts you in a wrong position as a recipient of somebody else's clever analysis. Which is almost entirely upside down from what you need: slowly growing towards understanding through, essentially, analysis of experience. So it seems to be diametrically opposite to what you need.

How would you categorise your role in NERF, the organisation, and its client group?

I am the programme leader of NERF. It is a unique role, not easy to generalise. The class of things NERF belongs to is best seen across all public policy areas, and internationally, across the developed world. So, across all public services, we are in a period where there is a concern about *evidence for policy and practice*. We share in common with many other countries the issue that the optimism about improving lives of people through public services, health, social care, education that we in the UK associate with the 1945 and 1944 Education Acts has given way to disillusionment that it didn't all work out. Poverty wasn't eliminated, people weren't able to reach their full potential educationally. Specific initiatives to do this, to put it mildly, didn't always work. So, trying to get it right for schools, colleges, children's homes and elderly care homes, we are making the same

> The vision is a clear, longstanding simple view of what users need. It does not change much. It is the view of what learners need, and an optimism to solve problems.
>
> *Dr Andrew Morris*

errors, going through a lot of the same difficulties we have done for decades. It's not just a kind of left/right ideological problem. More controversially, it is not just a money/resources problem, though all these things have a bearing on it. So I think, really, we are surrounded by a kind of disillusionment. It's not money, not politics, not optimism. It is not just goodwill.

The resort now is the concept of *evidence-informed* or *evidence-based action*. The optimistic call was that there would be evidence-based policy and practice. NERF is the way education in England responded, proposed in a report to Government. The Secretary of State, David Blunkett, set it up. Its remit is a very ambitious mission: to develop strategic coherence across research. On a more practical level, it works across the sector of education in a catalytic way, bringing together agents who could improve things, helping to formulate a plan of what they can do together, in the general view of developing coherence. That is our mission, and the assumption that this will lead to improved effectiveness.

What, in your experience, is the distinction, if any, between leadership and management in post-compulsory education?

Unusually, I have developed from the beginning a high regard for the concept of management. I see the word denoting something progressive and liberating. The quality of 'leading' is one of a number of qualities needed by good managers. There are other things like the quality of 'not leading'. The quality of letting others take over and holding back is an important thing. I don't think the verb 'to lead', or the noun 'leader' or the noun 'leadership' are particularly helpful. They seem to focus on areas to do with the individual, or to do with somehow being at the front of things, whereas I think the issues are to do with being in the middle of things, to be concerned with effectiveness and *systemic development*, not individual developments.

Andrew expressed his optimism that one can overcome obstacles and improve life:

My main aim as an education leader has been to improve the lot of the client. Another defining aim is to demonstrate that you really can do things. Things really can be good, you can overcome obstacles, you really can have excitement, quality and enrichment. And that a lot of the dullness of our experience of life is due to blockages, incompetencies, inefficiencies, ineffectiveness. Things that can be remedied: miscommunications, no communications.

Andrew explained how he saw life as a gradual unfolding of potentials:

I have those twofold aims: the main one is for the learner themselves; the second one is demonstration that difficulties can be overcome and things can be done better. It is very optimistic. The values I espouse are to do with people fulfilling themselves. I am a bit more towards the sort of Rousseau romantic view. My broad feelings are that people are born with enormous capabilities and potentials: very rarely do they get properly and fully expressed. I don't mean that pessimistically.

I see life as a gradual unfolding of potentials, rather like biological things, like flowers. I see learning rather like breathing. It's a very ordinary thing, very, very common, happens all the time, and is good for your health. So that's where the optimism is. I just see it as something . . . like we read books, or watch TV, or go for a walk, or see your grandma. This is what learning is. Then you find it doesn't always happen for everybody.

I came into all this because I wanted to be a teacher. I experienced exceptionally good teaching in a primary school when I was nine and ten, and basically thought that was what I wanted to do. Ironically, it was not so much to do with the subject, or with learning – it was really about the *art* of the teacher. It all goes back to Mr Thomas and Mr Ewart, my two junior school teachers.

I was very fortunate. I had a very, very liberal upbringing. So I just learned all day long, with toys, but none of it was pressurised, it wasn't 'performance improving' stuff, I just played. It was all playing: I just played, played, played. So learning and playing were indistinguishable to me. I was like that until I was about eight. I just played all through my life, with other children, on my own, with toys and with gadgets. Anyway, it was fantastic. There were absolutely no boundaries. I didn't have a thing called 'school', different from a thing called 'fun' at home, or fun in the street, it was all one thing. I just did project after project. I made puppets, made a theatre, did electrical wiring for the theatre, built a church out of matchboxes, wrote a book about Mozart, we did collages of fishes and the sea, I learned a poem by Keats, *Autumn of mists and summer fruitfulness*. I learnt maths without any problem, advanced decimals when I was ten. It was all an integrated project-based thing, the teacher was just hovering around, we had lots of resources and worked with each other.

> The short-termism induced by the political cycle means you can do something ineffective ten times over each year, but you can't do something effective over ten years . . . developing a *scientifically-understood* approach to how we help people learn is very difficult.
>
> *Dr Andrew Morris*

That was the best education I had in those two years. All of this would have scored very highly on league tables. The teachers would have got good performance measures. From my point of view, the activity was not divided into subjects or skills. It really was radical, I was in charge, empowered, I just got on with it, and so did my friends. So we just *did*. It was very much an empowering environment. The vital element is the extraordinary levels of *trust* that existed. Basically, I was constructing my own learning environment to a very, very high degree. I can still think of 25 projects I did. I must've been allowed to just beaver away, doing my own thing. I remember structured lessons in Maths, listening to a radio programme about Sunyat Sen, where I learned the word 'iconoclasm': I was ten. I remember dance, music, movement, gym. I remember structured things but, essentially, the overwhelming memories are of seemingly endless numbers of free-ranging projects.

This recurred when I did my PhD. When I did my PhD, I had resource areas, a computer, an X-ray diffractometer, and teams of colleagues in chemistry and biochemistry and molecular biology, and so on. And we all worked together, with these resources, to solve problems, but all the rest, the undergraduate degree, and the secondary education, did not work like this.

Then I think I probably began to realise it wasn't like that for everybody.

So my values are around trying to help out with what the obstruction is, like dealing with somebody who is not fully well, trying to find out what is ailing them, and doing something about it. I am not really comfortable with the whole kind of 'achievement culture'. My values are around playfulness, learning, getting a continuous enjoyment and satisfaction out of all that as part of your life. And getting involved when it doesn't happen for people. I think learning needs to take place. I think that values about learning in its own right are not deeply held very widely. I think this is profoundly problematic. The causes for this have a profoundly negative impact on what we do in education.

So as a child I developed views about things from very positive experiences and very negative experiences of teachers. That was extremely influential. But, as a professional, I was strongly influenced by the experience of poor management at all levels – high, medium and low. Then I found a fantastic job. Unrepeatable, really. I was in at the beginning of a new institution, from scratch, the second person appointed, as Deputy Head, and, remarkably, the Principal was brilliant. So I jumped from a situation where I had a pretty clear insight into what was going wrong, to a situation where I could just simply study excellence.

These things just do seem to go like London buses: they go in groups, you know. If you haven't got strong management, it's weak in every regard. And ironically, if it's good, it's good in almost every regard. It is certainly not the case that I have 'heroes' and 'villains', but these qualities we are after do group together. That explains the very clear, observed fact that organisations can transform, become quite different from the way they were, even with the same staff and the same funding. I have seen organisations where all-round poverty in leadership and management leads to an all-round weak institution. And the reverse, as well. That does clarify this high correlation between institutional performance and leadership: why schools and colleges can be made quite excellent from poor beginnings, and the reverse as well.

'Management' is a function: it is a role, a function. Scientifically, I would call it a 'second order' function. The 'first order' function is teaching in the classrooms, maintaining the buildings, running the office. The second order functions are enabling the first order functions to be carried out I see a logically layered relationship. First order activities can only happen to best effect if you have got the second order activities working well. This is what you see in a well-functioning organisation.

'Leadership' is categorically a completely different thing. Leadership is a personal quality exhibited in different ways by different kinds of people. It is more like the way you use your voice: it's an attribute, really, not a function. In terms of my own leadership, for me the word *facilitation* comes to mind, 'easing things', 'bringing together'. Also, 'investigating', or 'trying out': a kind of 'let's have a go kind of approach', seeing options for the way forward, seeing the way to do things, not *the* way – seeing *ways*. There are all sorts of different leadership 'styles'. There are a few nostrums everybody agrees – it is about 'facilitating', about 'seeing your way forward' and 'vision' – those sort of things, but they are rather vacuous statements really. I mean you could all sign up to them but it does not help you much.

My vision of 'mission' has been to help professionalise teaching, for the benefit of learning, through the most important missing element: good quality development of tools, processes, personal skills informed by rigorous research. It is all one story for me: I wanted to be a teacher because I thought learners needed that; then, when I saw teaching, I knew it needed to be good teaching. And to be good teaching, it needed to be developing, learning and improving. I saw poor quality development, so I could see helping develop staff, tools, curriculum, materials and management, developing all of that, needed to be improved. And the fundamental problem is that we didn't *know* the most effective way to do things, because it hadn't been researched. So we were improvising.

Andrew described his life as one single homogenous vision:

The mission is all the way through. Now I am in research, the mission is to make research better, much more effective, *so* that it can inform development, *so* it can inform teaching, *so* it can improve learning. I don't think learning or improving have end points: they are processes, like playing, learning and breathing. So the question is around the role of this playing, learning and breathing, in relation to vision. The whole of everything I do, or have done, is absolutely constantly all about vision. The whole of my life is one single homogenous thing about the vision. I haven't had to sit and construct it, because it was part of me when I was seven. I think there is a very strong relationship between having a vision, and between what you do, day-to-day or strategically.

Inducing systemic solutions

I have an insight into systemic solutions to individualised problems. If people confronting a difficulty are sensing the obstruction, I observe people in their different distresses, and *induce* a way forward. It is an 'engineering' or 'design approach'. I can *induce solutions* because I have a clear vision that has always been there, always consistent. So obstructions, difficulties with resources, individuals, management, are minor, transitory, *conditions of existence*, compared to the very huge vision of how it all could be. The induction of a way of progressing doesn't come with a compromise of all the problems, but comes from your vision. Most people have a catalogue of problems, think how they can minimise conflict, come up with a sticking plaster solution. The vision is a clear, longstanding simple view of what users need. It does not change much. It is the view of what learners need, and an optimism to solve problems.

Andrew described his belief in the importance of a long-term perspective:

To seriously improve things of any kind, you need a long term. Working in government offices, it is just absolutely palpable people hardly have time to even sit down and specify what needs to be done, let alone specify what needs to be done for the long term. The short-termism induced by the political cycle means you can do something ineffective once a year for ten years, but you can't do something effective over ten years. Our election cycle is quite long, so developing a *scientifically understood approach to how we help people learn* is very difficult. I mean 'scientifically' in the social sciences sense, the systematic approach to studying things, a scientific basis for education. If you look over the decades, what people talk about in FE now, we were talking about 30 years ago, are the same. We can work our way towards better ways of doing things, better lives by studying the problem, and dealing with it.

It is very important to make connections with external people, external organisations, allow light and fresh air to come into your unit from elsewhere. This is often lacking. More sophisticated things like knowledge, evidence, if you can bring these in, generate 'the whole thing moving forward, developing and growing', so, in the grandest sense of all, generate *learning*, a corporate learning experience. It is a sort of *learning paradigm* you are in, *working out together how to do things*. The analogy is a kind of horticultural, gardening analogy. What you will be doing is feeding and watering things that are growing, gradually designing how it will all be. You won't just be having one grand vision and putting it in place, it is not like 'Groundforce'. It is cultivation, feeding, caring about the individual, light and shade, and acidity for individuals, what they need. *And maintaining an open collaborative approach.*

Summary

A description of 'network leadership' introduces this interview with Dr Andrew Morris, Director of the National Educational Research Foundation (NERF). Andrew discusses the relatively weak evidence base for educational research in leadership, summing up NERF's role as an organisation providing a strategic coherence across research, working across sectors in a catalytic way to improve education. From extremely formative early positive experiences in learning, Andrew has drawn great strength in envisioning an organic paradigm of learning as continuous growth. He is optimistic that evidence-based research can provide ideas and networked leadership through systemic solutions and socially scientific designs for learning for the benefit of clients. He regards learning as being 'as natural as breathing' – throughout his life, this vision has progressively developed: his mission is to help people to learn.

Keywords

National education research organisation, London, international role evidence-based research, network leadership, organic, social sciences informed, learner-focused.

Further reading and resources

Hillier, Y. and Jameson J. (2003) *Empowering Researchers in FE*. Burton on Trent: Trentham.

Jameson, J. and Hillier, Y. (2003) *Researching Post-compulsory Education*. London: Continuum.

Senge, P.M. (1990) *The Fifth Discipline: The Art and Practice of the Learning Organisation*. London: Random House Business Books.

Senge, P.M. (1999) 'The Practice of Innovation', *Leader to Leader* 9, available at http://pfdf.org/leaderbooks/l2l/summer98/senge.html

Senge, P.M., Kleiner, A., Roberts, C., Ross, R., Roth, G. and Smith, B. (1999) *The Dance of Change: The Challenges of Sustaining Momentum in Learning Organizations*. New York: Doubleday/Currency.

Watts, D.J. (2004) *Six Degrees: The Science of a Connected Age*. London: Vintage.

Wenger, E. (1998) *Communities of Practice: Learning, Meaning and Identity*. Cambridge: Cambridge University Press.

The spread of leadership: distributed leadership

6 6Having worked for years with people who have had really bad experiences, I feel passionately education should be good. I feel very passionate about justice: social justice. 9 9
Wendy Moss

Distributed leadership

In her study of instructional change in an urban high school, Friedman (2004) notes:

> Leadership cannot lie solely on the shoulders of the principal; it must be shared, democratic, and collective. Leaders must design environments that allow people to learn what they need to learn. (Friedman, 2004, p.210)

The concept of designing an environment suitable for learning through 'distributed leadership' within an organisation relies on a mix of transformational and transactional roles.

Distributed leadership as a 'style' can involve leaders operating at all levels, including at first-line level in programme management, in the classroom with students, or at middle management level. Distributed leadership has the potential beneficially to improve organisational performance through delegation from more senior hierarchical staff to others lower down the system. Supportive staff development, advanced levels of personnel and human resources practice, effective appraisal systems and peer support are useful to implement distributed leadership effectively.

Frearson reports from Gronn's work in 2000, which indicated 'distributed leadership is an idea whose time had come' (Frearson, 2003, pp.8–9). In a post-heroic age, the distribution of leadership tasks between positional, emergent and informal leaders has seemed entirely appropriate for many.

The concept of distributed leadership has to some extent been regarded as a solution to the problem of transactional power being retained at the top of hierarchies by single people or small, elite teams. However, critique needs to be applied to this concept. The theory of distributed leadership is all very well, but in practice there is often only one person who is accountable legally when things go badly wrong. Hence the concept of 'distributed leadership' needs to be mediated, pragmatically, with the responsibilities people have at different levels in an organisation.

I selected the concept of distributed leadership to link with the case study interview with Wendy Moss, Manager of the Centre for Teacher and Management Training at City Lit in London, because Wendy's model of the 'circle of friendship' in adult education was a team-orientated approach closely resembling the concept of distributed leadership, and because adult education is intrinsically suited to concepts of distributed and team leadership.

Frearson notes that distributed leadership emerged from 'distributed cognition and activity theory' (Fearson, 2003, p.9, Leont'ev, 1981), in which the social context of thought is highly significant. The theory therefore stresses the interdependence of individuals within the context of activity, so that the interaction between peoples with situations are intrinsically linked. The theory is an attractive one at a time when there have been concerns about excessively transactional leadership styles and top-down systems of managerialist decision making. Distributed leadership is a particularly appropriate model in the context of adult education pedagogy and practice, the empowerment of communities of practice, and concepts of mediation and teamwork within adult education. The philosophy behind these ideas includes the work of many theorists on adult learning such as Paulo Freire and Carl Rogers, for whom further reading links and references are provided below.

When I met Wendy at the Centre for Teacher and Management Training at City Lit in London, a number of dilemmas about power in leadership emerged in the interview. These included the distribution of authority in teams, and individual responsibility in the context of maintaining good teamwork. Tensions between power and control, union leadership and institutional leadership were key issues in our discussion. Here I trace concepts emerging in the interview in the edited version of Wendy's replies to the questions I asked.

Case Study of Adult Education Distributed Leadership

Wendy Moss, Manager of the Centre for Teacher and Management Training, City Lit, London

How would you categorise the institution and client group in which you are currently a leader?

The City Lit is an adult education college, one of four designated colleges in inner London offering a very large liberal adult education programme. The vast majority of the courses are still not formally credited and are funded through the Learning and Skills Council. I think we're running at about 900 staff, 800 of whom are part time. We have around 35,000 students a year coming in, into five different schools – performing arts, humanities, visual arts, music, languages – and they can pick their subjects from a whole range. Our biggest use is evenings and weekends; we have a big daytime programme too.

My bit of it is the teacher and management training. We offer public courses where people can come to us to train part time, to be adult education teachers primarily, adult and community education teachers. The last phase they do at the Institute of Education: we work in partnership with them. Trainees do the first and second stage courses with us. We have five full time members of staff, an administrator and four other full time trainers/teachers. We're expanding our programme at the moment and working quite a lot with new organisations. We've run quite a few courses in the voluntary sector.

We've just been funded by the DfES to run a pilot in mentoring and coaching by subject expertise teachers. Besides the core teacher-training programme, we've run the Introductory Diploma in Management this year and last year. We've been developing a teacher-training programme for two years. All our qualifications match what are now Lifelong Learning UK Standards. We run one course at Level 3, the rest at Level 4.

What, in your experience, is the distinction, if any, between leadership and management in post-compulsory education?

Management is the operational side. The ability to *lead* in the sense of being able to think out of the box, think creatively and have a commitment to what people are doing and move people towards it, is almost essential in adult education. The whole function of adult education, in my life, has been to bring education and educational creative thinking, to reach people who may have been excluded from different ways or offer alternatives in some way . . . What's happened to me in the last few years is to realise that actually you need good management and leadership to be effective. A good manager can actually give people the space to do what they need to do and give people the sort of structured space they need.

> Very often teacher-training courses are life-changing for people, because the skills are very group based.
>
> *Wendy Moss*

I've got a very strong commitment to quality training. I think teachers can learn to teach, ought to learn to teach. Very often teacher-training courses are also life-changing for people, because the skills are very group based, so often getting people to look at themselves and what their own vision of education is and their own view of themselves is and how they are and how they behave. In a way, it often overlaps a little bit with management training and counselling actually, so they're not unrelated skills.

Being an effective teacher goes a long way beyond knowing your subjects and a range of teaching methods. Adult learners often don't need motivating but they do need to feel safe, they need to feel they can learn and need to be facilitated in that learning process. I believe very strongly that we need good teachers in adult education. Teachers in adult education are reaching people who are the most excluded in different ways. So it's particularly important that they learn to teach well, in student-centred ways, to deal with a very diverse learning. I believe teacher training is a huge contribution to the development of adult education. I believe that quite passionately.

We are particularly an adult continuing and community education unit. I believe very strongly what you experience here on our courses should be what you're aiming to try and create yourself, in your own place of work. Teachers for whom 'it's just a job' make me very angry. I understand it's not their fault, but I do feel like it's a gift, especially in adult education, to be able to do it and to do it well. Having worked for years with people who have had really bad experiences, being on the end of education, I feel quite passionately that it should be good and that people should be very respected and should have good experiences. I feel very passionate about justice, social justice. What makes me particularly angry with an organisation is when I see unjust things go on, at managerial level, between one person and another. You know, the organisation makes a decision which impacts badly on somebody and then everybody hides behind a policy. That particularly wound me up when I was in the union.

Wendy expressed her views of adult education as life-changing in the opportunities it offers:

I expect people mostly use adult education as a place to find out who they are and what they can do. That is how I see adult education. It's life-changing. It always has been and always will be and it's why it's such an exciting area to work in. If you have a good teacher who can help you pursue what you have in you, all sorts of things can happen with your life. Adult education is a huge, essential function. You know – the place where we can connect with other people in our lives, about real issues and new things and inspirational things – there aren't that many places of creativity like this.

Adult education thrives on attracting staff who are very committed, very engaged in a social justice agenda, are willing to work their socks off for very little money, because that's where they want to be. The people here are heroic in the things they do and the passion they put into their work. They do it because they believe in the work and if you take their work away from them or don't allow them to feel good about what they're doing or to feel they're doing the right things, you're taking away that goodwill. I think the government's got dangerously near it with us here sometimes.

Basically, now, if you want to be an adult literacy/numeracy or ESOL teacher, you not only have to have your PGCE or whatever any generic post-16 teacher has to have, but you have to have

> Adult education thrives on attracting people who are very committed, very engaged in social justice agendas, are willing to work their socks off for very little money, because that's where they want to be. The people here are heroic in the things they do and the passion they put into their work.
>
> *Wendy Moss*

an additional qualification. Most of this course is about the underpinning knowledge lying behind adult literacy or numeracy or ESOL teaching. Which is a problem because none of the methodology is in it: there's not enough theory about the pedagogy.

For the last 15 years, we've been through governments for whom lifelong learning has been relatively low down on the agenda, even though there's been a lot of rhetoric about it. And what we see now is a kind of imposition of the structures and attempt to organise and centralise adult education in a way that it's been relatively free of for years. And you know, in literacy it's the national tests, it's the teacher training qualifications. They're not necessarily a bad thing, but people who don't really know what they're doing have imposed these on us from above.

Wendy made it clear why she did not consider targets helpful:

And massive target setting stuff, which I think is deeply damaging in lots of ways. Targets to get these many learners through this by next week are not helpful in an under-funded workforce that has a very high turnover and has been under-trained for years; these are not helpful things, trying to do everything tomorrow. There's no sense of process or long-term developments, learning from experience or building up quality; it's, you know, churn out 40,000 basic skills qualifications by next week. So all those things are a worry.

I asked Wendy if her values had changed over the years:

I don't think my values have changed, I think the strategies and what has to be done to get there has changed. I think one of my strengths as a leader is that I feel very strongly about the importance of working to people's strengths and interests. One of the exciting things about the Talent Central Project was really bringing a whole pile of people together who were terribly enthusiastic and very committed and giving them the support and money to do what they wanted to do. And I

> I feel very strongly about the importance of working to people's strengths and interests . . . If you work as a team, you will have people who are strong at different things and the skill to allow them to run with that and to hold that . . .
>
> *Wendy Moss*

think I'm quite good at doing that, I'm sort of good at saying, this person is really good at this, let's run with them. This person doesn't like doing this you know, let's not go there, let's work to where the person is you know. I've become, now, a formal manager, and that's still one of my values.

If you work as a team, you will have people who are strong at different things and the skill is to allow them to run with that and to hold that and not to be you know, I'm the leader, so therefore I have to do everything or shine at everything. I think we're in a very different world from when I first started. I think my values of leadership are probably the same; I've stopped being frightened about being a leader.

I think the turning moment for me in leadership terms was when I took on the management of quite a big project. We had £1.5m over two years for that project. I had to work with people all over London, directly line manage some very good staff. And I did it without quite realising that's what I was doing, because it seemed sort of the stuff I did anyway. I had a label of being a project manager. But I've been doing that kind of stuff really, informally, since I was in community education. I was kind of thrown into leadership. I like to work with teams and I suppose have a democratic style. I like to feel there's a team, a lot of people working together, that's a very typical adult education sort of thing. You enjoy it because the people you work with, everyone's committed, everyone's throwing things in.

'Friendship rings'

I suppose it's like those kind of friendship rings. My ideal grounding sort of a leader would be somebody who would hold that kind of ring in a team. They're like little friendship rings – everybody's kind of standing in a circle, usually there's a candle in the middle and they go and bond together. So I would see my role would be to kind of hold that ring together, that my job will be to try and keep that ring going. We do have responsibility and I do have authority, but in a team that works well, that invaluable sense of mutual support and collaboration, commitment to supporting each other, not in competition, not trying to dump on each other, is there.

Wendy went on to describe her vision of a 'community of practice'

Because I think if you're a teacher, you need people to listen to what's going on for you – basically being a community of practice. And then you start to learn from each other and develop. I sometimes think having visions are good if you've got the right people. I'm quite good at teaming people. I'm reluctant to say, 'Oh, we're all the same and we all work together' because clearly, if you're in a leadership role, it's not good enough, really: you have to take the responsibility. But I would see it as encouraging, fostering and supporting that, facilitating it, I suppose. But also being willing, like any good group leader in adult education, being willing . . . to make the space for people to develop those kind of things and to support them. I think in adult education a lot of what you're doing is encouraging people to learn from each other. I think I'm having to refine what I always was. I don't think you can function well without distributed leadership, being willing to have people to take responsibility at every level. And my friendship circle, it's kind of iffy because it you know, I've been through enough collectives in my life to know what I'm talking about: people have to take responsibility. But leaders who separate themselves from people are a problem.

I don't have my career mapped out for the future. I have to believe what I'm saying. I will argue passionately for something I believe in. If you kind of hung round the 60s and 70s and 80s, there was something a bit politically unsound about being a leader. I was raised in the era of you know, total democracy and anarchy. There was something politically unsound about going into leadership. And there's a lot of me in that. I think lack of self-confidence really and fear of politics actually would stop me going any further, you know. I'm a sort of middle line manager.

'You can't teach someone to read in two hours a week in six months'

I find it irritating that in the current climate there's a lot of commitment to lifelong learning but two successive governments have felt that lifelong learning equals employment training. It's such a limited view, especially when there's research after research project saying the benefits of lifelong learning are endless but not simply that you go on a course and go into a job. In terms of enhancing the quality of the workforce, you might expect all sorts of things to happen. And if the Ford Motor Company knows this, why the British government doesn't, I don't know. There's endless evidence on what this does. So I think the drive for vocational training is a difficult one, it's got its pay-offs but basically I think it's quite limited. I don't know whether we'll ever persuade any government to think a bit out of the box about this you know. The other big drive is for expanding literacy, numeracy and ESOL provision at the moment. It's a mixed blessing. The funders often don't understand the field, don't really understand the demand on teachers round this. They don't really understand you can't teach somebody to read two hours a week in six months or to fundamentally develop their writing skills when they can only come for two hours a week.

You're talking about a big process and education, whereas the current drive is to reduce it to a set of skills. The LSCs have been quite good in supporting all sorts of providers, through different funds. But the range of things they're offering are largely shrinking. There are some creative projects – we've got a big peer education project for homeless people here. But you have to tie it up with vocational development and I think it's hugely limiting. A lot of money being spent on literacy, numeracy and ESOL resources is good though. There's a lot of good people involved and they will find good things coming out of it.

What you learn as you get older is not to take on faith the rhetoric that comes out of policy around lifelong learning, what the 'next education thing' is. It's about saying that you have to understand you don't have to totally believe whatever the rhetoric is about what you have to do. You have to trust your own judgement and your own experience.

Summary

A discussion of the distributed and team leadership model introduces the interview with Wendy Moss, Manager for the Centre for Teacher and Management Training at the City Lit in London. Wendy discusses leadership and management with reference to the 'circle of friendship' in adult education, and the group-based work in teacher training. She strongly believes that adult education can change people's lives for the better, and is in favour of providing high quality learning opportunities for students. She is critical of some government targets in relation to literacy training, and feels that leaders need to have faith in their own vision of education, and to be sceptical of the continual changes in lifelong learning and education policy.

Keywords

Adult Education Training Institute, London-based with a regional role, distributed and team leadership approach, circle of friendship, adult education pedagogy.

Further reading and resources

Collins, M. (1991) *Adult Education as Vocation. A critical role for the adult educator.* London: Routledge.

Freire, P. (1972) *Pedagogy of the Oppressed.* Harmondsworth: Penguin.

Friedman, A.A. (2004) 'Beyond mediocrity: transformational leadership within a transactional framework.' *International Journal of Leadership in Education*, 7, 3, pp.203–24, July–September.

Harrison, J.F.C. (1961) Learning and Living 1790–1960. 'A study in the history of the English adult education movement.' London: Routledge & Kegan Paul.

Jarvis, P. (ed.) (1987) *Twentieth Century Thinkers in Adult Education.* London: Routledge.

Kelly, T. (1992 [1970] [1962]) *A History of Adult Education in Great Britain.* Liverpool: Liverpool University Press.

Leont'ev, A.N. (1981) 'The problem of activity in psychology' in *The Concept of Activity in Soviet Psychology.* J.V. Wertsch (ed.), Armonk, NY: M.E. Sharpe, pp.37–71.

Rogers, C. and Freiberg, H.J. (1993) *Freedom to Learn* (third edition). New York: Merrill.

Stepping into the infinite cosmos: creative leadership

> ❝The journey is from where ever you are at. The starting point is wherever you are at . . . As you step into the world, it's an infinite cosmos. It's the principle of exploration and understanding and it's boundless.❞
> Talmud Bah

Creative leadership

Sternberg *et al.* (2003) developed a 'propulsion model of creative leadership' going beyond their earlier expression (1995) of 'an investment theory of creativity', which proposed that creative leaders bring forth ideas, like good investors, and treat these concepts like stocks which accrue gradually in value and are then sold to others (Sternberg *et al.* 1999, 2001, 2002). This idea is useful in considering the power of innovative creative works to change radically in value as they attract greater levels of public interest and acceptability. However, the later research by Sternberg *et al.* goes beyond this investment theory in recognising that not all creative leaders can be compared with investors, and that a more general theory of creative leadership is needed.

Sternberg *et al.* (2003, p.455) outline a number of other models which they term 'creative leadership', including theories put forward under the name of 'transformational leadership' (Bass and Avolio, 1994), 'emotionally intelligent leadership' (Goleman, 1998), 'visionary leadership' (Sashkin, 1988) and 'charismatic leadership' (Conger and Kanugo, 1998). Whether or not the original theorists would agree these are in fact models of 'creative leadership', there are undoubtedly elements of what could be broadly defined as 'creativity' within them. Defining more broadly some types of creative leadership, Sternberg *et al.* (2003) describe eight different ways of leading creatively in a 'propulsion model', to take followers forward:

1. replication
2. redefinition
3. forward incrementation
4. advance forward incrementation
5. redirection
6. reconstruction/redirection
7. reinitiation
8. synthesis.

They observe that organisations resisting change are more likely to accept conservative creative models (1–4), while organisations that welcome change will be more accepting of innovative models (5–8). This is a useful distinction, and Sternberg *et al.* (2003) also provide a helpful discussion of tests of creativity and the types of creative contributions individuals can make in a range of fields, including arts and sciences (pp.469–70).

Rickards and Moger (2000) consider creative leadership from the point of view of project team development, proposing a new conceptual framework for team formation and performance which goes beyond Tuckman's original team development model (Tuckman, 1965). Rickards and Moger's work is useful in considering mechanisms and protocols for improving the effectiveness of creative teams, and outlining the benefits of creative leadership approaches in facilitating enhanced performance (Rickards and Moger, 2000, pp.281–2).

Selection of case study: Talmud Bah at Second Wave Youth Arts

I selected the case study of Talmud Bah at Second Wave Youth Arts to link with the model of creative leadership because of the way Talmud works on the generation of vision and 'higher' ideals and values within the youth arts groups he leads at Second Wave. This application of creative leadership works at the level of the individual, the student group and the staff team. The staff team at Second Wave, with Talmud, have consistently achieved long-term beneficial results in which youngsters with serious, ongoing difficulties in their lives, often involving trauma, depression and a range of other more or less extreme hardships, are developed in confidence, and nurtured into a sense of community safety and belonging at Second Wave. The atmosphere at Second Wave is welcoming and inclusive for these young people, and long-term retention levels are very high. Some of the Second Wave clients have dropped out of school, are out of work, and are marginally if at all linked to stable family backgrounds.

Many of them have either come directly from or have been in Pupil Referral Units (PRUs), having been excluded from school. Their learning experiences have sometimes previously been extremely negative. The work done by Second Wave in providing creative and performing arts facilities and provision for these youngsters is highly effective, and has resulted in long-term membership of the group by a very high percentage (80%+) of youngsters who go there.

In his interview for this book, Talmud discussed his style of leadership and the way Second Wave operates. I trace below the links between his experiences of leadership at Second Wave and theories of creative leadership. The idea of 'white belt' leadership arises from martial arts. To wear a white belt signifies respect and willingness to learn. Openness to learning, boundless creativity and youthful energy in leadership in fact characterised this whole interview with Talmud Bah, whose role is as Assistant Director of Second Wave Centre for Youth Arts in Deptford, London. I went to see Talmud at Second Wave, and learnt about the way Talmud sees and practises leadership in a voluntary and community youth arts organisation dedicated to young people facing particular difficulties in their personal lives and in education in London. I found Talmud's description of Second Wave's long-term provision of activities for young people to be outstandingly inspiring for the voluntary arts leadership of future generations.

Case Study of Youth and Community Leadership

Talmud Bah, Assistant Director, Second Wave Centre for Youth Arts

The boundless creativity of white belt leadership

How would you categorise the institution and client group in which you are currently a leader?

> Second Wave works with young people aged from 13 to 24. Although it is funded for that age range, it continues to work with people who go past 24, normally on a voluntary or professional basis. The mission and purpose of the organisation is creating access to the arts and education for young people, who, because of being marginalised or being in some form of depression, haven't had access to the arts and education before or have been denied access or have been offered arts and education in a way which doesn't allow them to grow as people.
>
> Emotionally, artistically, educationally and culturally, it's about providing a safe environment for young people to take the necessary risks to discover who they are, to push their limitations, to raise the bar in terms of what they aspire to. The team at Second Wave have an expectancy of young people to be whatever they choose to be, and that is as small as an acorn or as big as an oak tree. That is the focus – not to

create young artists but to enable young people to express themselves and develop through the arts and being creative.

Students here study performing arts: drama, dance, sound, lighting, song writing, vocals and performance, connecting with an audience. On another level, it's problem-solving, behavioural education and emotional literacy. It's holistic. Students learn to formulate ideas, process information, deliver ideas constructively and find a language for them. Also to communicate their feelings, work creatively and collaboratively with other people, manage themselves in this context, and manage their feelings.

What, in your experience, is the distinction, if any, between leadership and management in post-compulsory education?

In terms of leadership, what it isn't is a 'lone commander kind of striving forward, with people following behind'. To truly lead or inspire leadership is to have an overview of the needs of the whole. So you look at what the needs of the young people are, what the needs of the organisation are. Then you make your judgments based on that and that alone. You also need to be aware of what your personal needs are, in a professional context, so what you need to best be effective in your role. On a personal level, what you need personally is to prepare yourself to be in a position to offer support, not only to young people but also to members of staff, and provide them with trust, for members of staff and young people to work effectively.

You have to be aware of 'ego' to put it to one side. It's not being a hollow shell. It's more about being clear about what the focus is. It's not about being 'singular'. My role and responsibility is to take things forward and offer encouragement and inspiration. It's important for me to know why I am achieving this, why is it important to me. If that isn't clear, then for me personally that which I do would become corrupt. If we have the feeling we've arrived, we stop growing. Even if you haven't got the necessary skills, you have the right intention. That always comes through if what you are trying to do is true. Management is about facilitating and providing structures which enable people to manage themselves. To offer support and guidance when they need a sounding board or advice, to encourage self-direction and offer support and provide structures to work within as well.

My intention is always to inspire and always to uplift but never by force. 'Not to enforce' is about being in a place which is responsive enough and sensitive enough to offer what is needed on many different levels. So, for that new young person coming into the organisation, it's about making them feel welcome, making them know this is a place where they can feel comfortable and letting them know the options and that whatever they choose to do in Second Wave is okay. It's very important not to become 'omnipotent' in what you do: that is the opposite of what we do here. Always remember there is a wider picture.

Young people come here at many different levels, in different ways. The arts provide the process and conduit for the young person to begin their journey. Through a process of self-discovery, interaction, networking and communicating with peers, they find out lots about themselves and their generation. They find language to communicate who they are, what they know, where they are, what they need.

The journey is from wherever you are at. The starting point is wherever you are at. So your journey begins, from your perspective, when your journey begins. From our perspective, when you step in Second Wave, we already see you are on your journey, be it here or not, because you are enquiring. You are taking an interest, you are looking into, you are trying to find out ways of expressing yourself as a human being. Your journey starts there.

Every young person, we meet them where they are. You may have had issues in the past with education, family, law. That is irrelevant to us. All you need to do is come as you are and we will take you as we find you. You come on the day, we meet you on the day and that's our starting point.

The journey has to be made and driven by the young person. We are guides and facilitators. We offer options, give structures, offer support. What we are trying to encourage is informed independence, a collaborative point of working and sharing ideas. When you have that informed confidence in what you feel and choose to do, you come to collaborate and share far easier, because you are not insecure and you are not precious about that which you have to offer. It's basically being in a place where people are all on journeys. This is just a beginning. So you don't have to be one particular thing, you don't have to fit into this box or this box, you can be many things.

One of the main components of being a human being is to be creative. We can't help but be creative. Your mind creates while you sleep, when you wake up you are creating, the structure of your day, organising when and at what time you are going to do things. Creativity is transferable, creativity is like an undefined conscious energy. Creativity kind of swallows and moves: it takes on the form of whatever it needs to take the form of. Like water, it's pliable. If it needs to be hot, it's hot. If it needs to be cold, it's cold. If it needs to be hard, it's hard. If it needs to evaporate, it evaporates. And it can take whatever shape it needs to take, depending on the intentions of the person that's using it, that's the beauty of it. You have skills and attributes and ideas which can be translated into whatever you choose to do. By realising that, you realise that you have no limit. When you take ownership of what you do, you are empowered. So if you change your perspective on life, it widens how you see things, widens your options. It's having perspective. If you are totally closed, you limit your experience of life and of people, your process of growing is kind of more limited.

> It's important to *come freshly to what you do*. Nurture yourself as a creative person if you are in the arts, as an artist. That way you come to your work fresh, ready to give, because your needs are being met.
>
> *Talmud Bah*

If you are in a role of responsibility, don't take it lightly. You have to be aware of what you are responsible for. There's the old saying power corrupts. So if you are in a role of responsibility, knowing why you are there, what your intentions are, what your role is, what is the actual agenda. You need to be aware of who you are as a person before you step into a role where you are going to interact and support and facilitate the emotions of other people. If you keep your needs and ego in context, keep focused on the job at hand, you don't have much trouble in terms of ego.

I believe the intention behind what you are trying to do always comes through. If you're in any area of work involved in supporting other people, taking care of other people, it's about doing your damned best. Don't take it lightly that what you do is important. You've got to be able to know yourself as a person the best you can and nurture yourself as a person and professional and as an artist; otherwise you get disgruntled. You could begin your journey having lots of ideas, lots of energy to bring to the role, and maybe because of commitment, time, restrictions in the context you're working in, you can easily become disheartened and disgruntled. It's important to nurture yourself. It's important to come freshly to what you do. Nurture yourself as a creative person if you are in the arts, as an artist. That way you come to your work fresh, ready to give, because your needs are being met. That's the first stage, know who you are, know where you're at, know where you fit, what you're feeling, what your needs are, do your best to meet those needs. And then you're in context.

> ... Far from being the antithesis of creativity, constraints on thinking are what make creativity possible ... Mozart is free to create things others cannot imagine, because he is bound by principles others cannot see ...
>
> *Margaret Boden*

Professionalism is key. Be professional. If you're working with a group of young people, you've got to be aware of your own personal boundaries in terms of how you behave and how you manage yourself with these young people and your language, at all levels. That's why you have to be aware of your needs. Professionalism is being aware of what your needs are and putting them in perspective, knowing your role, your personal boundaries and interacting with other professionals with professional courtesy. Respecting someone for who they are, whatever their background is.

The 'white belt mentality': always a beginner

When you acquire a certain wisdom, realise it's a two-way stream: so as you've acquired wisdom, you need to have a constant stream of new ideas and questions and learning. People are constantly evolving all the time. You can learn something in a five-minute conversation or interaction at a bus stop, you know. So you need to keep, I call it, like in martial arts, the white belt mentality. It's like you're always a beginner. You're always a white belt, a beginner. It's a martial arts description. It's like you're always a beginner, always learning. You've always got to learn, you've always got to be open. Have knowledge and expertise in what you do, but never close off and seal what you do. When you've created that shell, it becomes like a mental and emotional prison because you tie so many things up with that. The point is to keep open – remain open. Life is like a book that never closes and never ends – the pages are blank because it's for you to fill.

As you step into the world, it's an infinite cosmos. It's the principle of exploration and understanding and it's boundless. You learn about yourself through others, learn new things from others. Each day is a new experience, even if you're coming to the same place or you're working in the same area, each day is a new day. You might wake up a completely different person from the one you were the day before.

> Truly, a 'captain', or leader of any kind, puts the team first.
>
> *Talmud Bah*

My style is of someone who has begun a journey and through that journey has met and discovered many things. The gift of that process and journey is that I have learnt that knowledge, to truly know something, is to realise you really don't know anything at all. The more you find out, the more you realise there is to learn. It is about knowing your role, what you are responsible for, taking responsibility for that and facilitating the development of others, not being absolute in your role. Because truly a 'captain', or leader of any kind, puts the team first.

Leadership is organising yourself and your peers, being in a group and realising somebody is a bit anxious or feels uneasy. Leadership is putting in that time to organise the space before the workshop happens or prior to a performance. Leadership is fragmented: so that everyone is a leader at different levels, depending on who you are, where you are at, your stage of development and context: you are a leader for that context and for that experience. You should see a leader as someone who strides forwards and brings everyone along. The most important qualities of educational leadership for me are passion, good practice, personal self-development, understanding purpose, curiosity and creativity. I see creativity as energy unto itself, because of your passion, although when you feel it it's emotive but you think it as well, you think about something you are interested in and you have a passion.

> Life is like a book that never closes and never ends and the pages are blank because it's for you to fill.
>
> *Talmud Bah*

Sometimes a young person might be facing issues of eviction, homelessness. They may be having family problems, have money issues. You have got to be in the place to manage that, and not only manage that but manage the group. You could be in the workshop. That young person might be unnecessarily rude or aggressive or have an offensive manner. You've got to put that person at ease, contain it and put it to one side. It's about being able to manage that and having the training to manage that. It is challenging emotionally. Your interest in your work has to be your passion: you have to have emotional investment, but also emotional distance. So when a young person opens up to you, you don't get lost in the experience. You keep it clear, keep it in context, keep it in role, so you are the facilitator.

To manage that situation is emotionally demanding. That is why it is so important for you to know where you are at emotionally. That clear distinction in your mind helps you to manage those situations. The first thing is to hear them. They need you to hear it, but to acknowledge it at the same time. You can't make it better. They are not asking you to make it better. They just need you to hear it, and to acknowledge that you have heard it. You can then begin a process of exploration led by them. To facilitate them, I need to know how they are feeling, but it is more about them finding a language to communicate how they are feeling. Finding that language, they manage how they are feeling a lot better.

I believe life can't be extinguished, I don't believe in death, I believe we have different stages of life, and this is but one of them, and within this stage of life, we have different stages of development, and that continues until we go into a new experience of life. So death is but a doorway into another experience of life. So we are always beginning. I have learnt that as long as you take each day as it comes and you try and take an experience from each day and learn from each day and nurture your creativity, you always check your purpose, your passion and you always nurture yourself, you will continue to move forward. The only thing I can change is myself. Maybe through me changing myself, things around me begin to change: more often than not, that happens. So, part of it is about looking inwards to inspiration before looking outwards. Looking inwards, finding the God in you, then you look outwards, because the key is within yourself. Everything we need we have within us, we just don't know it or have forgotten it.

Summary

A discussion of creative leadership introduces the interview with Talmud Bah, Assistant Director of Centre for Youth Arts. Talmud sums up Second Wave's role as youth arts providers for young people aged 13–24. Second Wave provides a safe emotional, artistic, educational and cultural environment for young people to discover who they are, express themselves and develop through creative arts. Talmud has an optimistic and creative facilitative leadership role, believing leaders should nurture their creativity to ensure they can provide support to young people suffering problems in their lives. His values for educational leadership are passion, good practice, personal self-development, understanding purpose, curiosity and creativity.

Keywords

Youth Arts Organisation, Voluntary Group, London-based in Deptford, creative leadership approach, supportive, nurturing, facilitative, white belt leadership, always a beginner, optimistic, spiritual, creative.

Further reading and resources

Bass, B.M. and Avolio, B.J. (eds.) (1993) *Improving organizations through transformational leadership*. Beverly Hills, CA: Sage Publications.

Carnegie Council on Policy Studies in Higher Education (1979) *Giving Youth a Better Chance: Options for Education, Work, and Service*. San Francisco, CA: Jossey-Bass.

Chamberlin, J. (2003) 'Considering creativity: inspiring the masses through creative leadership.' *APA Online Monitor on Psychology*, 34, 10.

Harland, J., Kinder, K., Lord, P., Stott, A., Schagen, I. and Haynes, J. with Cusworth, L., White, R. and Paola, R. (2000) *Arts Education in Secondary Schools: Effects and Effectiveness*. Berkshire: National Foundation for Education Research.

Rickards, T. and Moger, S. (2000) 'Creative leadership processes in project team development: an alternative to Tuckman's stage model.' *British Journal of Management*, 11, pp. 273–83.

Sternberg, R.J., Kaufman, J.C. and Pretz, J.E. (2003) 'A propulsion model of creative leadership.' *Leadership Quarterly*, 14, pp.455–73.

Endnote

> **"I am more afraid of an army of 100 sheep led by a lion than an army of 100 lions led by a sheep."**
> Talleyrand

In this book, we have 'listened' to the voices of a number of leaders in post-compulsory education, exploring some theoretical and practical perspectives on leadership from different parts of the sector for the benefit of future leaders. In the Introduction we examined some issues about leadership in PCE which form the background to this book. In Part One, Chapter 1, we examined the 'State of play' in post-compulsory education, identifying a number of issues to be addressed in leadership and the need to investigate 'authentic' leadership through situated examples in case study interviews. In Chapter 2, we examined some different educational leadership theories, looking at a range of models, including transformational, charismatic and distributed leadership.

Then, in Chapter 3, we compared leadership and management in terms of their differences and similarities, rounding this up with a view that both good leadership and good management are needed in our organisations in the concept of the 'leader-manager'. In Chapter 4, we briefly examined the questions of equality and diversity in leadership in the sector, and the importance of ensuring that new PCE leadership is both more representative and more inclusive in the future.

> First they laugh at you, then they ignore you, then they fight you, then you win.
> *Mahatma Ghandi*

In Chapter 5, we considered the issue of continuous ongoing changes in post-compulsory education in relation to leadership, and the requirement to be adaptable and flexible in planning for the future. We moved on from this in Chapter 6 to examine 'Leaders in trouble', reflecting on the ways in which poor leaders sometimes operate, in an attempt to arm ourselves against poor quality and corruption in leadership and management.

Having briefly scanned this wide range of leadership issues affecting PCE, from factors affecting institutional change and problematic leadership to questions of diversity and equality, and differences between leadership and management, we rounded off our consideration of leadership in Part Two by considering lessons for future leaders, including the role of staff development and mentoring to encourage positive leadership. In Chapter 7, 'New leaders on the move', we reflected on the ways in which leadership might be taken forward positively in the sector in future. We were mindful, in this, of 'the succession crisis', the need to plan proactively for leadership developments in the future, and also of the impetus arising from the drive to implement *Success for All* (DfES, 2002). We then looked at the work of the Centre for Excellence in Leadership (CEL) in their *Leadership Qualities Framework*, providing this as an example of some highly positive new trends emerging in the sector.

After examining this useful *Framework*, we then looked at a new holistic model for the development of 'transforming leadership spaces', using a new framework based on prior research work done with the *Creative Learning Partnership* in London and on some ideas emerging in quantum and other new leadership theories. We considered leadership fields of influence as an apersonal distributed conception of leadership, and examined a new diagnostic model for leadership situations which we could use alongside the CEL *Leadership Qualities Framework*.

> You are here to enable the world to live more amply, with greater vision, and with a finer spirit of hope and achievement. You are here to enrich the world.
>
> *Woodrow Wilson*

Having put forward this model in Chapter 7, we then introduced Part Two. Chapter 8 began with a brief round-up of the range of different kinds of leadership roles we could identify in the sector, using this summary of leadership roles as a stepping stone to reflect, initially, on the model of 'servant leadership' and then to quote some extracts from an interview with Lynne Sedgmore, Chief Executive of the CEL, whose role gives her a wide-ranging perspective as a kind of implicit 'leader of leaders' for the sector. We noted the overall leadership responsibilities of CEL, reporting from a case study interview held with Lynne earlier in 2005. Following this reported interview, we then contemplated in turn (in Chapters 9–17) nine other case study interviews with leaders in the sector. Building on prior theoretical models and concepts of leadership that had been put forward in Part One, we considered, for each chapter, one

> The light is within us; let us work for our destiny-our destiny to better the human race. Let us become more aware of our actions; let us be more compassionate to our fellow human beings and to ourselves.
>
> *Carlos Barrios*

theoretical leadership model linked to each case study interview. These were as follows:

- servant leadership – Lynne Sedgmore
- guardianship and change agency – Dr John Guy
- quantum leadership – Dr David Collins
- systemic leadership – Ruth Silver
- inclusive leadership – Anne Morahan
- skills approaches in leadership – Professor Daniel Khan
- ethical leadership – Bob Challis
- networked and evidence-based research leadership – Dr Andrew Morris
- team leadership and distributed leadership – Wendy Moss
- creative leadership – Talmud Bah

A fascinating glimpse into the work of these leaders was captured in short edited excerpts from the transcripts of one-to-one interviews carried out with each person. Fuller transcripts of the text of these interviews will in due course be made available online through the publishers in selected cases, so that readers of this book who are interested in studying what these leaders said in full in the interviews can read the entire edited transcripts.

In finalising this book, we now draw together a range of reflections on leadership for the sector, beginning first of all with a story related during one of the interviews for this book, which links into future training for leaders in the sector.

Principals' induction by David Collins – the 'pictures on the walls' story

The CEL is currently running a number of programmes in leadership training for people throughout the learning and skills sector. One key programme is the 'Induction for new principals', led by Dr David Collins. In his interview with me, David made two main points in relation to this programme:

At the moment, I'm running a new principal's induction programme. Something I think that does make new principals think is, 'Are you aware of how long a shadow as a principal you cast?' Are you aware that, if you do put your values into action, show they are active, how well that will go down, and indeed the converse that, if you have words and actions not matching, how difficult it will be for staff to take you as seriously as you would like to be taken as a good leader?

I think it can be actively done – that's the important thing, it's trying to be a good leader. I think you do things that might look accidental, but frequently, if not always, they're by design.

I'll give you an example of something which probably of all the bits and pieces that I've done around the world, down through my life and wherever in the world, I'm probably most proud of, and it's just an idea that came to me in the middle of the night.

I was at one particular college as an acting principal to sort out or help them sort out, obviously, fairly major financial positions and some issues of quality, etc. I was brought in shortly before Christmas, about three weeks before Christmas, to an institution that was in a pretty big mess. Staff were very demoralised. In fact, I think the week before, they had had placards with the management team's (who were there, then) photographs on them being paraded around the building blaming them for the mess that the college was in.

I had a staff meeting straight away and outlined how bad the problem was and said, 'This is how much money we've got to save. Provided we've got co-operation and everybody is on the same side, we can do this without compulsory redundancies and we can make sure that the college has a firm future'. And then the idea which came to me in the middle of the night. I said, 'We can only do this if we've got everybody working in the same direction and everybody is part of that team, because it's not something that one person can do. It's something that needs all 380 of you', or whatever the number was, 'to do it.' So I said, 'I'm not in College tomorrow, I'm coming back on Thursday and I will tell you on Thursday what the percentage chances of this College surviving are – precisely. I will work this out to a figure out of a hundred percent and this is how I will do it. The walls of this campus . . .', and I was pointing particularly at one specific campus, ' . . . are completely bare. You all have in your garage or in your house somewhere a picture, which you do not want or you could do without. Tomorrow, put them on the walls of the College and I will come in on Thursday morning and count the number of pictures on the walls and the proportion out of 380 that we have on the walls will be our chances of survival.'

> I can do no great things, only small things with great love.
>
> *Mother Teresa*

I came in on the Thursday and there were something like 420 pictures on display, because some people had brought two just in case somebody had forgotten. So it was a fantastic opportunity and also a very visual opportunity of showing the importance of teamwork and how important it was for that particular organisation, for everybody to realise that yes, no matter how big the problem, if you've got 400 people trying to solve it, you can solve it.

> If your actions inspire others to dream more, learn more, do more and become more, you are a leader.
>
> *John Quincy Adams*

And over the rest of the year, people worked very hard, they were very flexible, and that particular College, as it now is, under its new principal is a successful and developing institution. (David Collins, 2005, Interview)

This story provides a remarkable example of effective translation of the vision of leadership into a whole-college reality. It gives useful insight for reflection for new principals, senior leaders and other leaders in the sector to consider 'How long a shadow as a leader do you cast?'

What have we learned about leadership in post-compulsory education?

The process of carrying out the interviews, studying and writing for this book has been an extraordinary journey. Worries and skepticism about leadership in the PCE sector from the reviewers marked the start of it. However, from the process of engaging in, transcribing and analysing interviews with ten successful leaders from a range of different situations and educational phases in the sector, I learned that in fact there existed much hope for future sectoral leadership. The interviewees here represented demonstrated extraordinary diligence, high quality provision, a passion for learning and for excellence, great concern for staff, and much skill, understanding and knowledge in leadership, education, social justice and equal opportunities, which I found both impressive and inspiring. I hope leaders of the future, also, may find in these leaders' examples hope and courage for the long and difficult journey of leadership ahead.

A new optimism for the future – principles of best practice in leadership

A new optimism about the potential for future PCE leadership therefore emerged as this book was completed. Some principles collected together for best practice in leadership in PCE from the interviews are shown in Figure 18.1. This is just a shortlist, but in these observations I pool together some reflections from the experience of all ten interviewees to arrive at a list characterising some

> The weak can never forgive. Forgiveness is the attribute of the strong.
> *Mahatma Ghandi*

aspects of good leadership derived from a summarised consideration of the interviews. To this should be added the model of the Transformational Leadership Framework proposed in Chapter 7.

Rounded, organic and authentic: communities of practice in leadership

This book has given a rounded human view of leadership in PCE from a variety of angles, perspectives and levels, forming what could be described as an organic 'authentic' view of a community of practice in leadership, operating from many points simultaneously in a distributed interconnected network. This could be contrasted with perspectives on leadership viewing power as the preserve of an elite operating only from the top of a more singular hierarchy downwards. It is time to share power out in our institutions, and to recognise that there are multiple leaderships operating at every level in PCE. This is both

1. CLEAR FOCUS ON HIGH ACHIEVEMENT (BALANCE INTELLECTUAL-EMOTIONAL-ENTERPRISE)

Leadership of all Nolan Principles, CEL – Focus to Achieve, Passion for Excellence, Mobilise to Impact, Sustain Momentum
Excellent at strategy, vision of high quality, focus on learner achievement – all Nolan Principles
Good leadership has a vision of excellence, a focus on attainable high quality, and developed strategy to implement this. A first priority is placed on learner achievement. This vision is consistent, durable and integral. It does not fade away as soon as inspectors or auditors leave. Good leaders are diligent and hardworking, making unremitting efforts to achieve excellence in provision.

2. EXCELLENT KNOWLEDGE MANAGEMENT (INTELLECTUAL-ENTERPRISE)

Accountability and Integrity Nolan Principles, CEL Focus to Achieve, Mobilise to Impact
Effective in navigation, adaptability and flexibility – Accountability Nolan Principle
Good leadership navigates the course of an institution effectively in a futures-centred adaptable and flexible way, is responsive to changing conditions, and always seeking to implement cost-effective, innovative solutions. Leaders keep up to date with the possibilities opened up by IC eLearning and systems improvement for effective learning environments.
Knowledgeable, practical and optimistic – Accountability and Integrity Nolan Principles
Good leadership cultivates excellent professional knowledge in the institution, and is practical at implementing solutions for problems creatively. Good leaders are pragmatic with a healthy approach to work. They demonstrate a powerful optimism and force for positivity.

3. VALUES-BASED INTEGRITY (EMOTIONAL-INTELLECTUAL)

Integrity, Honesty, Selflessness and Accountability Nolan Principles, CEL – Passion for Excellence, Mobilise to Impact
High in personal integrity and ethics – Selflessness Nolan Principle
Good leadership *always* upholds high standards of personal integrity and ethics in service of learners, avoiding many temptations to misuse power. Good leaders are professional, responsible, kind, courteous and considerate. They are also sincere, reliable, honest and hard-working. Good leaders communicate frequently and constantly nurture a good atmosphere.
Strong in an authentic sense of duty, truth and honour – Honesty Nolan Principle
Good leadership is both dutiful and honourable. It has a genuineness and authenticity which impresses others. If good leaders slip up, which even they sometimes do, they do not beat themselves or anyone else up about this, but accept their own and others' weaknesses, and work with these to transform organisations into better, more human, more forgiving places.
Values-driven, respectful of people, inspiring trust – Integrity and Selflessness Nolan Principles
Good leaders are committed to ensure beneficial values are 'lived' as the main 'drivers' of their organisation. Good leaders passionately uphold ethical standards, with a strong focus on values clarification in leadership, and, within this, a particular appreciation of the need for respect for learners and staff at all levels. Because they respect staff, they inspire trust throughout the institution.
Emotionally intelligent, knowledgeable and practical – Accountability and Integrity Nolan Principles
Good leadership is emotionally intelligent towards everyone in the organisation. Good leaders have a subtle, intuitive understanding of and response to the way 'institutions talk' to people.
Fully committed to the active implementation of equal opportunities, diversity and inclusion – Integrity Nolan Principle
Good leaders are not only aware of the importance, significance and benefits of being committed to equality of opportunity. They have an absolute commitment to diversity and equality, and are also aware of complex factors involved in implementing diversity, inclusion and equality at every level of the organisation. They are fully committed to ensuring that this is achieved.

4. EXCELLENT RESOURCES, SYSTEMS AND PERFORMANCE MANAGEMENT (ENTERPRISE-INTELLECTUAL)

Objectivity, Openness and Accountability Nolan Principles, CEL – Mobilise to Impact, Sustain Momentum, Passion for Excellence
Multilevelled leader-managers distributed in a heterarchy – Objectivity Nolan Principle
Good leadership recognises that leadership should be distributed at all levels of an organisation at a variety of levels in a heterarchy. They are also willing to take command of particular duties that come with occupying top roles. Good leaders demonstrate unexpected humility.
Effective communication processes, team-based – Openness Nolan Principle
Good leadership is best envisaged as a series of flexible, shared processes operating through many different levels in an interconnected network of effective relationships. Good communications assist 'great groups' in inclusive team-working. Good leaders have a strong allegiance to team-working and observe friendly styles of leadership, but they can also be tough in upholding standards of good conduct.
High 'people priority', concern for well-being and safety – Accountability Nolan Principle
Good leadership places a high priority on people in organisations. Good leaders have a sense of guardianship, caring for and protecting learners and staff. They place their first priority on learners and clients. They also prioritise the effective functioning of staff at all levels. Good leaders *always* demonstrate a concern for the well-being, benefit and happiness of people in their institution. This transcends and encompasses their focus on targets. A long-term, stable guardianship of people is in place.
High visibility, excellent systems management, beneficial impact of leadership field – Accountability Nolan Principle
Good leadership has a high visibility and powerful 'impact factor', implementing organisational mission, strategy and operations effectively. Good leaders have a deep understanding of management systems and theory, being excellent managers of people and resources.
Skilled in finance and evidence-based practice – Accountability and Leadership Nolan Principles
Good leadership is excellently skilled in finance, proactive in innovative enterprise based on evidence from successful practice and benchmarking for the organisation and ensures a flow of business generation activities, works well with employers, being responsive to needs.
Aware of the benefits of reflection – Objectivity Nolan Principle
Good leaders have an appreciation of the value of reflection and 'time out' for leaders, and they regularly update the education of themselves and others in leadership studies and theories an appreciation of the role of coaching, supervision and mentoring.

5. EFFECTIVE EXTERNAL NETWORKING AND PARTNERSHIPS (ENTERPRISE-INTELLECTUAL-EMOTIONAL)

Leadership, Selflessness, Objectivity, Openness, Accountability Nolan Principles, CEL – Focus to Achieve, Mobilise to Impact
Aware of 'the bigger picture', with an excellent outward-focus – Selflessness, Accountability and Openness Nolan Principles
Good leaders keep in touch with leaders in other organisations and remain abreast of new theroretical models for leadership. Creative networking with others outside the institution alleviates a sense of loneliness. They have a strong desire to share the role with others.
Skilled in innovative enterprise and business generation – Accountability and Leadership Nolan Principles
Good leadership is excellently skilled in finance, proactive in innovative enterprise for the organisation and ensures a continuous flow of appropriate business generation activities, works well with employers, being responsive to needs.

Figure 18.1 Five principles for good leadership in post-compulsory education

a challenge and a relief for staff – that leadership can be a shared task throughout our organisations, and that it works most effectively when it is. I have very much enjoyed writing and sharing these reflections on leadership with you, and I thank all the leaders who have taken part in the interviews.

Further research and reflection on leadership needed

Finally, in this endnote, we observe that considerable further research on, discussions with and development of leaders is needed in the sector, to take forward CEL's *Leadership Qualities Framework* and related models in ways beneficial to the achievement of future high quality in leadership. Research is in part the role of CEL, but further reflection and implementation of these models of good practice is also strongly the work of all future leaders in the PCE sector who read this book, the interviews, and related publications.

> After all this is over, all that will really have mattered is how we treated each other.
>
> *Anon*

Bibliography

Ackoff, R.L. (1998) 'A systemic view of transformational leadership.' *Systemic Practice and Action Research*, 11, 1, pp.23–36.

Adair, J. (2002) *Effective Strategic Leadership*. London: Pan Macmillan.

Adams, S. (1996) *The Dilbert Principle: A Cubicle's-Eye View of Bosses, Meetings, Management Fads and Other Workplace Afflictions*. New York: HarperCollins.

Ainley, P. (2003) 'Towards a seamless web or a new tertiary tripartism? The emerging shape of post-14 education and training in England.' *British Journal of Educational Studies*, 51, 4, p.390, December.

Ainley, P. and Bailey, B. (1997) *The Business of Learning: Staff and Student Experiences of Further Education in the 1990's*. London: Cassell Education.

ALI (Adult Learning Inspectorate) (2001–02) *Annual Report of the Chief Inspector 2001–02*. Coventry: ALI. Available at http://www.docs.ali.gov.uk/ciar/0102/info.htm, accessed 10 August 2005.

ALI/Ofsted (Office for Standards in Education) (2001) *The Common Inspection Framework for Inspecting Post-16 Education and Training*. Coventry: ALI and Ofsted.

Alimo-Metcalfe, B. and Alban-Metcalfe, J. (2005) 'Leadership: time for a new direction?' *Leadership*, 1, 1, 51–71.

AoC (Association of Colleges) (2001) *Association of Colleges and Joint Unions National Review of Staffing and Pay in Further Education*. London: OCR International.

AoC (2004) 'Ofsted college criticisms "inappropriate"'. Press release. London: AoC, 26 November.

Alvesson, M. and Sveningsson, S. (2003) 'Good visions, bad micro-management and ugly ambiguity: contradictions of (non-) leadership in a knowledge-intensive organization.' *Organization Studies*, 24, 6, pp.961–88.

Avis, J. (2002) 'Imaginary friends: managerialism, globalism and post-compulsory education and training in England.' *Discourse Studies in the Cultural Politics of Education*, 3, 3, pp.3–42.

Avis, J. (2003) 'Rethinking trust in a performative culture.' *Journal of Education Policy*, 18, pp.315–32.

Avis, J. and Bathmaker, A-M. (2004) 'Critical pedagogy, performativity and a politics of hope: trainee further education lecturer practice.' *Research in Post-Compulsory Education*, 9, 2, pp.301–12.

Ball, S. (2003) 'The teacher's soul and the terrors of performativity.' *Journal of Education Policy*, 18, pp.215–28.

Bascia, N. and Hargreaves, A. (eds) (2000) *The Sharp Edge of Educational Change: Teaching, Leading and the Realities of Reform.* London: Falmer Press.

Bass, B.M. and Avolio, B.J. (1990a) 'The implications of transactional and transformational leadership for individual, team, and organizational development' in *Research in Organizational Change and Development*, Vol 4, R.W. Woodman and W.A. Passmore (eds), Greenwich, CT: Jai Press, pp.231–72.

Bass, B.M. and Avolio, B.J. (1990b) 'Training and development of transformational leadership: looking to 1992 and beyond.' *Journal of European Industrial Training*, 14, 5, pp.21–37.

Bass, B.M. and Avolio, B.J. (eds) (1993) *Improving organizations through transformational leadership.* Beverly Hills, CA: Sage Publications.

Bass, B.M. and Avolio, B.J. (1994) *Improving organizational effectiveness through transformational leadership.* Thousand Oaks, CA: Sage Publications.

Bass, B.M. and Avolio, B.J. (1997) *Full Range Leadership Development, Manual for Multifactor Leadership Questionnaire.* San Francisco, CA: Mind Garden Inc.

Bass, B.M. and Avolio, B.J. (2000 [1995]) *Technical Report for the Multifactor Leadership Questionnaire.* San Francisco, CA: Mind Garden Inc.

Bass, B.M. and Steidlmeier, P. (1998) *Ethics, Character, and Authentic Transformational Leadership.* Binghamton, NY: Center for Leadership Studies, School of Management, Binghamton University. Available at http://www.cls.binghamton.edu/BassSteid.html, accessed 5 August 2005.

Bauman, Z. (2001) *The Individualized Society.* Cambridge: Polity Press.

Beck, U. and Beck-Gernsheim, E. (2002) *Individualization.* London: Sage Publications.

Bedeian, A.G. and Armenakis, A.A. (1998) 'The cesspool syndrome: how dreck floats to the top of declining organizations.' *Academy of Management Executive*, 12, pp.58–63.

Bennis, W.G. and Nanus, B. (1985) *Leaders: The Strategies for Taking Charge.* New York: Harper and Row.

Bernstein, B. (1996) *Pedagogy Symbolic Control and Identity.* London: Taylor and Francis.

Bettelheim, B. (1976) The Uses of Enchantment. New York: Knopf.

Binney, G., Wilke, G. and Williams, C. (2005) *Living Leadership: A Practical Guide for Ordinary Heroes.* Harlow: Pearson Education.

Blackmore, J. (2004) 'Leading as emotional management work in high risk times: the counterintuitive impulses of performativity and passion.' *School Leadership and Management*, 24, 4, pp.440–59, London: Carfax.

Blake, R.R. and Mouton, J.S. (1964) *The Managerial Grid.* Houston, TX: Gulf Publishing.

Blake, R.R. and Mouton, J.S. (1978) *The New Managerial Grid.* Houston, TX: Gulf Publishing.

Blake, R.R., Mouton, J.S. and McCanse, A.A. (1989) *Change by Design.* Reading, MA: Addison-Wesley.

Blanchard, K. and Johnson, S. (1983) *The One Minute Manager.* London: Fontana.

Blanchard, K., Zigarmi, P. and Zigarmi, D. (1986) *Leadership and the One Minute Manager* (first published 1985). London: HarperCollins.

Blank, W. (1995) *The Nine Natural Laws of Leadership.* New York: AMACOM.

Blase, J. and Anderson, G.L. (1995) *The Micropolitics of Educational Leadership: From Control to Empowerment.* London: Cassell.

Block, P. (1987) *The Empowered Manager: Positive Political Skills at Work.* San Francisco, CA: Jossey-Bass.

Block, P. (1993) *Stewardship: Choosing service over self-interest.* San Francisco: Berrett-Koehler.

Bloomer, M. and Hodkinson, P. (1997) *Moving into FE: The Voice of the Learner.* London: Further Education Development Association.

Bloomer, M. and Hodkinson, P. (1999) *College Life: The Voice of the Learner.* London: Further Education Development Association.

Blunt R. (2001) *Organisations Growing Leaders: Best Practices and Principles in the Public Service.* The Price Waterhouse Coopers Endowment for the Business of Government. Washington DC: CEL, p.7.

Boje, D.M. (1991) 'The storytelling organization: a study of story performance in an office-supply firm.' *Administrative Science Quarterly*, 36, 1, pp.106–26, March.

Boje, D.M. (1995) 'Stories of the storytelling organization: a postmodern analysis of Disney as Tamara-land.' *Academy of Management Journal*, 38, pp.997–1035. Available at http://cbae.nmsu.edu/˜dboje/papers/DisneyTamaraland.html, accessed 20 May 2005.

Boje, D.M. (2001a) 'Carnivalesque resistance to global spectacle: a critical postmodern theory of public administration.' *Administrative Theory and Praxis*, 23, 3, pp.431–58. Available at http://cbae.nmsu.edu/~dboje/papers/carnivalesque_resistance_to_glob.htm, accessed 20 May 2005.

Boje, D.M. (2001b) *Network Leadership* in Boje's teaching pages, available at http://cbae.nmsu.edu/~dboje/388/, accessed 20 May 2005.

Bolden, R. (ed.) (2005) *What is Leadership Development? Purpose and Practice*, Leadership South West Research Report 2, June, Exeter: University of Exeter.

Bolman, L.G. and Deal, T.E. (1993) *The Path To School Leadership: A Portable Mentor*. Newbury Park, CA: Corwin Press.

Bolman, L.G. and Deal, T.E. (1995) *Leading With Soul: An Uncommon Journey of Spirit*. San Francisco, CA: Jossey-Bass.

Bolman, L.G. and Deal, T.E. (1997) *Reframing Organizations: Artistry, Choice, and Leadership*. San Francisco, CA: Jossey-Bass.

Bosworth, D. (1999) *Empirical Evidence of Management Skills in the UK*. National Skills Task Force. Research paper 18, Department for Education and Employment.

Brennan, J. (2004) 'Letter to David Bell, HMCI, on "Why Colleges succeed" and "Why Colleges Fail".' AoC Briefing CE 24/04, London: AoC.

Briggs, A.R.J. (2001a) 'Academic managers in further education: reflections on leadership.' *Research in Post-Compulsory Education*, 6, 2, pp.223–36.

Briggs, A.R.J. (2001b) 'Middle managers in further education: exploring the role.' *Management in Education*, 15, 4, pp.12–15.

Briggs, A.R.J. (2002) 'Facilitating the role of middle managers in further education.' *Research in Post-compulsory Education*, 7, 1, pp.63–78.

Briggs, A.R.J. (2005a) 'Middle managers in English further education colleges: understanding and modelling the role.' *Educational Management and Administration*, 33, 1, pp.27–50.

Briggs, A.R.J. (2005b) 'Making a difference: an exploration of leadership roles within sixth form colleges in maintaining ethos within a context of change.' *British Educational Research Journal*, 31, 2, pp.223–8.

Briggs, A.R.J. (2005c) 'Modelling the muddle – making sense through research' in *Readings in post-compulsory education*, Y. Hillier and A. Thompson (eds), London: Continuum, pp.109–25.

Bruner, J.S. (1986) *Actual Minds, Possible Worlds*. Cambridge, MA: Harvard University Press.

Bruner, J. (1996) *The Culture of Education*. Cambridge, MA: Harvard University Press.

Bryant, H. (2004) 'Ask who is in charge', transcript segment 1, interview with Professor Keith Grint: *Take me to your leader*. Small Business School

Series, PBS, Worldnet and the web, television interview responses online, 30 June.

Brymann, A. (1996) 'Leadership in organizations' in *Handbook of Organization Studies*, S.R. Clegg, C. Hardy and W.R. Nord (eds). London: Sage Publications, pp.276–92.

Burchill, F. (1998) *Five Years of Change: A Survey of Pay*, Terms and Conditions in FE Five Years after College Incorporation. London: NATFHE (The University and College Lecturers' Union).

Burgoyne, J. (2004) 'How certain are we that management and leadership development is effective?' Presentation at the *Centre for Excellence in Leadership First Annual Conference*, 30–31 March.

Burgoyne, J., Hirsh, W. and Williams, S. (2004) *The Development of Management and Leadership Capability and its Contribution to Performance: The Evidence, the Prospects and the Research Need.* DfES Research Report 560, Lancaster: Lancaster University. Available at www.dfes.gov.uk/research/data/uploadfiles/RR560.pdf, accessed 6 August 2005.

Burns, J.M. (1978) *Leadership*. New York: Harper and Row.

Bush, T. (2003) *Theories of Educational Leadership and Management* (third edition). London: Paul Chapman Publishing and Sage Publications.

Bush, T. and Bell, L. (eds) (2002) *The Principles and Practice of Educational Management.* London: Paul Chapman Publishing and Sage Publications.

Bush, T. and Glover, D. (2003) *Leadership Development: Evidence and Beliefs*, Nottingham: National College for School Leadership.

Bush, T. and West-Burnham, J. (1994) *The Principles of Educational Management.* London: Pearson Education.

Busher, H. and Harris, A. (2000) *Leading Subject Areas Improving Schools.* London: Paul Chapman.

Caldwell, B.J. and Spinks, J.M. (1992) *Leading the Self-Managing School.* London: Falmer Press.

Campbell M. (2001) *Skills in England 2001: Key Messages*. Department for Education and Skills.

Campbell M. (2002) *Learn to Succeed: The Case for a Skills Revolution*. Bristol: Policy Press.

Carnegie Council on Policy Studies in Higher Education (1979) *Giving Youth a Better Chance: Options for Education, Work, and Service*. San Francisco, CA: Jossey-Bass.

CEL (Centre for Excellence in Leadership) (2004a) *Leading Learning and Skills.* Newsletter. London: CEL, autumn.

CEL (2004b) *Leading the Way 2004–06: Leadership for the Learning and Skills Sector.* London: CEL.

CEL (2005) *Hints and Tips: career insights from successful leaders in the learning and skills sector.* London: CEL.

CEML (Council for Excellence in Management and Leadership) (2002) *Managers and Leaders; Raising our Game.* Final report. London: CEML.

Chamberlin, J. (2003) 'Considering creativity: inspiring the masses through creative leadership.' *APA Online Monitor on Psychology,* 34, p.10.

Clancy, J. (2005) 'Race chief threat to colleges', *TES (Times Educational Supplement),* 28 January. Available at http://www.tes.co.uk/search/story/ ?story_id=2069038, accessed 5 August.

Clarke, C. (2004) 'Developing the learning and skills sector – next stage of reform.' Keynote address presented to the *Learning and Skills Development Agency Summer Conference,* 15 June.

Clements, C. and Washbush, J.B. (1999) 'The two faces of leadership: considering the dark side of leader-follower dynamics.' *Journal of Workplace Learning,* 11, 5, pp.170–1.

Codd, J. (1999) 'Educational reform, accountability and the culture of distrust.' *New Zealand Journal of Educational Studies,* 34, pp.45–53.

Cohen, S. and Eimicke, W. (1995) *The New Effective Public Manager: Achieving Success in a Changing Government.* San Francisco, CA: Jossey-Bass.

Cole, M. (2000) 'Learning through reflective practice: a professional approach to effective continuing professional development among health care professionals.' *Research in Post-Compulsory Education,* 5, 1, pp.23–38.

Coleman, M. and Briggs, A.R.J. (eds) (2002) *Research Methods in Educational Leadership and Management.* London: Paul Chapman Publishing and Sage Publications.

Colley, H. (2002) 'From childcare practitioner to FE tutor: biography, vocational culture and gender in the transition of professional identities.' Paper presented to the *British Education Research Conference,* University of Exeter, 12–14 September.

Collins, M. (1991) *Adult Education as Vocation. A critical role for the adult educator.* London: Routledge.

Commission for Black Staff in Further Education (2002a) *Challenging Racism: Further Education Leading the Way.* London: AoC.

Commission for Black Staff in Further Education (2002b) *Black Staff in Further Education: An Agenda for Action?* London: AoC.

Covey, S.R. (1991) *Principle-Centered Leadership.* New York: Summit Books.

Crowther, F. and Olsen, P. (1997) 'Teachers as leaders – an exploratory framework.' *International Journal of Educational Management,* 11, 1, pp.6–13.

Cummings, T.G. and Worley, C.G. (2001) *Organization Development and Change* (seventh edition). Cincinnati, OH: South-Western College Publishing.

Curtis, P. (2004) 'Colleges branded a "national disgrace".' *Guardian*, 29 November. Available at http://www.education.guardian.co.uk/ofsted/story/0,7348,1362030,00.html, accessed 12 June 2005.

Davidson, M. (1997) *The Black and Ethnic Minority Woman Manager: Cracking the Concrete Ceiling*. London: Paul Chapman.

Dawoody, A. (2003) *The Matriarch as a Leader and the Metaphors of Chaos and Quantum Theories*. Bloomington, IN: 1st Books.

Deem R., Ozga J.T. and Pritchard G. (2000) 'Managing further education: is it still men's work too?' *Journal of Further and Higher Education*, 24, 2, pp.231–51.

De Pree, M. (1989) *Leadership is an Art*. New York: Doubleday.

DfES (Department for Education and Skills) (2002) *Success for All: Reforming Further Education and Training*. London: DfES.

Dourado, P. and Blackburn, P. (2005) *Seven Secrets of Inspired Leaders: How to Achieve the Extraordinary . . . by the Leaders Who Have Been There and Done it*. Chichester: Capstone.

Doyle, M.E. and Smith, M.K. (2001) 'Classical leadership' in *The Encyclopaedia of Informal Education*. Available at http://www.infed.org/leadership/traditional_leadership.htm, accessed 14 May 2005.

Downton, J.V. (1973) *Rebel Leadership: Commitment and Charisma in the Revolutionary Process*. New York: The Free Press.

Duigan, P.A. and Macpherson, R.J.S. (eds) (1992) *Educative Leadership: A Practical Theory for New Administrators and Managers*. London: The Falmer Press.

Eagly, A.H. and Carli, L.L. (2003) 'The female leadership advantage: an evaluation of the evidence.' *Leadership Quarterly*, 14, pp.807–34.

Ecclestone, K. (2003) 'From Freire to fear: the rise of low self-esteem in British post-16 education.' Paper presented to the *British Educational Research Association Annual Conference*, Heriot-Watt University, Edinburgh, 11–13 September.

English, F.W. (1994) *Theory in Educational Administration*. New York: Harper Collins College Publisher.

FEFC (Further Education Funding Council) (1998) *Management Statistics 1995–96*. Coventry: FEFC.

FENTO (Further Education National Training Organisation) (1999) *Standards for Teaching and Supporting Learning in Further Education in England and Wales*. London: FENTO.

FENTO (2002) *Skills Foresight for Further Education in 2002: England Supplement.* Available at http://www.lifelonglearninguk.org/research/skills_foresight_and_dev_plans.html Accessed 23 August 2005.

Fiedler, F.F. (1964) 'A contingency model of leadership effectiveness' in *Advances in Experimental Social Psychology*, vol 1, L. Berkowitz (ed.), New York: Academic Press.

Fiedler, F.E. (1967) *A Theory of Leadership Effectiveness.* New York: McGraw Hill.

Fiedler, F.E. (1997) 'Situational control and a dynamic theory of leadership' in *Leadership: Classical, Contemporary and Critical Approaches*, K. Grint (ed.), Oxford: Oxford University Press, pp.126–48.

Fiedler, F.E. and Garcia, J.E. (1987) *New Approaches to Effective Leadership.* New York: John Wiley.

Field, R.H.G. (2002) 'Leadership defined: web images reveal the differences between leadership and management.' Paper submitted to the Administrative Sciences Association of Canada annual meeting in Winnipeg, Manitoba, January.

Fisher, D. and Torbert W.R. (1995) *Personal and Organisational Transformation: The True Challenge of Continual Quality Improvement.* London: McGraw Hill.

Fisher, J.L.(1994) 'Reflections of transformational leadership.' *Educational Record*, 75, 3, pp.60–5.

Frearson, M. (2002) *Tomorrow's Learning Leaders: Developing Leadership and Management for Post-compulsory Learning: 2002 Survey Report.* London: Learning and Skills Development Agency (LSDA).

Frearson, M. (2003a) *Tomorrow's Learning Leaders: Developing Leadership and Management for Post-compulsory Learning.* London: LSDA.

Frearson, M. (2003b) *Leading Learning Project, Work Package 1: International Comparator Contexts*, LSRC – Research findings report. London: LSDA. Available at http://www.lsda.org.uk/pubs/dbaseout/download.asp?code=LSRC533RF1, accessed 8 August 2005.

Freire, P. (1972) *Pedagogy of the Oppressed.* Harmondsworth: PenguinBooks.

Friedman, A.A. (2004) 'Beyond mediocrity: transformational leadership within a transactional framework.' *International Journal of Leadership in Education*, 7, 3, pp.203–24, July–September.

Funk, M.M. (2004) Book review of M. Buber (2003) ' "I and Thou": practicing living dialogue', *Monastic Interreligious Dialogue Bulletin*, 73, p.15. Monastic Dialogue, Booklight Inc. Available at http://monasticdialog.com/b.php?id=42, accessed 14 May 2005.

Gardner, H. (1993 [1983]) *Frames of Mind: The Theory of Multiple Intelligences.* New York: Basic Books.

Gardner, H. (1995) *Leading Minds: An Anatomy of Leadership*. London: HarperCollins.

Gardner, W.L. and Schermerhorn, J.R., Jnr. (2004) 'Unleashing individual potential: performance gains through positive organisational behavior and authentic leadership.' *Organizational Dynamics*, 33, 3, pp.270–81.

Gilbert T. (2001) 'Reflective practice and clinical supervision: meticulous rituals of the confessional.' *Journal of Advanced Nursing*, 36, 2, pp.199–205.

Glatter, R. and Kydd, L. (2003) ' "Best practice" in educational leadership and management: can we identify and earn from it?' *Educational Management and Administration*, 31, 3, pp.231–43.

Gleeson, D. (2001) 'Style and substance in education leadership: further education (FE) as a case in point.' *Journal of Education Policy*, 16, 3, pp.181–96.

Gleeson, D. and Shain, F. (1999) 'Managing ambiguity: between markets and managerialism – a case study of "middle" managers in further education.' *Sociological Review*, 47, pp.461–90.

Glover, D. and Law, S. (2000) *Educational Leadership and Learning*. Milton Keynes: Open University Press.

Goldstein, H. (1990) *Problem-oriented policing*. New York: McGraw Hill.

Greenleaf, R.K. (1970) *The Servant as Leader*. Newton Centre, MA: Robert K. Greenleaf Center.

Greenleaf, R.K. (1977) *Servant Leadership: A Journey into the Nature of Legitimate Power and Greatness*. New York: Paulist.

Gregory, M. (1996) 'Developing effective college leadership for the management of educational change.' *Leadership and Organization Development Journal*, 17, 4, pp.46–51.

Grint K. (2000) *The Arts of Leadership*. Oxford: Oxford University Press.

Grint, K. (2005a) *Leadership: Limits and Possibilities*. Basingstoke: Palgrave Macmillan.

Grint, K. (2005b) 'Leadership limited: white elephant to wheelwright.' *Ivey Business Journal*, 69, 3, pp.1–4.

Gronn, P. (1995) 'Greatness re-visited: the current obsession with transformational leadership.' *Leading and Managing*, 1, 1, pp.14–27.

Guardian (2003) 'FE college managers given pay cut.' 3 January.

Gunter, H.M. (2001) *Leaders and Leadership in Education*. London: Paul Chapman Publishing and Sage Publications.

Hall, L. (2000) 'Electricity', from *Billy Elliot: The Screenplay*. London: Faber and Faber.

Handy, C. (1981 [1976]) *Understanding Organizations.* Harmondsworth: Penguin Books.

Handy, C. (1989) *The Age of Unreason.* London: Pan Books.

Handy, C. (1994) *The Empty Raincoat: Making Sense of the Future.* London: Hutchinson.

Handy, C. (1995) *The Age of Paradox.* Cambridge, MA: Harvard Business School Press.

Hargreaves, D. (2003) *Education Epidemic: Transforming Secondary Schools through Innovative Networks.* London: Demos.

Harland, J., Kinder, K., Lord, P., Stott, A., Schagen, I. and Haynes, J. with Cusworth, L., White, R. and Paola, R. (2000) *Arts Education in Secondary Schools: Effects and Effectiveness.* Berkshire: National Foundation for Education Research.

Harper, H. (2000) 'New college hierarchies: towards an examination of organisational structures in further education in England and Wales.' *Educational Management and Administration*, 28, pp.433–46.

Harrison, J.F.C. (1961) *Learning and Living 1790–1960. A Study in the History of the English Adult Education Movement.* London: Routledge and Kegan Paul.

Hay Group (2002) *Further Lessons of Leadership: How does Leadership in Further Education Compare to Industry.* London: Hay Group.

Hay McBer (2000a) *Models of Excellence for School Leadership: Raising Achievement in Our Schools: Models of Excellence for Headteachers in Different Settings, Parts 1 and 2*: Hay Group for the National College for School Leadership. Available online at: http://www.ncsl.org.uk/the_knowledge_pool/foundations/kpool-foundations-index.cfm *Part 3*: Hay Group for the National College for School Leadership. Available online at: http://www.ncsl.org.uk/media/F7B/52/kpool-hay-models-of-excellence-part-3.pdf Accessed 9 September 2005.

Hay McBer (2000b) *Research into Teacher Effectiveness: A Model of Teacher Effectiveness* (DfEE Research Report 216). London: DfEE. Available online at http://www.teachernet.gov.uk/teachinginengland/detail.cfm?id-521 Accessed 9 September 2005.

Hayes, D. (2003) 'New Labour, New Professionalism' in *Discourse, Power Resistance: Challenging the Rhetoric of Contemporary Education.* J. Satterthwaite, E. Atkinson and K. Gale (eds), Stoke-on-Trent: Trentham Books: pp.27–42.

Heifetz, R.A. (1994) *Leadership without Easy Answers.* Cambridge, MA: Harvard University Press.

Heifetz, R. and Laurie, D.L. (1997) 'The work of leadership.' *Harvard Business Review*, 75, 1, pp.124–34, January.

Heron, J. (1981) 'Philosophical basis for a new paradigm' in Caring Labor, P. Reason and S. Himmelweit (1999), *Annals of the American Academy of Political and Social Science*, 561, pp.27–36, January.

Hill, R. (2000) 'A study of the views of full-time further education lecturers regarding their college corporations and agencies of the further education sector.' *Journal of Further and Higher Education*, 24, 1, pp.67–75.

Hillier, Y. and Jameson J. (2003) *Empowering Researchers in FE*. Stoke-on-Trent: Trentham Books.

Hochschild, A.R. (1983) *The Managed Heart: Commercialisation of Human Feeling*. Berkeley: University of California Press.

Hochschild, A.R. (2003) *The Commercialisation of Intimate Life: Notes from Home and Work*. Berkeley: University of California Press.

Hodge, M. (1998) *House of Commons Select Committee on Education and Employment: Sixth Report (Further Education)*. London: HMSO.

Hollinshead, A. (2003) 'Quality control autonomy accountability: lecturers' perception of their working lives in the changing context of HE.' Unpublished EdD thesis, Open University.

Horsfall, C. (ed.) (2001) *Leadership Issues: Raising Achievement*. Learning and Skills Development Agency.

House, R. (1971) 'A path-goal theory of leadership effectiveness.' *Administrative Science Quarterly*, 16, pp.321–38, September.

House, R.J. and Baetz, M.L. (1979) *Leadership: Some Empirical Generalizations and New Research Directions*. New York: Academic Press.

House, R. and Baetz, J. (1979) 'Leadership: some empirical generalizations and new research directions' in Yammarino, F.J., Spangler, W.D., & Bass, B.M. (1993) Transformational leadership and performance: A longitudinal investigation. *The Leadership Quarterly*, 4(1): 81–102.

Howell, J.M. and Hall-Meranda, K.E. (1999) 'The ties that bind: the impact of leader-member exchange, transformational and transactional leadership, and distance on predicted follower performance.' *Journal of Applied Psychology*, 84, 5, pp.680–94.

Howells, R. (2000) *Team Management Profile and Emotional Intelligence: More than the Sum of their Parts*. Available at http://www.tms.com.au/tms12-1s.html, accessed 9 August 2005.

Hughes, C. (2003) *LSDA Briefing: Editorial*. London: LSDA, October.

Hughes M. (2002) *Making the Grade: A Report on Standards in Work-based Learning for Young People*. London: LSDA.

Irby, B.J., Brown, G., Duffy, J. and Trautman, D. (2002) 'The synergistic leadership theory.' *Journal of Educational Administration*, 40, 4, pp.304–22.

Jameson, J. and Hillier, Y. (2003) *Researching post-compulsory education*. London, Continuum.

Jameson, J. (2005a) 'Inspiring leaders for the future of lifelong learning.' Paper presented at the *Twelfth International Conference on Learning*, University of Granada, Spain, 11–14 July.

Jameson, J. (2005b) 'Metaphors of leadership in post-compulsory education.' Paper presented at the *Re-thinking Leadership: New Directions in the Learning and Skills Sector? Research Conference*, CEL, University of Lancaster, 26–27 June.

Jameson, J. and McNay, I. (forthcoming) *The Ultimate FE Leadership and Management Handbook*, Book. 9 in *The Essential FE Toolkit Series* for senior and middle managers, Series editor: J. Jameson. London: Continuum.

Jarvis, P. (ed.) (1987) *Twentieth Century Thinkers in Adult Education*. London: Routledge.

Johnson, J. and Winterton, J. (1999) *Management Skills*. National Skills Task Force. Research paper 3, Department for Education and Employment, p.35.

Katz, R.L. (1955) 'Skills of an effective administrator.' *Harvard Business Review*, 33(1), pp.33–42.

Keith, K.M. (2003 [1968]) *The Silent Revolution: Dynamic Leadership in the Student Council* (revised edition). Madison, WI: University of Wisconsin Press, Terrace Books.

Kellerman, B. (2004) *Bad Leadership: What it is, How it Happens, Why it Matters*. Boston, MA: Harvard Business School Press.

Kelly, S., White, M.I., Randall, D. and Rouncefield, M. (2004) 'Stories of educational leadership.' *CCEAM Conference on Educational Leadership in Pluralistic Societies*, Hong Kong and Shanghai, October.

Kelly, T. (1992 [1970] [1962]) *A History of Adult Education in Great Britain* (revised edition). Liverpool: Liverpool University Press.

Kennedy, H. (1997) *Learning Works: Widening Participation in FE*. Coventry: Further Education Funding Council.

Kerfoot, D. and Whitehead, S. (1998) ' "Boys own stuff": masculinity and the management of further education.' *Sociological Review*, 46, 3, pp.436–55.

Killian, R. (2004) *Ethical Leadership*. Professional MBA Leeds School of Business presentation at the University of Colorado, J. Luftig (ed.). Boulder, CO: University of Colorado. Available at http://www.leeds-faculty.colorado.edu/luftig/Past_Course_Websites/Ethics_and_Decision_Making/Presentations/Ethics_and_Leadership.ppt, accessed 10 August 2005.

Kilmann, R.H. (2001) *Quantum Organizations: A New Paradigm for Achieving Organizational Success and Personal Meaning*. Palo Alto: CA: Davies-Black.

Kingston, P. (2003) 'Has the FE management crisis solution come too late?' *Guardian*, 15 July.

Kotter, J.P. (1990) *A Force for Change: How Leadership Differs from Management*. New York: Macmillan.

Kugelmass, J.W. (2003) *Inclusive Leadership; Leadership for Inclusion*. International Practitioner Inquiry Report, Nottingham: National College for School Leadership.

Lave, J. and Wenger, E. (1990) *Situated Learning: Legitimate Peripheral Participation*. Institute for Research on Learning (IRL) report 90-0013, Palo Alto, CA: IRL.

Leader, G. (2004) Further Education Middle Managers: Their Contribution to the Strategic Management Decision Process. *Educational Management and Administration*, 32, 1, pp.67–79.

Leonard, L. and Leonard, P. (1999) 'Reculturing for collaboration and leadership.' *Journal of Educational Leadership*, 92, 4, pp.235–42.

Leonardo, Z. (2003) 'Discourse and critique: outlines of a post-structural theory of ideology.' *Journal of Education Policy*, 18, pp.203–14.

Leont'ev, A.N. (1981) 'The problem of activity in psychology' in *The Concept of Activity in Soviet Psychology*, J.V. Wertsch (ed.), Armonk, NY: M.E. Sharpe, pp. 37–71.

Lester, S. (1994) 'Management standards: a critical approach.' *Competency*, 2, 1, pp.28–31, October.

Lingard, B., Hayes, D., Mills, M. and Christie, P. (2003) *Leading Learning*. Maidenhead: Open University Press and McGraw-Hill Education.

Loots, C. and Ross, J. (2004) 'From academic leader to Chief Executive: altered images.' *Journal of Further and Higher Education*, 28, 1, pp.19–34.

LSC (Learning and Skills Council) (2002) *Leadership and Management in Work Based Learning*, Coventry: LSC.

LSDA (Learning and Skills Development Agency) (2003) *Leading Learning Project Work Package 1: International Comparator Contexts*. Research findings report, London: LSDA, July.

Lucas, N. (2004) 'The "FENTO Fandango": national standards, compulsory teaching qualifications and the growing regulation of FE college teachers.' *Journal of Further and Higher Education*, 28, 1, pp.35–51.

Lumby, J. (1997a) 'Developing managers in further education. Part 1: the extent of the task.' *Journal of Further and Higher Education*, 21, 3, pp.345–54.

Lumby, J. (1997b) 'Developing managers in further education. Part 2: the process of development.' *Journal of Further and Higher Education*, 21, 3, pp.355–64.

Lumby, J. (1999) 'Strategic planning in further education: the business of values.' *Educational Management and Administration*, 27, 1, pp.71–83.

Lumby, J. (2000) 'Funding Learning in Further Education' in *Managing Finance and Resources in Education*, M. Coleman and L. Anderson (eds), London: Paul Chapman, pp.81–98.

Lumby, J. (2001) *Managing Further Education: Learning Enterprise*. Education management: research and practice series. London: Paul Chapman.

Lumby, J. (2002) 'Distributed leadership in colleges: leading or misleading?' Keynote paper presented at the *British Educational Leadership and Management Association Annual Conference*, 'Leaders and leadership: leadership teams, team leaders and middle managers', 20–22 September, Birmingham.

Lumby, J. (2003a) 'Distributed leadership in colleges? Leading or misleading?' *Educational Management and Administration*, 31, 3, pp.283–93.

Lumby, J. (2003b) 'Constructing culture change: the case of sixth form colleges.' *Educational Management and Administration*, 31, 2, pp.157–72.

Lumby, J. and Simkins, T. (2002) 'Editorial: Researching Leadership and Management.' *Research in Post-Compulsory Education*, 7, 1, p.5.

Lumby, J. and Tomlinson, H.T. (2000) 'Principals speaking: managerialism and leadership in further education.' *Research in Post-Compulsory Education*, 5, 2, pp.139–151.

Lumby J., Briggs, A.R.J. with Wilson, M., Glover, D. and Pell, A. (2002) *Sixth Form Colleges: Policy, Purpose and Practice*. Research report, Leicester: Leicester University.

Lumby, J., Harris, A., Morrison, M., Muijs, D. and Sood, K. with Briggs, A., Glover, D., Middlewood, D. and Wilson, M. (2004) *Leadership, Development and Diversity in the Learning and Skills Sector*. London: LSRC (draft copy).

Lumby, J., Harris, A., Morrison, M., Muijs, D. and Sood, K. with Briggs, A., Glover, D., Middlewood, D. and Wilson. M. (2005) *Leadership, Development and Diversity in the Learning and Skills Sector*. London: LSRC.

McGregor, D. (1960) *The Human Side of Enterprise*. New York: McGraw Hill.

Maccoby, M. (2005) 'Narcissistic leaders: the incredible pros, the inevitable cons' in *Harvard Business Review on The Mind of the Leader*. Boston, MA: Harvard Business School Publishing Corporation.

Maginn, A. and Williams, W. (2002) *An assessment of skill needs in post-16 education and training*. London: Institute for Employment Studies, Department for Education and Skills.

Marshall, S. (1995) 'Appraisal in a decentralised school system.' Research reports, *Hot Topics*, 1, pp.1–4.

Matteson, J.A. and Irving, J.A. (2005) *Servant versus Self-Sacrificial Leadership: Commonalities and Distinctions of Two Follower-Oriented Leadership*

Theories. Servant Leadership Research Roundtable, Regent University, August.

MCI (Management Charter Initiative) (1997) *National Occupational Standards in Management.* London: MCI. Available at http://www.management-standards.org.uk, accessed 19 May 2005.

Méndez-Morse, S. (1992) *Leadership Characteristics that Facilitate Change.* Online electronic research report, ID: CHA-02, SEDL (Southwest Educational Development Laboratory). Available at http://www.sedl.org/pubs/index.cgi?l=itemandid=cha02, accessed 5 August 2005.

Merrick, N. (2004) *Lessons learnt? Independent* newspaper news item, © 2004 Independent Digital (UK) Ltd, 01 July 2004.

Michie, S. and Gooty, J. (2005) 'Values, emotions and authenticity: will the real leader please stand up?' *Leadership Quarterly,* 16, 3, pp.441–57.

Millar, M. (2005) 'Lack of faith in senior managers is exposed.' *Personnel Today,* 12, 22 February.

Moore, A., Edwards, G., Halpin, D. and George, R. (2002) 'Compliance, resistance and pragmatism: the (re)construction of schoolteacher identities in a period of intense educational reform.' *British Educational Research Journal,* 28, pp.551–65.

MSC (Management Standards Centre) (2004) *Draft National Occupational Standards in Management and Leadership.* Working document. Available at http://www.management-standards.org, accessed 19 May 2005.

Mullen, C.A. and Kochan, F.K. (2000) 'Creating a collaborative leadership network: an organic view of change.' *International Journal of Leadership in Education,* 3, 3, pp.183–200.

Mumford, M.D., Zaccaro, S.J., Connelly, M.S. and Marks, M.A. (2000) 'Leadership skills: Conclusions and future directions.' *Leadership Quarterly,* 11(1), pp.155–70.

NAO (National Audit Office) (1999) *Value for Money Report: Education and Employment: Investigation of Alleged Irregularities at Halton College.* House of Commons paper no. HC 357 1998–99. Crown copyright. London: The Stationery Office.

NAO (2005) *Securing Strategic Leadership for the Learning and Skills Sector in England.* Report by the Comptroller and Auditor General, HC 29 Session 2005–06, 18 May 2005.

NCSL (National College for School Leadership) (2003) *Leadership Development Framework.* Available at http://www.ncsl.org.uk/index.cfm?pageid=ldf, accessed 19 May 2005.

Northouse, P.G. (2004) *Leadership Theory and Practice* (third edition). London: Sage Publications.

OECD (Organisation for Economic Cooperation and Development) (2001) 'Investment in human capital through post compulsory education and training.' *Economic Outlook*, 70, Chapter V.

Ofsted (2003) *Annual Report of Her Majesty's Chief Inspector of Schools 2001/02*. Norwich: The Stationery Office.

Ofsted (2004a) *Chief Inspector's report*, London, Ofsted, *Annual report of Her Majesty's Chief Inspector of Schools 2003/04*. Norwich: The Stationery Office.

Ofsted (2004b) *Why Colleges Succeed*. London: Ofsted.

Ofsted (2004c) *Why Colleges Fail*. London: Ofsted.

Ofsted (2004d) *The Common Inspection Framework for Inspecting Education and Training*, HMI 2434. London: Ofsted.

Ofsted (2005) *Annual Report of Her Majesty's Chief Inspector of Schools 2003/04*, p.9. Norwich: The Stationery Office.

Ogawa, R.T. and Bossert, S.T. (1997) 'Leadership as an organisational quality' in M. Crawford, L. Kydd and C. Riches (eds) *Leadership and Teams in Educational Management*. Buckingham: Open University Press, pp.9–23.

Olssen, M. (2003) 'Structuralism, post-structuralism, neo-liberalism: assessing Foucault's legacy.' *Journal of Education Policy*, 18, pp.189–202.

Pattakos, A. (2004) *Prisoners of Our Thoughts: Viktor Frankl's Principles at Work*. San Francisco, CA: Berrett-Koehler.

Patterson, K. (2003) 'Servant leadership: a theoretical model.' *Dissertation Abstracts International*, 64, 2, p.570 (UMI 3082719).

Peters, L.J. and Hull, R. (1969) *The Peter Principle: Why Things Always Go Wrong*. New York: Morrow.

Pfeffer, J. and Viega, J.F. (1999) *Putting people first for organizational success*. Academy of Management Executive, 13, pp.37–48.

Podsakoff, P.M., Todor, W.D., Grover, R.A. and Humber, V. (1984) 'Situational moderators of leader reward and punishment behaviours: factor or fiction?' *Organizational Behavior and Human Performance*, 34, pp.21–63.

Powell, S. (2000) 'Great Groups and Leaders'; Warren Bennis *Team Performance Management*, 6, 1–2, p.34.

Preedy, M., Glatter, R. and Wise, C. (2003) *Strategic Leadership and Educational Improvement*. London: Paul Chapman Publishing and Sage Publications.

Price, H. (2001) 'Emotional labour in the classroom: a psychoanalytic perspective.' *Journal of Social Work Practice*, 15, pp.161–80.

Price, T.L. (2003) 'The ethics of authentic transformational leadership.' *Leadership Quarterly*, 14, pp.67–81.

Prince, L. (2005) 'Eating the Menu Rather than the Dinner: Tao and Leadership.' *Leadership*, 1, 1, pp.105–26.

Pritchard, C., Deem, R. and Ozga, J. (1998) 'Managing Further Education: Is it still Men's Work too?' Paper presented at *Gender, Work and Organisation Conference*, UMIST and Manchester Metropolitan University, January.

PWC (Price Waterhouse Coopers) (2002) *Leadership and Management in Further Education and Work-based Learning: Final Summary Report to the Department for Education and Skills*, London: PWC.

Radin, M.J. (1996) *Contested Commodities*. Cambridge: Harvard University Press.

Randle, K. and Brady, N. (1997a) 'Managerialism and professionalism in the "Cinderella service".' *Journal of Vocational Education and Training*, 49, pp.121–40.

Randle, K. and Brady, N. (1997b) 'Further education and the new managerialism.' *Journal of Further and Higher Education*, 21, pp.229–38.

Reason, P. and Rowan, J. (ed.) (1981) *Human Inquiry: A Source Book of New Paradigm Research*. Chichester: John Wiley.

Richmon, M.J. and Allison, D.J. (2003) 'Toward a conceptual framework for leadership inquiry.' *Educational Management and Administration*, 31, 1, pp.31–50.

Rickards, T. and Moger, S. (2000) 'Creative leadership processes in project team development: an alternative to Tuckman's stage model.' *British Journal of Management*, 11, pp.273–83.

Rilke, R.M. (1939) *Duino Elegies* (trans. J.B. Leishman and S. Spender). New York: W.W. Norton.

Rogers, C. and Freiberg, H.J. (1993) *Freedom to Learn* (third edition). New York: Merrill.

Rodgers, H., Frearson, M., Gold, J. and Holden, R. (2003) *International Comparator Contexts*. London: LSRC.

Rubenstein, H. (2004) *Ethical Leadership: The State of the Art*. Article in the CEO Refresher Archives, Toronto: Refresher Publications. Available at http://www.refresher.com/!hrrethical.html, accessed 31 July 2005.

Russell, M. (2004) 'The importance of the affective domain in further education classroom culture.' *Research in Post-Compulsory Education*, 9, 2, pp.249–70.

Ryan, J. (2006) *Inclusive Leadership*. San Francisco, CA: Jossey-Bass.

Sachs, J. (2003) Keynote speech, presented to the *British Educational Research Association Annual Conference*, Heriot-Watt University, Edinburgh, 11–13 September.

Salo, F. (2002) *Leadership in Education: Effective UK College Principals*. McClelland Centre, Hay Group.

Schön, D.A. (1983) *How Professionals Think in Action*. New York: Basic Books.

Schön, D.A. (1987) *Educating the Reflective Practitioner.* San Francisco, CA: Jossey-Bass.

Sedgmore, L. (2002) 'Learning excellence: towards a learning skilled age.' *People and Organisations* 9, 3, pp.1–12.

Sedgmore, L. (2003) 'Transformational Leadership', in *Human Resources*.

Senge, P.M. (1990) *The Fifth Discipline: The Art and Practice of the Learning Organisation*. London: Random House Business Books.

Senge, P.M. (1998) 'The Practice of Innovation', *Leader to Leader* 9, available at http://www.pfdf.org/leaderbooks/l2l/summer98/senge.html, accessed 31 July 2005.

Senge, P.M.(1999) *The Dance of Change*. New York: Currency Doubleday.

Senge, P.M., Kleiner, A., Roberts, C., Ross, R., Roth, G. and Smith, B. (1999) *The Dance of Change: The Challenges of Sustaining Momentum in Learning Organizations*. A Fifth Discipline Resource. London: Nicholas Brealey Publishing.

Shain, F. (1999) 'Managing to lead: women managers in the further education sector.' Paper presented at the *British Educational Research Association Annual Conference*, University of Sussex at Brighton, 2–5 September.

Shain, F. and Gleeson, D. (1999) 'Under new management: changing conceptions of teacher professionalism and policy in further education.' *Journal of Education Policy*, 14, 4, pp.445–62.

Shelton, C.K. and Darling, J.R. (2001) 'The quantum skills model in management: a new paradigm to enhance effective leadership.' *Leadership and Organizational Development Journal*, 22, 6, pp.264–73.

Shelton, C.D., McKenna, M.K. and Darling, J.R. (2002) 'Leading in the age of paradox: optimizing behavioural style, job fit and cultural cohesion.' *Leadership and Organization Development Journal*, 23, 7, pp.372–9.

Siegrist, G. (1999) 'Educational leadership must move beyond management training to visionary and moral transformational leaders.' *Education*, 120, pp.297–303, Winter.

Simkins, T. (2000) 'Education reform and managerialism: comparing the experience of schools and colleges.' *Journal of Education Policy*, 15, 3, pp.317–32.

Simkins, T. (2003) 'Reform, accountability and strategic choice in education' in *Strategic Leadership and Educational Improvement*, M. Preedy, R. Glatter and C. Wise (eds), London: Paul Chapman, pp.215–32.

Simkins, T. (2005) 'Leadership in education: "What works" or "What makes sense"?' *Educational Administration and Leadership*, 33, 1, pp.9–26.

Simkins, T. and Lumby, J. (2002) 'Cultural transformation in further education? Mapping the debate', *Research in Post-Compulsory Education* 7, 1, pp.9–25.

Smith, C., Gidney, M., Barclay, N. and Rosenfield, R. (2002) 'Dominant logics of strategy in further education colleges.' *Research in Post-compulsory Education*, 7, 1, pp.45–61.

Spears, L.C. (ed.) (1998) *Insights on Leadership: Service, Stewardship, Spirit, and Servant-leadership.* New York: John Wiley and Sons.

Spears, L.C. (2005) 'On character and servant-leadership: ten characteristics of effective, caring leaders.' Indianapolis, IN: The Robert K. Greenleaf Center for Servant-Leadership. Available at http://www.greenleaf.org/leadership/read-about-it/Servant-Leadership-Articles-Book-Reviews.html, accessed 10 August 2005.

Stanton, G. (1997) 'Patterns in development' in *Education 14–19: Critical Perspectives*, S. Tomlinson (ed.), London: Athlone Press.

Stanton, G. (2000) 'Research' in *Further Education Re-Formed*, P. Smithers and P. Robinson (eds), London: Falmer Press.

Stanton, G. and Morris, A. (2000) 'Making R&D more than research plus development.' *Higher Education Quarterly*, 54, 2, pp.127–46.

Sternberg, R.J., Kaufman, J.C. and Pretz, J.E. (2003) 'A propulsion model of creative leadership.' *Leadership Quarterly*, 14, pp.455–73.

Storey, J. (2005) 'What next for strategy-level leadership research?' *Leadership*, 1, 1, pp.89–104.

Stott, C. and Lawson, L. (1997) *Women at the Top in Further Education.* Bristol: Further Education Development Agency.

Summerhayes, P. (2005) *Hints and Tips: Career Insights from Successful Leaders in the Learning and Skills Sector.* London: Careers Development Service, CEL.

Tenbrunsel, A.E. and Messick, D.M. (2004) 'Ethical fading: the role of self-deception in unethical behavior.' *Social Justice Research*, 17, 2, June.

Thompson, L., Aranda, E. and Robbins, S.P. (2000) *Tools for Teams.* Boston: Pearson Custom Publishing.

Tomlinson Committee Report. Great Britain. Department for Education and Skills (DfES) (2004) *Final Report of the Working Group on 14–19 Reform.* Report 0976-2004, Annesley: DfES Publications.

Torbert, W.R. (1981a) 'Why educational research has been so uneducational: the case for a new model of social science based on collaborative inquiry' in *Human Inquiry: A Sourcebook of New Paradigm Research*, P. Reason and J. Rowan (eds), Chichester: John Wiley and Sons.

Torbert, W.R. (1981b) 'Interpersonal Competence' in *The Modern American College*, A.W. Chickering and Associates. San Francisco, CA: Jossey-Bass.

Torbert, W.R. (1991) *Power of Balance:Transforming Self, Society and Scientific Inquiry.* London: Sage Publications.

Tressell, R. (1971) *The Ragged Trousered Philanthropist.* London: Lawrence and Wishart.

Trevino, L.K., Brown, M. and Hartmann, L.P. (2003) 'A qualitative investigation of perceived executive ethical leadership: perceptions from inside and outside the executive suite.' *Human Relations*, 56, 1, pp.5–37, the Tavistock Institute.

Tuckman, B.W. (1965) 'Developmental sequence in small groups.' *Psychological Bulletin*, 63, pp.384–99, reprinted in *Group Facilitation: A Research and Applications Journal* 3, Spring, 2001. Available as a Word document at http://www.dennislearningcenter.osu.edu/references/GROUP%20DEV%20ARTICLE.doc, accessed 19 May 2005.

Tuckman, B.W. and Jensen, M.A.C. (1977) 'Stages of small group development revisited.' Group and Organizational Studies, 2, pp.419–27.

Turner, F. (2005) 'Poor ethics in organizations – how to avoid fleas coming back.' Research report in *LeaderValues* online leadership resource centre, article accessible at http://www.leader-values.com/Content/detail.asp?ContentDetailID=966, accessed 5 August 2005.

Vaill, P.B. (1989) *Managing as a Performing Art: New Ideas for a World of Chaotic Change*. San Francisco, CA: Jossey-Bass.

Vaill, P. (1996) *Learning as a Way of Being*. San Francisco, CA: Jossey-Bass.

Vasager, J. (2003) 'Embezzling headmistress found in hospital.' *Guardian*, 23 August. Available at http://www.guardian.co.uk/crime/article/0,2763,1028121,00.html, accessed 3 June 2005.

Vecchio, R. (2002) 'Leadership and gender advantage.' *Leadership Quarterly*, 13, pp.643–71.

Walker, R. and Adelman, C. (1975) *A Guide to Classroom Observation*. London: Methuen.

Waters, T., Marzano, R.J., and McNulty, B. (2003) *Balanced Leadership: What 30 Years of Research Tells us about the Effect of Leadership on Student Achievement*. Information Analysis Report, Aurora, CO: Mid-Continent Regional Educational Lab., available from ERIC Clearing House on Educational Management.

Watson, G. and Crossley, M. (2001) 'The strategic management process: an aid to organisational learning in further education?' *Research in Post-Compulsory Education*, 6, 1, pp.19–29.

Watts, D.J. (2004) *Six Degrees: The Science of a Connected Age*. London: Vintage.

Weber, M. (1947) *Max Weber: The Theory of Social and Economic Organization* (trans. A.M. Henderson and T. Parsons). New York: The Free Press.

Wenger, E. (1998) *Communities of Practice: Learning, Meaning and Identity*. Cambridge: Cambridge University Press.

Wheatley, M.J. (1999) *Leadership and the New Science: Discovering Order in a Chaotic World* (second edition). San Francisco, CA: Berrett-Koehler.

Williams, R. (1977) *Marxism and Literature*. Oxford: Oxford University Press.

Williams, S. (2002) 'Individual agency and the experience of New Deal.' *Journal of Education and Work*, 15, 53–74.

Wilson, A. (2003) *Inclusive Leadership*. Berkhamsted: Ashridge Centre for Business and Society. Available at http://www.ashridge.org.uk/www/ ACBAS.nsf/web/Publications/$file/InclusiveLeadership.pdf, accessed 30 July 2005.

Woods, P. (1983) *Sociology and the School*. London: Routledge & Kegan Paul.

Wren, H.D. (1999) 'A profile of community college presidents' leadership styles.' *Dissertation Abstracts International*. Mississippi State University, 36.

Yammarino, F.J., Spangler, W.D. and Bass, B.M. (2003) 'Transformational leadership and performance: a longitudinal investigation.' *Leadership Quarterly*, 4, 1, pp.81–102, Spring.

Yukl, G. (1999) 'An evaluation of conceptual weaknesses in transformational and charismatic leadership theories.' *Leadership Quarterly*, 10, 2, pp.285–305.

Yukl, G. (2002) *Leadership in Organizations* (fifth edition). Upper Saddle Creek, NJ: Prentice-Hall.

Zaleznik, A. (1990) 'Managers and leaders: are they different?' in *Harvard Business Review on Leadership*. Boston, MA: Harvard Business School Publishing.

Zeldin, T. (1998) *An Intimate History of Humanity*. New York: Vintage Books.

Zukas, M. and Malcom, J. (1999) 'Models of the educator in Higher Education.' Paper presented at the *British Educational Research Association Conference*, University of Sussex, Brighton, 2–5 September. Available at http://www.leeds.ac.uk/educol, accessed 6 August 2005.

Index

Titles of publications appear in *italics*.